AMERICAN POPULISM

AMERICAN POPULISM

Edited, Selected, and with Introductions by

GEORGE McKENNA

Capricorn Books
G. P. PUTNAM'S SONS, *New York*

Capricorn Books Edition, 1974

Copyright © 1974 by George McKenna

SBN: 399-11116-6
Capricorn Books SBN: 399-50316-1
*Library of Congress Catalog
Card Number: 72-97303*

PRINTED IN THE UNITED STATES OF AMERICA

To Sylvia

Acknowledgments

I am grateful to the staffs of the New York City, Boston, and Vermont public libraries for their assistance in locating some of the material in this collection of readings. I also want to express my gratitude to Mr. Billy Joe Camp, Press Secretary to Governor George Wallace, for supplying me with texts of Governor Wallace's speeches.

The views expressed in the introductory essays are, of course, my own. But I want to extend particular thanks to Charles M. Sherover, Department of Philosophy, Hunter College, for valuable editorial assistance, for suggestions, encouragement, and dogged support; also to Mr. Walter Betkowski of Putnam's whose support for the idea of this reader helped make it possible, and to Mrs. Renate Murry for assistance in the preparation of this volume.

And thanks, as always, to my dear Sylvia, who sustains me, who props me up.

Contents

Populism:
The American Ideology

This is a presentation, not of Populism, but of populism. Populism with a capital *P*, populism as an organized political party, enjoyed a very short life-span, extending roughly over the last decade of the nineteenth century. It was considered a subject of historical interest until the 1950's, when a group of liberal historians and sociologists, notably Daniel Bell and Richard Hofstadter, began to find in it some of the roots of contemporary McCarthyism. But with the fifties safely behind, and McCarthyism itself a topic of history, populism, defused again, became once more of mainly academic interest. All during the 1960's academicians milled and re-milled the data and hypotheses that students of populism had produced a decade earlier. Was McCarthyism populist or not? As the debate warmed, the arguments became increasingly subtle and the factual grist exceedingly fine.

While the scholars were thus occupied, some curious events were occurring on the hustings, far from the halls of ivy. A Southern governor came north and began to make speeches before increasingly receptive audiences. Following a warm-up that included blue-grass guitar and banjo selections, the governor would step forward and deliver a speech attacking pointy-headed intellectuals, bureaucrats with briefcases, and, in one breath, socialists and the privileged rich. Claiming to speak for all "average" Americans, he urged them to desert the major parties for his "new party of the people." Meanwhile, one of the major party candidates could be seen riding on a flatbed truck with striking farm workers, appealing to blue-collar workers in steel mill towns, and claiming that he was the candidate who could unite all Americans. And in the next election another candidate from the same party promised to bring the troops home in ninety days, close tax loopholes, make the rich pay their share.

The point is not merely that populism enjoyed a revival in America at the end of the 1960's—for all of the themes touched on are explicitly populistic—but that populism never died in the first place. True, historic Populism lasted no more than a decade, but the soil that nourished it was rich enough to support other strains of populism, and these have cropped up with seasonal regularity down to our present time. Populism, then, is not a sometime thing which puts in an occasional appearance in America. It is the perennial American "ism," with its roots extended at least as far back as the American Revolution and a development which, while directed toward different objects at different times, has never obliterated the essential qualities which stamp it as a uniquely American movement.

The first of these is a lack of class consciousness. Like socialism and communism, populism raises the question of income distribution and protests against economic privilege. (This is true even of right-wing populism, which manages to associate subversion and lawlessness with those born, as McCarthy used to say, "with silver spoons in their mouths.") But, unlike socialism or communism, populism proceeds not on the basis of class analysis but on the division of the nation into an overwhelming majority of "plain people," on the one hand, and a relative handful of very un-plain, very sophisticated, very scheming conspirators, on the other.

To see concretely this lack of class consciousness we might compare the Populist platform of 1892 with the formulation by an American socialist twelve years later. Note the simplicity—some would say simplemindedness—of the populist formulation:

> Assembled on the anniversary of the birthday of the nation, and filled with the spirit of the grand general and chief who established our independence, we seek to restore the government of the Republic to the hands of "the plain people," with which class it originated.*

*See below, p. 89.

Now here is Eugene Debs, a former populist turned socialist:

> Socialism is first of all a political movement of the
> working class, clearly defined and uncompromising,
> which aims at the overthrow of the prevailing capitalist
> system by securing control of the national government
> and by the exercise of the public powers, supplanting the
> existing capitalist class government with Socialist
> administration—that is to say, changing a republic in
> name into a republic in fact.*

The Debs formulation sounds shrill and somehow "alien" to
the populist ear. Populist demonology centers its enmity not upon
a whole social class but a relative handful of *big* business conspirators (or their spoiled sons and daughters). Everyone else,
from small businessmen, to farmers, to workers, are "the plain
people." (William Jennings Bryan considered everyone as a kind
of small businessman, and American workers today seem to agree:
They like to be considered "middle class.") True, American
socialists such as Debs and Norman Thomas were far less rigorous
than their European counterparts in the matter of class analysis, but
they still insisted upon a minimum recognition, to use Thomas'
language, of "the exploitation of the masses by an owning class."
This the populists refused to provide, if for no other reason than
that the farmer—backbone of vintage populism—was himself part
of an "owning class."

But beyond this reason was a deeper one, connected with a
central assumption of the populist credo. The populist believes that
the "plain people" of America, which for him includes almost
everyone, are in basic agreement with one another about what is
right and wrong, fair and foul, legitimate and crooked. Fancy
dialectics are unnecessary to discover these kinds of truths: we
need only search our hearts. And our hearts are basically the same.
The populist cannot bring himself to believe that the social environments of different Americans can set them thinking differently
about fundamentals. Economic determinism is anathema to him.
So is anything, *e.g.*, black power, which might divide his coun-

*From *Writings and Speeches of Eugene V. Debs* (New York: Hermitage Press, 1948).

trymen by ethnic or racial lines. (This does not mean that there were not racists in the People's Party, but that their racism was a social prejudice which they attempted to isolate from their political goals. Needless to add, the effort was not wholly successful—Tom Watson, for example, who once labored for a black-white alliance, ended up being honored at graveside by the Ku Klux Klan—but to that extent they proved untrue to their own populist principles.) As an editorial in the *Farmer's Alliance*, newspaper of the movement which culminated in the People's Party, put it in 1891:

> The people's party has sprung into existence not to make the black man free, but to emancipate all men; not to secure political freedom to a class, but to gain for all *industrial* freedom, without which there can be no political freedom; no lasting people's government.*

Even the name, People's Party, is significant. At about the time when British social democrats were building a party with a name, Labour, calculated to appeal to class interests, American populists were aiming at nothing less than the whole nation.

According to one view this is the cardinal error of the populists. The critic of populism will argue that it is a naive doctrine which has never progressed beyond the eighteenth century in its view of the nation. For all the boldness of populists in action, the critic will say, they have been extremely timid theoreticians. And it is unquestionably true that Thomas Jefferson, the father of populism, was an unoriginal thinker whose formulations, for all their elegance, did not go much beyond the commonplaces of Enlightenment republicanism: The majority ought at all times to prevail; the people should be ever watchful of the attempts by irresponsible elites to sneak back into power, and they have the right to overthrow them if they do. (Madison, and later Calhoun, sought to modify this simple elite/mass dichotomy, but neither had any influence on populist thinking.) Populism as a protest movement starts with the assumption that an elite has indeed taken power, and that the remedy is "to restore" the Republic back into the hands of the majority, "with which class it originated." Marx, even Debs,

*From *Farmer's Alliance*, October 22, 1891.

would never talk that way. For the socialist the golden age lies ahead, and the task is to push toward it or, in Debs' words, to change "a republic in name into a republic in fact." Even if we wanted to, says the socialist, we could never restore the past: Too many changes have occurred since the Industrial Revolution, the most important being the appearance of intense class struggle. The classes, each pursuing what it conceives to be its legitimate self-interest, have sharpened their conflict to the point of crisis. From this crisis there can be no turning back; the old forms of republicanism no longer fit our economic situation.

The populist disagrees with this analysis for a number of reasons. First of all, he cannot bring himself to imagine that the normal pursuit of self-interest has to lead to exploitation. "Real Americans," said a farm leader quoted by Senator William Borah in the 1930's, "have no desire to take away the property that honestly belongs to others." But in socialist analysis "desires" are of little relevance to objective behavior. Whether societal actors are subjectively "good" or "bad" is quite beside the point. They are fated by the laws of history and economics to act out their roles until the final denouement comes in the form of a seizure of power (whether violent or parliamentary) by the workers. This is a tragic view of human affairs not shared by the populist. He prefers melodrama. For him, exploitation is not the result of normal self-interest but of an unnatural appetite for something far in excess of self-interest—a lust for unlimited control over the lives of others. Jefferson pictured governmental elites as a pack of wolves, and this metaphor was enlarged by later populists to include economic elites.

Is this melodrama warranted? Is the populist naive to see reform as chastening villains instead of restructuring the system? Hasn't industrialism made obsolete a hazy doctrine of "plain people," born long before our present arrangement of social classes had appeared?

The populist answer is that, while changes have indeed occurred, none of them have radically changed the American's image of himself in society. Socialists can talk all they please about "the proletariat," but what if the American worker obstinately refuses to see himself as a member of that class? As for the wealthy, Alexis de Tocqueville, a French visitor in Jacksonian

America, noted that they lock their finery behind closed doors and pretend to be sturdy democrats—the same pretense affected a century later by the young Nelson Rockefeller, who wanted to wait tables at Dartmouth so as to be "a regular fellow." The point here is that American society seems to lack the subjective basis for any rigorous definition of social class. Louis Hartz has described the American democrat as a unique hybrid of petit bourgeois, peasant, and proletariat, without being distinctly any of these classes. If William Jennings Bryan was confused about classes, so were his constituents. And if Joe McCarthy was able successfully to appeal to workers, small businessmen, and farmers, does not this tell us a great deal about America's fluid class structure—or rather lack of structure? If populism lacks class consciousness, so does America.

Yet the socialist may take some vengeful satisfaction from this central weakness running through the development of American populism: It may not be class conscious, but it is class *un*conscious. Populism, in other words, historically has carried with it a largely unconscious class bias. Sometimes, as with Jefferson's declaration that farmers are a "chosen people," or Bryan's prediction that grass would grow in the streets of the cities if it were not for the farmers, these biases are brought into the open. But more often they remain under the surface of grand universal rhetoric, hedging it with cultural prejudice. Vintage populism was born in the East, but it underwent its critical period of growth on the Western frontier of the nineteenth century, and during that time it developed in an ambience of rural Protestant evangelism. Despite earnest efforts, despite platforms which linked the cause of the farmer with that of the worker, the old populists were never able to break through to the Catholic working class of the cities. The People's Party was snubbed by the developing labor unions and rejected at the polls by urban workers, and the reason had less to do with platform than with what we now call life-style. A typical populist gathering resembled nothing so much as a camp meeting: inspired oratory, laced with Biblical allusions, aimed at "elevating" the audience and transmuting mundane questions of politics and economics into grand moral issues. All of this ran contrary to the political style of Catholics, who were not Bible readers and had little impulse to explore the social meaning of the gospel. Vintage populism could claim some Catholic adherents in the West —notably Ignatius Donnelly in Minnesota—but in the East, where Catholics best preserved their culture, its support from the Catholic working class was almost nil. Jews, blacks, atheists, immigrants, Unitarians, and people who saw nothing wrong in drinking whiskey or teaching Darwin, also found themselves outside the cultural perimeter of vintage populism in its declining years. The old populism claimed to speak for all "the plain people" of America, but it spoke with the twang of rural and small-town "WASP"—an element of the nation well on its way to becoming a minority group.

But modern populism, both left and right, has broken through the old cultural compartments. When George Wallace came North to win the Michigan Democratic primary in 1972 it was clear that he had discovered an issue—busing—broad enough to unite "plain people" regardless of region, class, and religion (though not race). And George McGovern attempted to forge a link between the traditional populist state of South Dakota and the cities and campuses of America. His failure can be ascribed to a number of factors, but certainly not to rural provincialism.

At any rate, whatever goes on in the unconscious mind of populism, its avowed aim is to speak not for any class or group but for the entire nation. From its inception populism has been integrally related to patriotism, and this is another factor that distinguishes it from some, though not all, kinds of social democracy. It would unite not "workers of the world" but "workers—and farmers, and small businessmen, firemen and policemen, barbers and beauticians, secretaries and schoolteachers and just about everyone else except the idle rich—of America." And since that is hardly a very ringing slogan, the Populist converts it to, "It's time for the *real* people of America to stand up." The reason for the dogged "Americanism" in populism is closely related to its mythology. Every political movement is based upon a controlling myth, by which, without any disparagement, is meant an idealized history or genealogy. The populist myth is that America is where the decisive revolution took place, a revolution to end all revolutions. The populist looks back on the event with the spectacles provided by Paine and Jefferson: It was not simply a revolt over commerce or taxes or continental autonomy. Beyond these questions was the decisive test of whether anyone is the natural superior of another. It decided forever that people without titles or inherited wealth were able to run their own affairs without interference. America does not need a revolution for the simple reason that it has already had one. What it does need is a restoration. America needs to put the plain people, "from which class it originated," back into power. This means that we first must throw the rascals out, the rascals being the economic royalists, the Harvard intelligensia, the effete snobs, or the Communists. (Joe McCarthy managed to lump them all together—Dean Acheson was "the great Red Dean of fashion," a member of "the lace handkerchief crowd.") America, then, does not need to link up with any world revolution; all it needs to do is rediscover its own roots. "We have lost our way," say the authors of *A Populist Manifesto*. But this assumes that there is an American "way" to be found again.

Populist nationalism is almost always tinged with isolationism. Jefferson warned that we must neither imitate nor get involved in the affairs of Europe, and subsequent populists have echoed this theme with various degrees of stridency, from the "America first" of Borah and Nye to the "Come home America" of McGovern. An offshoot, seemingly contradictory, of this isolationism is jingoism, which usually crops up in the right-wing variety. It would indeed be contradictory if jingoism were identical with imperialism; but the two must not be confused. The imperialist will go to war for territorial gain—for markets, to "civilize" the natives, to insure that the sun never sets on his country's flag. The jingoist wants none of these things. He may even, as Bryan did, argue strenuously against imperial adventures. But once the country already finds itself at war in another land, then, by jingo. . . . Today the right-wing populist will usually admit that our involvement in Vietnam was a terrible mistake, but once we were in it "we have to get the job done." Then he invariably adds something that no imperialist would ever say—"and bring the boys home." The imperialist knows that the moment the boys are brought home the natives will reassert their independence, but the populist believes that the natives are really on our side. All populists, right and left, are uneasy about military expeditions abroad, but this does not prevent the jingoist variety from wishing the very worst upon those who protest too much. Civil liberties have never been an obsession with populists, and some of them are inclined to forget about constitutional safeguards during wartime. On the very eve of American entry into World War I Bryan was opposed to it, but once the war began . . . ''I thought that citizens should not obstruct the government in the prosecution of the war by the exercise of freedom of speech and press. I thought that they should suspend the right to such criticism rather than risk prolonging the war.'' If you want peace, stop criticizing the war. The formula is Orwellian, but it flows from the jingoist impatience to ''get the job done.''

We should not detain ourselves too long in examining populist nationalism during wartime, because its main stem grew during a century of international peace. Its real preoccupations, consequently, are in the domestic sphere, and they center on the problem of irresponsible elites, elites that rob the people of the products which are rightly theirs. ''This land is your land, this land is my land,'' a Woody Guthrie line quoted by George McGovern in his acceptance speech, is, of course, a populist statement. It is also a statement of economic nationalism because it insists that the land and commodities of America belong not to some but to all the American people. Yet this does not mean that populism is identical with what might be called, except for its unfortunate connotations, national socialism. Let us call it national supervision. Edward Bellamy wrote a utopian novel about it in 1887, Theodore Roosevelt preached a variant of it in his unsuccessful second bid for the Presidency, and F.D.R. experimented with it during the 1930's. The argument for it goes like this: The populists are right in declaiming against the evils of big business. But the solution to the problem of big business is not to make it small again—which would be inefficient and reactionary—but to control it and make it serve the nation. Toward this end we need to balance big business by big government or, in the more radical variant of national supervision, absorb it into the government.

The populist replies that the cardinal error of the national supervisionists is the assumption that bigness equals efficiency and progress. ''The evidence,'' say the authors of A Populist Manifesto, ''proves very much the opposite.'' They then go on to cite examples of how big companies have retarded progress by rejecting innovations which would require them to retool, in some cases buying patents only to lock them in their safes. They conclude that General Motors could be broken into competing units with possibly a gain in efficiency.

Whether these points can be sustained is beyond the scope of this discussion. I bring them up only to introduce a central feature of populism: its fear of bigness. Populist economics never wander very far from Adam Smith's laissez-faire; this is not, however, because of any love for competition (survival of the fittest was just as objectionable in economics as it was in biology to vintage populists) but because the remedy of government supervision seems only to compound the problem. Who will supervise the supervisors? Government supervision is also government permission, and what invariably happens is that the agencies set up to regulate big business end up being its allies and co-conspirators.* Even the more radical schemes of government supervision, which do away entirely with businessmen, do not solve the problem of elite irresponsibility but merely transfer it to a different set of elites. Big businessmen are replaced by big commissars, a new class of exploiters is put into power, and a new round of exploitation is begun. To the argument that this can never happen in a democracy the populist replies that democracy itself is enervated by bigness. As government becomes gargantuan, it becomes remote.

> We are not Luddites; we do not propose to smash the machines and turn America into an agrarian society. . . . But the constant yearning of Americans—of all ages, races, and classes—for a sense that *some* part of our lives be closer to human scale must be counted when figuring the enormous cost of centrated power.**

The authors of the *Populist Manifesto* are expressing a fear shared by all populists, left and right. When the political process

---

*C. Wright Mills' contention in the 1950's that America was controlled by an alliance of generals, big businessmen, and government administrators provoked the most spirited reaction not from conservatives but from New Dealers like Arthur Schlesinger and A. A. Berle. Had the New Deal administrators tamed big business, or was it the other way around? Was big government part of the solution or part of the problem? These are the basic issues that have always divided populists from national supervisors.

**Jack Newfield and Jeff Greenfield, *A Populist Manifesto: The Making of a New Majority* (New York: Praeger Publishers, 1972), p. 44.

loses the intimacy of face-to-face contact, then democracy becomes largely ritualized; the people are provided with pageantry but little real control over their nominal servants. (From the standpoint of populist sensibilities George Wallace's caricature of "bureaucrats with briefcases" is at least as potent as the older cartoon of capitalists in spats.) The populists have been ready to advocate nationalization in some cases, such as the railroads, but they regard with great suspicion any grand schemes for government ownership. They prefer homely solutions: Bust the trusts into small units; establish a truly progressive income tax without loopholes; give plain people a chance to participate in politics by means of open primaries, the initiative and referendum; reform the rules for selecting convention delegates. The point is not to build a new ship of state but to make the old one work again by scrubbing off all the barnacles of accumulated privilege.

It is in the context of anti-elitism that we ought to examine a charge frequently leveled at populists, that of "anti-intellectualism." The label is accurate if "intellectual" is used as a noun, designating those professional wise men in universities or "think tanks" who make their living as advisers to the powerful. But the charge is misleading and unfair if it means that the populist is necessarily opposed to the use of the intellect. Here is a typical populist statement from Professor George McGovern: "It was not the American worker who designed the Vietnam war or our military machine. It was the establishment wise men, the academicians of the center." Is this an "anti-intellectual" statement? Perhaps, but certainly not an assault on the intellect so much as a criticism of those who make a craft of it—or, more accurately, a criticism of the presumptuousness, the vanity, and the lust for power which frequently hide behind the façade of intellectualism. What the populists resent are not intellectuals but "pseudo-intellectuals," to use a Wallacite term, who pretend that their education has exempted them from the passions of ordinary men. What Jefferson said of judges sums up the populist attitude toward all intellectual elites: "Our judges are as honest as other men and not more so. They have with others the same passions for party, for power, and the privilege of their corps."

The "anti-intellectualism" of the populist, then, is really an aspect of his anti-elitism. He believes that the great political problems of America require the application not so much of brains as of moral sensitivity, and he knows that no one is an expert on morals. If, as William Jennings Bryan said, "What this country needs is not more brains but more heart," then the people who work with their hands are at least the equals of those who work with books or slide rules. Indeed, the professional conceptualizers may, in their obsession with research and theorizing, become desensitized to moral issues. One of McCarthy's defenders saw his whole performance as a kind of protest against moral relativism.* Bryan, for his part, fought the evolutionists because "their creed denudes life of its spiritual elements and makes man a brother of the beast." Misguided, yes. But the spirit behind these attacks on intellectuals is not a perverse opposition to learning as such but a fear that the cultural elites may be bent upon dehumanizing man's concept of himself and his relations with others. And today—with our Pentagon game theorists who " orchestrate" bombing attacks, our city planners who destroy neighborhoods in the name of "urban renewal," our sex researchers who mechanize the act of love, our "behavioral scientists" who persist, even after the Nazi experience, in viewing man as a laboratory animal—the point may at least be arguable.

Arguable or not, populist "anti-intellectualism" is one prominent feature which sets it apart from liberalism. The term "liberal" first came into widespread use in the nineteenth century, and while it had a variety of meanings one of its most persistent was the conviction that free and open discussion was the best way to reach truth. This conviction, which John Stuart Mill defended so eloquently in his famous *On Liberty*, became the bedrock of Anglo-American liberalism. Sir Ernest Barker, a twentieth-century British liberal, defined democracy as "government by discussion" and saw "the grand dialectic of public debate" as the

---

*"Joe McCarthy became the center of the century's most scandalous fracas because he had the strength and the defects of organic innocence. When his day of destiny came, he looked around, innocently, saw the gargoyles of Anti-Christ staring and sneering at him from everywhere, and innocently reached out to crush them. Now others had seen the gargoyles before him, and some had even visibly shuddered. But, at mid-century, everyone who spoke or wrote or emoted before the public had gone through the post-graduate school of relativism (which is the insolent denial of the free will that chooses between right and wrong). And so the speakers and the writers and the emoters, who among them are the true rulers of our society, kept constantly changing the subject." William S. Schlamm, "Across McCarthy's Grave," *National Review*, III (May 18, 1957), p. 469.

nation's best means of policymaking. In America, liberalism has a somewhat different nuance. This country's variant of Western liberalism translates a love for discussion into a love of academia. And perhaps with justification, since the American classroom has become the real center of discussion in America (the floor of Congress, unlike that of Parliament, is mainly for prepared speeches which nobody bothers to answer). Justifiably or not, the American liberal tends to equate debate and discussion with a preference for the academic style. Thus Democratic liberals worked for and celebrated the nomination of the donnish Adlai Stevenson in 1952 and 1956—even though, in the former year, he was outpolled in the primaries by Estes Kefauver, who investigated monopolies and wore a coonskin cap. Like populists and unlike socialists, liberals have tended to play down class interests and avoid schemes for wholesale government ownership. But the distinguishing mark of the liberal is his partiality to academic styles and personalities, and for academic structures like Harvard "brain trusts" in government. The liberal tends to place a high value on wit and verbal agility, and to make heros of those, like Stevenson, or John F. Kennedy, or Joseph Welch (McCarthy's opponent in the Army-McCarthy hearings of the 1950's), who have mastered the art of the quick thrust.

Populists are unenthusiastic about these skills. Brain trusts, like any other elite, are suspect. As for discussion, the populist knows that it can be used as often to obfuscate as to clarify an issue. The Kennedy-Nixon debates of 1960 taught the voters little about any important issues, and President Kennedy's many press conferences actually enabled him to brush off serious questions with his quick wit. Both "left" and "right" populists have belittled the liberal preoccupation with First Amendment freedoms, both have criticized the university and the communications media for their servility to "the establishment," and neither is convinced that the "free trade in ideas," to use the expression of Oliver Wendell Holmes, will benefit anyone except the craftiest trader.

The populist's cynicism about words does not lead him to counsel silence. On the contrary, he likes words and may use them profusely—not, however, to exchange ideas but to conjure up an emotional mood so that the hearer may better receive, "in his heart," an essentially nonverbal and nonintellectual message.

Populism has never quite lost the flavor of revivalism. William Jennings Bryan's "Cross of Gold" speech is, of course, the classic example, but even the young SDSers of the 1960's, seemingly the antithesis of Bryan's followers, turned with relief to the revivalistic style of Southern blacks as an antidote to "academic bullshit."

Even the prerevivalistic Jefferson was populistic, not liberal, in his attitude toward words and ideas. Of the Declaration of Independence John Adams complained "that it contained no new ideas, that it is a commonplace compilation, its sentiments hackneyed in Congress for two years before." Jefferson replied that the object of the Declaration was "not to find out new principles or new arguments never before thought of, not merely to say things which had never been said before, but to place before mankind the common sense of the subject in terms so plain and firm as to command their assent, and to justify ourselves in the independent stand we are compelled to take. Neither aiming at originality of sentiment, nor yet copied from any particular and previous writing, it was intended to be an expression of the American mind, and to give to that expression the proper tone and spirit called for by the occasion." Note these typical populist tenets: the faith in a homely "common sense" understandable by all; the belief in a homogeneous "American mind"; the emphasis on "tone" and "spirit." Here Jefferson seeks no new ideas; what he wants to do instead is to drive the old ones into our hearts by the force of his rhetoric. The "tone" or "spirit" which he seeks is not bantering or discursive, but earnest and solemn.

Populists, like other social democrats, start from a position of popular sovereignty and seek to end the domination of the masses by economic and social elites. Unlike socialists, they tend to blur class distinctions, lumping all, or nearly all, together into the category of "plain people." Unlike other economic nationalists, they are chary of state ownership or supervision. Unlike liberals—with whom they agree in their reluctance to accept nationalization—they prefer plain people to experts, familiar beliefs to unconventional opinions, the heart (or "soul") to the head, the inspirational to the syllogistic.

These generalizations, like all generalizations, are necessarily overdrawn and, to that extent, unfair. To be a populist one does not have to sacrifice substance to style, nor to be utterly unconcerned about the intellect. We speak here only of relative emphases, useful in comparing populism to other American "isms." Nor should anyone expect that all the individuals represented in this volume fit perfectly into the populist model. Some of them —George Norris, for example—occasionally shade off into liberalism, and others, like La Follette, lean toward national supervision. Human beings are not zoological specimens; their opinions cannot be sealed in airtight categories. What can be said, though, is that the populist spokesmen tend, more often than not, in the direction of the populist model outlined above.

When all is said and done, however, populism remains more a mood than a doctrine. Trust in the simple people; faith in America; scorn for the privileged. All of this is fine, but, we finally ask, who are the plain people and who are the privileged, whose America are we to honor, and how are we to honor it? Populism seems to leave everyone free to fill the blanks with their favorite heroes, villains, and solutions. The same doctrinal fluidity which enables populism to appeal to such a broad spectrum of opinion also contains the fatal seeds of factionalism and reductionism. The great vintage populist movement of the 1890's was reduced to absurdity when it finally pinned the whole salvation of America on the issue of free silver. More recently, SDS was split into a rainbow of factions, from morose Stalinists to manic Weathermen, after it was discovered that terms like "participatory democracy" meant so many things to so many different people.

But these vacuities in populism—are they not also in the fabric of American political society? Americans have always understood one another in their major premises ("equal opportunity" is a good example) even while fighting one another over the contents of the premises. Populism's weakness, if it is a weakness, lies in its fidelity to the spirit of the nation in which it was born. Within that nation it remains, after two centuries, the most durable expression of its yearnings and dreams.

Part One

Vintage Populism

I.   THE ROOTS OF POPULISM

The doctrinal ingredients of populism are products of the Enlightenment. Although the tenets of Enlightenment thought had been ripening for centuries, they reached their fullest development during the period of the American Revolution, which seemed to many a successful test of their validity. Three of these tenets are very closely related to populism.

1. *The deification of nature*. Deism, which was fashionable among intellectuals of the eighteenth century, insisted that man's knowledge of God could best be secured by a study of His grand work: the physical universe. The distinction, therefore, between the natural and the artificial assumed great importance because the natural provided the only real clue to God's intentions. Consequently, anything close to the soil, to the smell of God's earth, was to be preferred to the merely artificial or man-made. Here, then, is the doctrinal underpinning for Jefferson's claim that farmers are God's "chosen people" and his preference for agriculture over industry. It also underlies the doctrine of laissez-faire, which Jefferson carried almost (but not quite) to the point of anarchy. Government, as a man-made contrivance, is at best a necessary evil. Paine compared it with clothing, another artifice, and considered it a "badge of lost innocence." Necessary though it is, it is a clumsy contrivance, and a corrupting one, so it should be avoided wherever possible in favor of spontaneous and uncoerced cooperation. Jefferson preferred the primitive ways of the Indians to the sophisticated over-government which he associated with Europe, and this preference for society over the state, citizen over

politician, amateur over professional, has been a staple of populist speech-making down to the present day.

The natural/artifical dichotomy, one suspects, also underlies much of the emotional reaction of populism to such things as banks, gold, Eastern manners, lace cuffs, tie wigs, and foppery of all kinds. To be sure, there were hard economic reasons why later populists should resent the gold standard, and equally hard sectional and political reasons why Jacksonians should fear the Bank of the United States. But the emotional intensity of these reactions, and the lurid colors they paint, suggest more than a pragmatic opposition to the offending institutions and practices. The impression is conveyed that everything good, decent, homely, simple, honest, in a word *natural*, is about to be felled, murdered, raped, crucified by something phony, mannered, effete, superfluous, in a word *artificial*.

2. *A relatively optimistic view of human nature*. If nature is deified, it follows that human nature is also entitled to great respect. The men of the Enlightenment had argued that human nature, while perhaps not angelic, is at least capable of grasping certain ''self-evident'' truths without benefit of clergy or scripture. Of course men need education (of this Jefferson was a staunch proponent), but this education should consist not of indoctrination but of razing barriers to the mind—barriers *created* by centuries of indoctrination—in order that it may freely, through its own nature, discover moral truth. The mind's natural ally in this quest is the heart, that most innocent and artless of faculties, which follows the moral commandments of the universe without questioning or quibbling. The early populists saw this partnership as one of equals; only later, especially after the infusion of fundamentalism and the trauma caused by the Darwinian revolution, did populism incline toward making the heart a senior partner.

Since orders and classes among men seemed ''artificial'' to the Enlightenment mind, it follows that, if human nature is essentially moral and rational, then *all* men must be so. Thus populist egalitarianism is a logical concomitant of populist optimism concerning human nature. There is no reason, then, why aristocrats and bishops, lawyers and judges for that matter, are better able to discern right and wrong than the average man. Andrew Jackson's defense of the spoils system took its root in the conviction that, since the tasks of government could be performed by any man, they should be undertaken by those men who had won the election. Other things being equal, the majority should run the machinery of government. And for the populist, the other things in question —morality and brains—*are* equal.

3. *Contract theory*. As an egalitarian, the populist must reject any paternalistic justification for authority—that men require "natural" superiors to rule them, that some men are "born" to lead, and so on. To derive authority the populist falls back on the assumption, already commonplace in the eighteenth century (although its origins go back at least two centuries earlier) that government results from a contract in which men provisionally give up some of their freedom, the provision being that the government serves the ends toward which the parties to the contract have ordained it. It is evident that contract theory leaves a convenient loophole for revolution: Most populists since the eighteenth century have closed it by reasoning that America has already had its revolution and needs no more, since the Constitution permits a kind of legal revolution through the amendment process. Populists are reformists rather than revolutionaries, and here contract theory assumes its greatest importance. The underlying strategy for change, as the populist sees it, is to "let the people decide." The thrust is toward conventions instead of "king caucus," direct elections instead of appointments, and initiative and referendum, at least on important issues, instead of merely representation. Populists take the myth of the contract seriously enough to insist that the people should be given the means of rewriting it or adding new clauses whenever the occasion warrants.

Contract theory also affects the populist's attitude toward business. While pro-business interests have tried to use contract theory to justify monopoly and exploitation, populists have replied by pointing to an important corollary: Contracts must not be signed under duress. "You can rob a person with a gun and you can rob him with a fountain pen," said Woody Guthrie. If, to take one example, a worker has no other place to go for a job, his contract to work for a subsistence wage is not really free, since the alternative is death. This is why so many populists finally supported labor unions, even while recognizing the essentially feudal character of unions. At least, by balancing the scales already tipped by big business, they might serve to restore some measure of equality to the bargaining process and thus help to eliminate duress.

But the sweep of the corollary can go much further. If duress can be present during the time of contract-signing, it can also be injected much earlier: by a bad education, by a poor environment, by slums, by racial prejudice, by anything that could scar the mind or will of the potential contract-signer. Here the populist slogan of "equal opportunity for all, special privileges for none" brings us to the threshold of the Great Society. If "special privileges" include the privilege of being born in a middle-class neighborhood, then all kinds of social programs, from counseling to busing, may be necessary to reverse the damage of a slum environment so that all the competitors in the economic race may truly have an "equal opportunity."

But the populist shrinks from this extension in his logic. Social engineering requires a large governmental bureaucracy, which the populist fears as much as he fears big business. Worse, these attempts to change the "culture" of poverty probe the very nerve of the populist assumption that men are "naturally" endowed with intelligence and common sense. Behind the good intentions of the social planners the populist sees, or thinks he sees, the return of medieval paternalism. This is why he clings to simpler solutions to the poverty problem: provide jobs, eliminate the scandalous *disproportion* of wealth by taxing the rich; invigorate the market by breaking up monopolies. But social engineering seems to him an unwarranted and, finally, futile extension of the principle of "equal opportunity."*

The greatest problem in contract theory, all aside from its logical extensions, is whether it makes any kind of sense as a model for viewing man and society. Historically and anthropologically it is nonsense, for no nation ever established its governing

---

*Another embarrassing extension of "equal opportunity" is found in the area of trust-busting. How often will the government have to intervene in the economic game and restore "equal opportunity"? If competition itself leads to economic concentration, then constant governmental intervention will become necessary—requiring a well-staffed governmental bureaucracy to oversee and intervene. In this instance, the populist seems to be prepared to accept governmental machinery, if only because the role of government in trust-busting is essentially negative (preventing, rather than steering or directing) and neutral (not preferring any industry over another). As to whether untrammeled competition *must* lead to concentration, the populist could reply that the proposition has never been fairly tested.

organs by unanimous covenant. Psychologically it is also dubious, since it assumes a kind of rationality, individuality, and public spirit seldom found among people at large—who seem most often ruled by unthinking habits, traditions, and sentiments.

All of these flaws are easily, perhaps too easily, pointed out. The real challenge today is to find something to put in the place of contract theory. The conservative alternative, that some men are the "natural" superiors of others, seems wholly unacceptable. Marxist and Hegelian alternatives, which find the justification for authority in the historical process, have demonstrated their own pitfalls. Pragmatists tend to dismiss the whole question of justification as "ideology," but this dismissal is itself a kind of ideology, usually an ideology of the *status quo*. So, again, if contract theory is nonsense, what do we put in its place?

Perhaps nothing. It may well be, as the anarchists have concluded, that there is no justification for governmental authority. Such a conclusion puts an end to one search but opens up another one, a far more difficult one, and one far less certain of success: the search for our lost innocence.

A. *Thomas Jefferson:*
"We Hold These Truths . . ."

Like most populists, Thomas Jefferson (1743-1826) was not a systematic political writer, nor did he claim to be. Some of his most memorable political statements are found in his personal correspondence, which he attended to religiously despite the demands of an active political life. From the many fragments of his writings, we can piece together the general picture of his thought: a belief in a transcendent body of natural laws understandable to all men, a willingness to trust in the wisdom and goodness of the numerical majority, coupled with an almost anarchistic suspicion of government; an insistence upon the sovereignty of each generation's majority, an impatience with all traditional ways and institutions, a seemingly boundless confidence in the future of America.

Jefferson belongs at the heart of the populist tradition. No other Founder is more frequently invoked by latter-day populists, and with good reason, for none of the Founders had put the case for "our common people" with greater eloquence.

And who were these "common people" in whom Jefferson reposed his ultimate faith? In his later life Jefferson admitted that his dream of a wholly agrarian republic was no longer realistic, but he never abandoned his conviction that honesty and incorruptibility were the special properties of those who till the soil. This rural romanticism, which provided so much verbal fodder to the agrarian populists at the end of the nineteenth century, has even managed to survive the collapse of the old populism and find a new home in the ecology movement of today. To a generation bone-weary of the machine Jefferson's agrarian bias may even seem timely again.

But the perennial quality of Jefferson's appeal results from much more than the durability of the rural myth in America. More important is the masterly way in which Jefferson expressed this appeal. Paradoxically, in spite of his rural bias, Jefferson was able—as most subsequent populists were not—to rise above the immediate concerns of class and section and state his case in universal terms.

Here, then, are models of populist thought, models which have been endlessly reapplied and reinterpreted by later populists, but never equaled in force or brilliance.

The selections are taken from Andrew A. Libscomb, ed., *The Writings of Thomas Jefferson* (Washington: Thomas Jefferson Memorial Association, 1903). I have added some minor changes in punctuation.

ON REVOLUTION

When in the Course of human events it becomes necessary for one people to dissolve the political bands which have connected them with another, and to assume among the powers of the earth, the separate and equal station to which the Laws of Nature and of

Nature's God entitle them, a decent respect to the opinions of mankind requires that they should declare the causes which impel them to the separation.

We hold these truths to be self-evident, that all men are created equal, that they are endowed by their Creator with certain unalienable Rights, that among these are Life, Liberty and the pursuit of Happiness.—That to secure these rights, Governments are instituted among Men, deriving their just powers from the consent of the governed.—That whenever any Form of Government becomes destructive of these ends, it is the Right of the People to alter or to abolish it, and to institute new Government, laying its foundation on such principles, and organizing its powers in such form, as to them shall seem most likely to effect their Safety and Happiness. Prudence, indeed, will dictate that Governments long established should not be changed for light and transient causes; and accordingly all experience hath shewn, that mankind are more disposed to suffer, while evils are sufferable, than to right themselves by abolishing the forms to which they are accustomed. But when a long train of abuses and usurpations, pursuing invariably the same Object, evinces a design to reduce them under absolute Despotism, it is their right, it is their duty, to throw off such Government, and to provide new Guards for their future security.

From *Declaration of Independence*

I am impatient to learn your sentiments on the late troubles in the Eastern States. So far as I have yet seen, they do not appear to threaten serious consequences. Those States have suffered by the stoppage of the channels of their commerce, which have not yet found other issues. This must render money scarce and make the people uneasy. This uneasiness has produced acts absolutely unjustifiable, but I hope they will provoke no severities from their governments. A consciousness of those in power that their administration of the public affairs has been honest may, perhaps, produce too great a degree of indignation, and those characters wherein fear predominates over hope may apprehend too much from these instances of irregularity. They may conclude too hastily that nature has formed man insusceptible of any other government than that of force, a conclusion not founded in truth nor experience. Societies exist under three forms, sufficiently distinguishable: (1) without government, as among our Indians; (2) under governments wherein the will of everyone has a just influence, as is the case in England in a slight degree and in our States in a great one; (3) under governments of force, as is the case in all other monarchies and in most of the other republics. To have an idea of the curse of existence under these last, they must be seen. It is a government of wolves over sheep. It is a problem, not clear in my mind, that the first condition is not the best. But I believe it to be inconsistent with any great degree of population. The second state has a great deal of good in it. The mass of mankind under that enjoys a precious degree of liberty and happiness. It has its evils, too, the principal of which is the turbulence to which it is subject. But weigh this against the oppressions of monarchy and it becomes nothing. *Malo periculosam libertatem quam quietam servitutem.** Even this evil is productive of good. It prevents the degeneracy of government and nourishes a general attention to the public affairs. I hold it that a little rebellion, now and then, is a good thing, and as necessary in the political world as storms in the physical. Unsuccessful rebellions, indeed, generally establish the encroachments on the rights of the people which have produced them. An observation of this truth should render honest republican governors so mild in their punishment of rebellions as not to discourage them too much. It is a medicine necessary for the sound health of government.

To James Madison, Paris, January 30, 1787.

I own, I am not a friend to a very energetic government. It is always oppressive. It places the governors indeed more at their ease at the expense of the people. The late rebellion in Massachusetts has given more alarm than I think it should have done. Calculate that one rebellion in thirteen States in the course of eleven years is but one for each State in a century and a half. No country should be so long without one. Nor will any degree of

---

*"I prefer hazardous liberty to quiet servitude."—*Editor's translation.*

power in the hands of government prevent insurrections. In England, where the hand of power is heavier than with us, there are seldom half a dozen years without an insurrection. In France, where it is still heavier but less despotic, as Montesquieu supposes, than in some other countries and where there are always two or three hundred thousand men ready to crush insurrections, there have been three in the course of the three years I have been here, in every one of which greater numbers were engaged than in Massachusetts and a great deal more blood was spilt. In Turkey, where the sole nod of the despot is death, insurrections are the events of every day. Compare again the ferocious depredations of their insurgents with the order, the moderation, and the almost self-extinguishment of ours. And say, finally, whether peace is best preserved by giving energy to the government or information to the people. This last is the most certain and the most legitimate engine of government. Educate and inform the whole mass of the people. Enable them to see that it is their interest to preserve peace and order, and they will preserve them. And it requires no very high degree of education to convince them of this. They are the only sure reliance for the preservation of our liberty.

To James Madison, Paris, December 20, 1787.

The commotions that have taken place in America, as far as they are yet known to me, offer nothing threatening. They are a proof that the people have liberty enough, and I could not wish them less than they have. If the happiness of the mass of the people can be secured at the expense of a little tempest now and then, or even of a little blood, it will be a precious purchase.

To Ezra Stiles, Paris, December 24, 1786.

God forbid we should ever be twenty years without such a rebellion [Shays's Rebellion]. The people cannot be all, and always, well-informed. The part which is wrong will be discontented in proportion to the importance of the facts they misconceive. If they remain quiet under such misconceptions, it is a lethargy, the forerunner of death to the public liberty. We have had thirteen States independent for eleven years. There has been one rebellion. That comes to one rebellion in a century and a half for each State. What country before ever existed a century and a half without a rebellion? And what country can preserve its liberties if its rulers are not warned from time to time that this people preserve the spirit of resistance? Let them take arms. The remedy is to set them right as to facts, pardon and pacify them. What signify a few lives lost in a century or two? The tree of liberty must be refreshed from time to time with the blood of patriots and tyrants. It is its natural manure. Our convention has been too much impressed by the insurrection of Massachusetts; and on the spur of the moment they are setting up a kite to keep the hen yard in order.

To William S. Smith, Paris, November 13, 1787.

"THE CHOSEN PEOPLE"

We have now lands enough to employ an infinite number of people in their cultivation. Cultivators of the earth are the most valuable citizens. They are the most vigorous, the most independent, the most virtuous, and they are tied to their country, and wedded to its liberty and interests, by the most lasting bonds. As long, therefore, as they can find employment in this line, I would not convert them into mariners, artisans, or anything else. But our citizens will find employment in this line, till their numbers, and of course their productions, become too great for the demand, both internal and foreign. This is not the case as yet, and probably will not be for a considerable time. As soon as it is, the surplus of hands must be turned to something else. I should then, perhaps, wish to turn them to the sea in preference to manufactures; because, comparing the characters of the two classes, I find the former the most valuable citizens. I consider the class of artificers as the panders of vice, and the instruments by which the liberties of a country are generally overturned.

However, we are not free to decide this question on principles of theory only. Our people are decided in the opinion, that it is necessary for us to take a share in the occupation of the ocean, and their established habits induce them to require that the sea be kept open to them.

But what will be the consequence? Frequent wars without a doubt. Their property will be violated on the sea, and in foreign ports, their persons will be insulted, imprisoned, &c., for pretended debts, contracts, crimes, contraband, &c., &c. These insults must be resented, even if we had no feelings, yet to prevent their eternal repetition; or, in other words, our commerce on the ocean and in other countries, must be paid for by frequent war. The justest dispositions possible in ourselves, will not secure us against it. It would be necessary that all other nations were just also. Justice indeed, on our part, will save us from those wars which would have been produced by a contrary disposition. But how can we prevent those produced by the wrongs of other nations? By putting ourselves in a condition to punish them. Weakness provokes insult and injury, while a condition to punish, often prevents them.

To John Jay, Paris, August 23, 1785.

Those who labor in the earth are the chosen people of God, if ever He had a chosen people, whose breasts He has made His peculiar deposit for substantial and genuine virtue. It is the focus in which he keeps alive that sacred fire, which otherwise might escape from the face of the earth. Corruption of morals in the mass of cultivators is a phenomenon of which no age nor nation has furnished an example. It is the mark set on those, who, not looking up to heaven, to their own soil and industry, as does the husbandman, for their subsistence, depend for it on casualties and caprice of customers. Dependence begets subservience and venality, suffocates the germ of virtue, and prepares fit tools for the designs of ambition. . . .

Generally speaking, the proportion which the aggregate of the other classes of citizens bears in any State to that of its husbandmen, is the proportion of its unsound to its healthy parts, and is a good enough barometer whereby to measure its degree of corruption. While we have land to labor then, let us never wish to see our citizens occupied at a work-bench, or twirling a distaff. Carpenters, masons, smiths, are wanting in husbandry; but, for the

general operations of manufacture, let our workshops remain in
Europe. It is better to carry provisions and materials to workmen
there, than bring them to the provisions and materials, and with
them their manners and principles. The loss by the transportation
of commodities across the Atlantic will be made up in happiness
and permanence of government. The mobs of great cities add just
so much to the support of pure government, as sores do to the
strength of the human body.

From *Notes on Virginia*.

ELIMINATING "ARTIFICIAL" CLASS DISTINCTIONS

An industrious farmer occupies a more dignified place in the
scale of beings, whether moral or political, than a lazy lounger,
valuing himself on his family, too proud to work, and drawing out
a miserable existence by eating on the surplus of other men's labor,
which is the sacred fund of the helpless poor.

To Jean Nicolas de Meusnier, 1786.

It should be further considered, that in America no other distinction between man and man had ever been known, but that of
persons in office, exercising powers by authority of the laws, and
private individuals. Among these last, the poorest laborer stood on
equal ground with the wealthiest millionaire, and generally on a
more favored one, whenever their rights seemed to jar. It has been
seen that a shoemaker or other artisan, removed by the voice of his
country from his work bench into a chair of office, has instantly
commanded all the respect and obedience which the laws ascribe
to his office. But of distinction by birth or badge, they had no more
idea than they had of the mode of existence in the moon or planets.
They had heard only that there were such, and knew that they must
be wrong. A due horror of the evils which flow from these
distinctions, could be excited in Europe only, where the dignity of
man is lost in arbitrary distinctions, where the human species is
classed into several stages of degradation, where the many are

crushed under the weight of the few, and where the order established, can present to the contemplation of a thinking being, no
other picture than that of God Almighty and his angels, trampling
under foot the host of the damned.

To Jean Nicolas de Meusnier, 1786.

I agree with you that there is a natural aristocracy among men.
The grounds of this are virtue and talents. Formerly, bodily powers
gave place among the *aristoi*. But since the invention of gunpow-
der has armed the weak as well as the strong with missile death,
bodily strength like beauty, good humor, politeness, and other
accomplishments has become but an auxiliary ground of distinction. There is also an artificial aristocracy, founded on wealth and
birth, without either virtue or talents; for with these it would
belong to the first class. The natural aristocracy I consider as the
most precious gift of nature for the instruction, the trusts, and
government of society. And, indeed, it would have been inconsistent in creation to have formed man for the social state and not to
have provided virtue and wisdom enough to manage the concerns
of the society. May we not even say that that form of government is
the best which provides the most effectually for a pure selection of
these natural *aristoi* into the offices of government? The artificial
aristocracy is a mischievous ingredient in government, and provision should be made to prevent its ascendency. On the question
what is the best provision, you and I differ, but we differ as rational
friends, using the free exercise of our own reason and mutually
indulging its errors. You think it best to put the pseudo-*aristoi* into
a separate chamber of legislation, where they may be hindered
from doing mischief by their co-ordinate branches and where,
also, they may be a protection to wealth against the agrarian and
plundering enterprises of the majority of the people. I think that to
give them power in order to prevent them from doing mischief is
arming them for it and increasing instead of remedying the evil.

To John Adams, Monticello, October 28, 1813.

* * *

WISDOM OF "OUR COMMON PEOPLE"

Our act for freedom of religion* is extremely applauded. The ambassadors and ministers of the several nations of Europe, resident at this Court have asked of me copies of it to send to their sovereigns, and it is inserted at full length in several books now in the press—among others, in the new *Encyclopédie*. I think it will produce considerable good even in these countries where ignorance, superstition, poverty, and oppression of body and mind in every form are so firmly settled on the mass of the people that their redemption from them can never be hoped. If all the sovereigns of Europe were to set themselves to work to emancipate the minds of their subjects from their present ignorance and prejudices, and that as zealously as they now endeavor the contrary, a thousand years would not place them on that high ground on which our common people are now setting out. Ours could not have been so fairly placed under the control of the common sense of the people had they not been separated from their parent stock and kept from contamination, either from them or the other people of the old world, by the intervention of so wide an ocean. To know the worth of this, one must see the want of it here. I think by far the most important bill in our whole code is that for the diffusion of knowledge among the people. No other sure foundation can be devised for the preservation of freedom and happiness. If anybody thinks that kings, nobles, or priests are good conservators of the public happiness, send him here. It is the best school in the universe to cure him of that folly. He will see here with his own eyes that these descriptions of men are an abandoned confederacy against the happiness of the mass of the people. The omnipotence of their effect cannot be better proved than in this country particularly, where, notwithstanding the finest soil upon earth, the finest climate under heaven, and a people of the most benevolent, the most gay and amiable character of which the human form is susceptible—where such people, I say, surrounded by so many blessings from nature, are loaded with misery, by kings, nobles, and priests, and by them alone. Preach, my dear Sir, a crusade against ignorance. Establish and improve the law for educating the

---

*Statute of Virginia for Religious Freedom, 1786.

common people. Let our countrymen know that the people alone can protect us against these evils, and that the tax which will be paid for this purpose is not more than the thousandth part of what will be paid to kings, priests, and nobles, who will rise up among us if we leave the people in ignorance.

To George Wythe, Paris, August 13, 1786.

The doctrines of Europe were that men in numerous associations cannot be restrained within the limits of order and justice but by forces physical and moral wielded over them by authorities independent of their will—hence their organization of kings, hereditary nobles, and priests. Still further, to constrain the brute force of the people, they deem it necessary to keep them down by hard labor, poverty, and ignorance; and to take from them, as from bees, so much of their earnings as that unremitting labor shall be necessary to obtain a sufficient surplus barely to sustain a scanty and miserable life. And these earnings they apply to maintain their privileged orders in splendor and idleness, to fascinate the eyes of the people, and excite in them a humble adoration and submission, as to an order of superior beings. Although few among us had gone all these lengths of opinion, yet many had advanced, some more, some less, on the way. And in the convention which formed our government, they endeavored to draw the cords of power as tight as they could obtain them, to lessen the dependence of the general functionaries on their constituents, to subject to them those of the States, and to weaken their means of maintaining the steady equilibrium which the majority of the convention had deemed salutary for both branches, general and local. To recover, therefore, in practice, the powers which the nation had refused, and to warp to their own wishes those actually given, was the steady object of the federal party. Ours, on the contrary, was to maintain the will of the majority of the convention and of the people themselves. We believed, with them, that man was a rational animal, endowed by nature with rights, and with an innate sense of justice; and that he could be restrained from wrong and protected in right by moderate powers confided to persons of his own choice and held to their duties by dependence on his own will. We believed that the complicated organization of kings, nobles, and priests was not the wisest nor best to effect the happiness of associated man, that wisdom and virtue were not hereditary, that the trappings of such a machinery consumed by their expense those earnings of industry they were meant to protect and by the inequalities they produced exposed liberty to sufferance. We believed that men, enjoying in ease and security the full fruits of their own industry, enlisted by all their interests on the side of law and order, habituated to think for themselves and to follow their reason as their guide, would be more easily and safely governed than with minds nourished in error and vitiated and debased, as in Europe, by ignorance, indigence, and oppression. The cherishment of the people then was our principle, the fear and distrust of them that of the other party.

To William Johnson, Monticello, June 12, 1823.

The storm through which we have passed has been tremendous indeed. The tough sides of our argosy have been thoroughly tried. Her strength has stood the waves into which she was steered with a view to sink her. We shall put her on her republican tack, and she will now show by the beauty of her motion the skill of her builders. Figure apart, our fellow citizens have been led hoodwinked from their principles by a most extraordinary combination of circumstances. But the band is removed, and they now see for themselves. I hope to see shortly a perfect consolidation, to effect which nothing shall be spared on my part short of the abandonment of the principles of our revolution. A just and solid republican government maintained here will be a standing monument and example for the aim and imitation of the people of other countries, and I join with you in the hope and belief that they will see, from our example, that a free government is of all others the most energetic, that the inquiry which has been excited among the mass of mankind by our revolution and its consequences will ameliorate the condition of man over a great portion of the globe. What a satisfaction have we in the contemplation of the benevolent effects of our efforts, compared with those of the leaders on the other side, who have discountenanced all advances in science as dangerous inno-

vations, have endeavored to render philosophy and republicanism
terms of reproach, to persuade us that man cannot be governed but
by the rod, etc. I shall have the happiness of living and dying in the
contrary hope.

To John Dickinson, Washington, March 6, 1801.

In the great work which has been effected in America, no
individual has a right to take any great share to himself. Our people
in a body are wise because they are under the unrestrained and
unperverted operation of their own understandings. Those whom
we have assigned to the direction of their affairs have stood with a
pretty even front. If any one of them was withdrawn, many others
entirely equal have been ready to fill his place with as good
abilities. A nation composed of such materials and free in all its
members from distressing wants furnishes hopeful implements for
the interesting experiment of self-government, and we feel that we
are acting under obligations not confined to the limits of our own
society. It is impossible not to be sensible that we are acting for all
mankind; that circumstances denied to others but indulged to us
have imposed on us the duty of proving what is the degree of
freedom and self-government in which a society may venture to
leave its individual members.

To Joseph Priestley, Washington, June 19, 1802.

I have no fear but that the result of our experiment will be that
men may be trusted to govern themselves without a master. Could
the contrary of this be proved, I should conclude either that there is
no God or that he is a malevolent being.

To David Hartley, Paris, July 2, 1787.

Convinced that the republican is the only form of government
which is not eternally at open or secret war with the rights of
mankind, my prayers and efforts shall be cordially distributed to

the support of that we have so happily established. It is indeed an animating thought that, while we are securing the rights of ourselves and our posterity, we are pointing out the way to struggling nations who wish like us to emerge from their tyrannies also. Heaven help their struggles and lead them, as it has done us, triumphantly through them.

To William Hunter, Alexandria, March 11, 1790.

The spirit of 1776 is not dead. It has only been slumbering. The body of the American people is substantially republican.

To Thomas Lomax, Monticello, March 12, 1799.

We think, in America, that it is necessary to introduce the people into every department of government as far as they are capable of exercising it, and that this is the only way to insure a long continued and honest administration of its powers.

1. They are not qualified to exercise themselves the executive department, but they are qualified to name the person who shall exercise it. With us, therefore, they choose this officer every four years. 2. They are not qualified to legislate. With us, therefore, they only choose the legislators. 3. They are not qualified to judge questions of *law*, but they are very capable of judging questions of *fact*. In the form of juries, therefore, they determine all matters of fact, leaving to the permanent judges to decide the law resulting from those facts. But we all know that permanent judges acquire an *esprit de corps*; that, being known, they are liable to be tempted by bribery; that they are misled by favor, by relationship, by a spirit of party, by a devotion to the executive or legislative power; that it is better to leave a cause to the decision of cross and pile than to that of a judge biased to one side; and that the opinion of twelve honest jurymen gives still a better hope of right than cross and pile does. It is left, therefore, to the juries, if they think the permanent judges are under any bias whatever in any cause, to take on themselves to judge the law as well as the fact. They never exercise this power but when they suspect partiality in the judges, and by the exercise

of this power they have been the firmest bulwarks of English liberty. Were I called upon to decide whether the people had best be omitted in the legislative or judiciary department, I would say it is better to leave them out of the legislature. The execution of the laws is more important than the making of them. However, it is best to have the people in all the three departments, where that is possible.

To the Abbé Arnoud, Paris, July 19, 1789.

You seem . . . to consider the judges as the ultimate arbiters of all constitutional questions, a very dangerous doctrine indeed and one which would place us under the despotism of an oligarchy. Our judges are as honest as other men and not more so. They have with others the same passions for party, for power, and the privilege of their corps. Their maxim is *boni judicis est ampliare jurisdictionem*,* and their power the more dangerous as they are in office for life and not responsible, as the other functionaries are, to the elective control. The constitution has erected no such single tribunal, knowing that, to whatever hands confided, with the corruptions of time and party its members would become despots. It has more wisely made all the departments co-equal and co-sovereign within themselves. If the legislature fails to pass laws for a census, for paying the judges and other officers of government, for establishing a militia, for naturalization as prescribed by the constitution, or if they fail to meet in congress, the judges cannot issue their mandamus to them; if the President fails to supply the place of a judge, to appoint other civil or military officers, to issue requisite commissions, the judges cannot force him. They can issue their mandamus or distringas to no executive or legislative officer to enforce the fulfillment of their official duties, any more than the President or legislature may issue orders to the judges or their officers. . . .

The judges certainly have more frequent occasion to act on constitutional questions, because the laws of mine and thine and of criminal action forming the great mass of the system of law

---

*"A good judge expands his jurisdiction."—*Editor's translation*.

constitute their particular department. When the legislative or executive functionaries act unconstitutionally, they are responsible to the people in their elective capacity. The exemption of the judges from that is quite dangerous enough. I know no safe depository of the ultimate powers of the society but the people themselves, and, if we think them not enlightened enough to exercise their control with a wholesome discretion, the remedy is not to take it from them but to inform their discretion by education. This is the true corrective of abuses of constitutional power.

To William C. Jarvis, Monticello, September 28, 1820.

The tumults in America [Shays's Rebellion] I expected would have produced in Europe an unfavorable opinion of our political state. But it has not. On the contrary, the small effect of these tumults seems to have given more confidence in the firmness of our governments. The interposition of the people themselves on the side of government has had a great effect on the opinion here. I am persuaded myself that the good sense of the people will always be found to be the best army. They may be led astray for a moment but will soon correct themselves. The people are the only censors of their governors, and even their errors will tend to keep these to the true principles of their institution. To punish these errors too severely would be to suppress the only safeguard of the public liberty. The way to prevent these irregular interpositions of the people is to give them full information of their affairs through the channel of the public papers, and to contrive that those papers should penetrate the whole mass of the people. The basis of our governments being the opinion of the people, the very first object should be to keep that right; and were it left to me to decide whether we should have a government without newspapers or newspapers without a government I should not hesitate a moment to prefer the latter. But I should mean that every man should receive those papers and be capable of reading them.

To Edward Carrington, Paris, January 16, 1787.

* * *

A METHOD OF SELF-GOVERNMENT: THE WARD SYSTEM

If it is believed that these elementary schools will be better managed by the governor and council, the commissioners of the literary fund, or any other general authority of the government, than by the parents within each ward, it is a belief against all experience. Try the principle one step further and amend the bill so as to commit to the governor and council the management of all our farms, our mills, and merchants' stores. No, my friend, the way to have good and safe government is not to trust it all to one but to divide it among the many, distributing to everyone exactly the functions he is competent to. Let the national government be entrusted with the defense of the nation and its foreign and federal relations; the State governments with the civil rights, laws, police, and administration of what concerns the State generally; the counties with the local concerns of the counties, and each ward direct the interests within itself. It is by dividing and subdividing these republics from the great national one down through all its subordinations until it ends in the administration of every man's farm by himself, by placing under everyone what his own eye may superintend, that all will be done for the best. What has destroyed liberty and the rights of man in every government which has ever existed under the sun? The generalizing and concentrating all cares and powers into one body, no matter whether of the autocrats of Russia or France, or of the aristocrats of a Venetian senate. And I do believe that if the Almighty has not decreed that man shall never be free (and it is a blasphemy to believe it), that the secret will be found to be in the making himself the depository of the powers respecting himself, so far as he is competent to them, and delegating only what is beyond his competence by a synthetical process to higher and higher orders of functionaries, so as to trust fewer and fewer powers in proportion as the trustees become more and more oligarchical. The elementary republics of the wards, the county republics, the State republics, and the republic of the Union would form a gradation of authorities, standing each on the basis of law, holding every one its delegated share of powers, and constituting truly a system of fundamental balances and checks for the government. Where every man is a sharer in the direction of his ward-republic, or of some of the higher ones, and feels that he is a participator in the government of affairs, not merely at an election one day in the year but every day; when there shall not be a man in the State who will not be a member of some one of its councils, great or small, he will let the heart be torn out of his body sooner than his power be wrested from him by a Caesar or a Bonaparte. How powerfully did we feel the energy of this organization in the case of embargo? I felt the foundations of the government shaken under my feet by the New England townships . . . As Cato, then, concluded every speech with the words, *"Carthago delenda est,"* so do I every opinion with the injunction, "divide the counties into wards." Begin them only for a single purpose; they will soon show for what others they are the best instruments.

To Joseph C. Cabell, Monticello, February 2, 1816.

At the first session of our legislature after the Declaration of Independence we passed a law abolishing entails. And this was followed by one abolishing the privilege of primogeniture and dividing the lands of intestates equally among all their children or other representatives. These laws, drawn by myself, laid the axe to the foot of pseudo-aristocracy. And had another which I prepared been adopted by the legislature, our work would have been complete. It was a bill for the more general diffusion of learning. This proposed to divide every county into wards of five or six miles square, like your townships; to establish in each ward a free school for reading, writing, and common arithmetic; to provide for the annual selection of the best subjects from these schools, who might receive at the public expense a higher degree of education at a district school; and from these district schools to select a certain number of the most promising subjects to be completed at a University, where all the useful sciences should be taught. Worth and genius would thus have been sought out from every condition of life and completely prepared by education for defeating the competition of wealth and birth for public trusts. My proposition had, for a further object, to impart to these wards those portions of self-government for which they are best qualified, by confiding to them the care of their poor, their roads, police, elections, the nomination of jurors, administration of justice in small cases, elementary exercises of militia; in short, to have made them little republics with a warden at the head of each for all those concerns which, being under their eye, they would better manage than the larger republics of the county or State. A general call of ward meetings by their wardens on the same day through the State would at any time produce the genuine sense of the people on any required point and would enable the State to act in mass, as your people have so often done and with so much effect by their town meetings. The law for religious freedom, which made a part of this system, having put down the aristocracy of the clergy and restored to the citizen the freedom of the mind, and those of entails and descents nurturing an equality of condition among them, this on education would have raised the mass of the people to the high ground of moral respectability necessary to their own safety and to orderly government, and would have completed the great object of qualifying them to select the veritable *aristoi* for the trusts of government.

To John Adams, Monticello, October 28, 1813.

Virginia, of which I am myself a native and resident, was not only the first of the States, but, I believe I may say, the first of the nations of the earth, which assembled its wise men peaceably together to form a fundamental constitution, to commit it to writing, and place it among their archives, where every one should be free to appeal to its text. But this act was very imperfect.

My own State . . . is now proposing to call a convention for amendment. Among other improvements, I hope they will adopt the subdivision of our counties into wards. The former may be estimated at an average of twenty-four miles square; the latter should be about six miles square each, and would answer to the hundreds of your Saxon Alfred. In each of these might be: 1st. an elementary school; 2nd. a company of militia with its officers; 3rd. a justice of the peace and constable; 4th. each ward should take care of their own poor; 5th. their own roads; 6th. their own police; 7th. elect within themselves one or more jurors to attend the courts of justice; and, 8th. give in at their Folkhouse their votes for all functionaries reserved to their election. Each ward would thus be a small republic within itself, and every man in the State would thus become an acting member of the common government, transacting in person a great portion of its rights and duties, subordinate indeed, yet important, and entirely within his competence. The wit of man cannot devise a more solid basis for a free, durable, and well administered republic.

To John Cartwright, Monticello, June 5, 1824.

MAJORITY RULE, MINORITY RIGHTS: A SUMMARY

Friends and Fellow Citizens:

Called upon to undertake the duties of the first executive office of our country, I avail myself of the presence of that portion of my fellow citizens which is here assembled to express my grateful thanks for the favor with which they have been pleased to look toward me, to declare a sincere consciousness that the task is above my talents, and that I approach it with those anxious and awful presentiments which the greatness of the charge and the weakness of my powers so justly inspire. A rising nation, spread over a wide and fruitful land, traversing all the seas with the rich productions of their industry, engaged in commerce with nations who feel power and forget right, advancing rapidly to destinies beyond the reach of mortal eye—when I contemplate these transcendent objects and see the honor, the happiness, and the hopes of this beloved country committed to the issue and the auspices of this day, I shrink from the contemplation and humble myself before the magnitude of the undertaking. Utterly indeed should I despair did not the presence of many whom I here see remind me that in the other high authorities provided by our Constitution I shall find resources of wisdom, of virtue, and of zeal on which to rely under all difficulties. To you then, gentlemen, who are charged with the sovereign functions of legislation, and to those associated with you, I look with encouragement for that guidance and support which may enable us to steer with safety the vessel in which we are all embarked amidst the conflicting elements of a troubled world.

During the contest of opinion through which we have passed, the animation of discussions and of exertions has sometimes worn an aspect which might impose on strangers unused to think freely and to speak and to write what they think. But this being now decided by the voice of the nation, announced according to the rules of the Constitution, all will of course arrange themselves under the will of the law and unite in common efforts for the common good. All, too, will bear in mind this sacred principle that, though the will of the majority is in all cases to prevail, that will, to be rightful, must be reasonable; that the minority possess their equal rights, which equal laws must protect and to violate which would be oppression. Let us then, fellow citizens, unite with one heart and one mind; let us restore to social intercourse that harmony and affection without which liberty, and even life itself, are but dreary things. And let us reflect that, having banished from our land that religious intolerance under which mankind so long bled and suffered, we have yet gained little if we countenance a political intolerance as despotic, as wicked, and capable of as bitter and bloody persecutions. During the throes and convulsions of the ancient world, during the agonizing spasm of infuriated man, seeking through blood and slaughter his long-lost liberty, it was not wonderful that the agitation of the billows should reach even this distant and peaceful shore, that this should be more felt and feared by some and less by others, and should divide opinions as to measures of safety.

But every difference of opinion is not a difference of principle. We have called by different names brethren of the same principle. We are all republicans; we are all federalists. If there be any among us who would wish to dissolve this Union or to change its republican form, let them stand undisturbed as monuments of the safety with which error of opinion may be tolerated, where reason is left free to combat it. I know, indeed, that some honest men fear that a republican government cannot be strong; that this government is not strong enough. But would the honest patriot, in the full tide of successful experiment, abandon a government which has so far kept us free and firm, on the theoretic and visionary fear that this government, the world's best hope, may by possibility want energy to preserve itself? I trust not. I believe this, on the contrary, the strongest government on earth. I believe it the only one where every man, at the call of the law, would fly to the standard of the law and would meet invasions of the public order as his own personal concern. Sometimes it is said that man cannot be trusted with the government of himself. Can he then be trusted with the government of others? Or have we found angels, in the form of kings, to govern him? Let history answer this question.

Let us then, with courage and confidence, pursue our own federal and republican principles, our attachment to Union and representative government. Kindly separated by nature and a wide ocean from the exterminating havoc of one quarter of the globe; too high-minded to endure the degradations of the others; possessing a chosen country, with room enough for our descendants to the thousandth and thousandth generation; entertaining a due sense of our equal right to the use of our own faculties, to the acquisitions of our own industry, to honor and confidence from our fellow citizens, resulting not from birth but from our actions and their sense of them; enlightened by a benign religion, professed indeed and practiced in various forms, yet all of them including honesty, truth, temperance, gratitude, and the love of man; acknowledging and adoring an overruling Providence which, by all its dispensations, proves that It delights in the happiness of man here and his greater happiness hereafter; with all these blessings, what more is necessary to make us a happy and a prosperous people? Still one thing more, fellow citizens—a wise and frugal government which shall restrain men from injuring one another, shall leave them otherwise free to regulate their own pursuits of industry and improvement, and shall not take from the mouth of labor the bread it has earned. This is the sum of good government, and this is necessary to close the circle of our felicities.

About to enter, fellow citizens, on the exercise of duties which comprehend everything dear and valuable to you, it is proper you should understand what I deem the essential principles of our government and, consequently, those which ought to shape its administration. I will compress them within the narrowest compass they will bear, stating the general principle but not all its limitations: Equal and exact justice to all men, of whatever state or persuasion, religious or political; peace, commerce, and honest friendship with all nations, entangling alliances with none; the support of the State governments in all their rights, as the most competent administrations for our domestic concerns and the surest bulwarks against anti-republican tendencies; the preservation of the general government in its whole constitutional vigor, as the sheet anchor of our peace at home and safety abroad; a jealous care of the right of election by the people, a mild and safe corrective of abuses which are lopped by the sword of revolution where peaceable remedies are unprovided; absolute acquiescence in the decisions of the majority, the vital principle of republics from which there is no appeal but to force, the vital principle and immediate parent of despotism; a well-disciplined militia, our best reliance in peace and for the first moments of war till regulars may relieve them; the supremacy of the civil over the military authority; economy in the public expense, that labor may be lightly burdened; the honest payment of our debts and sacred preservation of the public faith; encouragement of agriculture, and of commerce as its handmaid; the diffusion of information, and arraignment of all abuses at the bar of the public reason; freedom of religion; freedom of the press; freedom of person, under the protection of the habeas corpus; and trial by juries, impartially selected. These principles form the bright constellation which has gone before us and guided our steps through an age of revolution and reformation. The wisdom of our sages and blood of our heroes have been devoted to their attainment; they should be the creed of our political faith, the text of civic instruction, the touchstone by which to try the services of those we trust; and should we wander from them in moments of error or of alarm, let us hasten to retrace our steps and to regain the road which alone leads to peace, liberty, and safety.

I repair then, fellow citizens, to the post you have assigned me. With experience enough in subordinate offices to have seen the difficulties of this, the greatest of all, I have learned to expect that it will rarely fall to the lot of imperfect man to retire from this station with the reputation and the favor which bring him into it. Without pretensions to that high confidence you reposed in our first and great revolutionary character, whose pre-eminent services had entitled him to the first place in his country's love and destined for him the fairest page in the volume of faithful history, I ask so much confidence only as may give firmness and effect to the legal administration of your affairs. I shall often go wrong through defect of judgment. When right, I shall often be thought wrong by those whose positions will not command a view of the whole ground. I ask your indulgence for my own errors, which will never be intentional, and your support against the errors of others who may condemn what they would not if seen in all its parts. The approbation implied by your suffrage is a great consolation to me for the past, and my future solicitude will be to retain the good opinion of those who have bestowed it in advance, to conciliate that of others by doing them all the good in my power, and to be instrumental to the happiness and freedom of all.

Relying then on the patronage of your good will, I advance with obedience to the work, ready to retire from it whenever you become sensible how much better choice it is in your power to make. And may that Infinite Power which rules the destinies of the universe lead our councils to what is best and give them a favorable issue for your peace and prosperity.

First Inaugural Address, March 4, 1801.

B. *Thomas Paine:* "The Last Cord Now Is Broken . . ."

The place of Thomas Paine (1737-1809) in the tradition of American populism is less secure than that of Jefferson, who can be safely quoted or eulogized by anyone identified with "the plain people." In contrast, Paine's reputation has never quite shed the stigma of disreputability given it by his political opponents: "The filthy Tom Paine." John Adams' epithet opened a wound which has still not completely healed, despite the fact that Paine, befriended by Jefferson in his later life, professed a political credo almost identical with that of Jefferson. Paine, to be sure, was less specifically "American," much more sanguine in his cosmopolitanism, than Jefferson. He saw the American Revolution as a spark for world revolution; one of his longest works was a defense of the ill-fated French Revolution. Paine has thus suffered from the nativist backlash against things "alien," especially alien revolutions. But even here the difference between Paine and Jefferson is one more of emphasis than principle; Jefferson was hardly less enthusiastic about the French Revolution, and equally full of "decent respect to the opinions of mankind." The question remains, then, why Paine should be less securely a populist figure, less esteemed by the "plain people" as an unchallengeable spokesman for their interests.

The main reason, surely, is Paine's outspoken hostility to Christianity, especially fundamentalist Christianity. The Western farmers who gave populism its name in the nineteenth century were nothing if not religious, and their religion consisted not of abstract hypothesizing but passionate affirmation—in the literal truth of Scripture, in divine intervention, in the divinity of Jesus, in mystery and mysticism. When Paine scornfully attacked all these aspects of Christianity in *The Age of Reason*, a pamphlet published in 1794, he provided his enemies with a perfect weapon for character assassination, and they used it so well that a century later Paine was still being called a "filthy little atheist." Actually Paine was not an atheist but a deist, but this distinction seemed excessively fine to those who could not forget his anti-Christian polemic. Certainly the Western farmer could not be expected to take kindly to such bohemian types.

And yet Paine, by his life and his writings, can claim membership in the American populist tradition as well as anyone else. Like Jefferson, he preached the rights of the common man, whose intelligence and dignity he believed to be the equal of any nobleman. Unlike Jefferson, he was himself of humble origin, and remained poor his entire life. The son of a corset-maker, he eked out a precarious existence in England as a stay-maker, a sailor, and a tax collector until he lost his job and almost landed in a debtor's prison. His flight to America brought somewhat better times, but he still endured privation with a ragged Revolutionary army, voluntarily waived royalties from his enormously popular pamphlets, finally died a poor man in a miserable rooming house. Paine's style of writing, like his style of living, was simple, unassuming, perfectly suited to the mass audience to which it appealed.

The selection is taken from *Common Sense* which was first published in January, 1776. It became an instant best-seller and had much to do with the radicalization of American attitudes which culminated in Jefferson's dramatic Declaration six months later. Starting from the basis of republican principles, it systematically demolished all the claims which Britain had made upon America. In its avoidance of legalistic arguments, in its favoring of "simple facts, plain arguments, and common sense," in its majoritarianism, in its shrewd appeal both to the nationalism and self-interest of Americans, *Common Sense* remains a classic populist tract.

ON THE ORIGIN AND DESIGN OF GOVERNMENT IN GENERAL, WITH CONCISE REMARKS ON THE ENGLISH CONSTITUTION

Some writers have so confounded society with government, as to leave little or no distinction between them; whereas they are not only different, but have different origins. Society is produced by our wants and government by our wickedness; the former promotes our happiness *positively* by uniting our affections, the latter *negatively* by restraining our vices. The one encourages intercourse, the other creates distinctions. The first is a patron, the last a punisher.

Society in every state is a blessing, but government, even in its best state, is but a necessary evil; in its worst state an intolerable one: for when we suffer, or are exposed to the same miseries *by a government*, which we might expect in a country *without government*, our calamity is heightened by reflecting that we furnish the means by which we suffer. Government, like dress, is the badge of lost innocence; the palaces of kings are built upon the ruins of the bowers of paradise. For were the impulses of conscience clear, uniform and irresistibly obeyed, man would need no other law-giver; but that not being the case, he finds it necessary to surrender up a part of his property to furnish means for the protection of the rest; and this he is induced to do by the same prudence which in every other case advises him, out of two evils to choose the least. Wherefore, security being the true design and end of government, it unanswerably follows that whatever form thereof appears most likely to ensure it to us, with the least expence and greatest benefit, is preferable to all others.

In order to gain a clear and just idea of the design and end of government, let us suppose a small number of persons settled in some sequestered part of the earth, unconnected with the rest; they will then represent the first peopling of any country, or of the world. In this state of natural liberty, society will be their first thought. A thousand motives will excite them thereto; the strength of one man is so unequal to his wants, and his mind so unfitted for perpetual solitude, that he is soon obliged to seek assistance and relief of another, who in his turn requires the same. Four or five united would be able to raise a tolerable dwelling in the midst of a wilderness, but one man might labor out the common period of life without accomplishing any thing; when he had felled his timber he could not remove it, nor erect it after it was removed; hunger in the mean time would urge him to quit his work, and every different want would call him a different way. Disease, nay even misfortune, would be death; for though neither might be mortal, yet either would disable him from living, and reduce him to a state in which he might rather be said to perish than to die.

Thus necessity, like a gravitating power, would soon form our newly arrived emigrants into society, the reciprocal blessings of which would supersede, and render the obligations of law and government unnecessary while they remained perfectly just to each other; but as nothing but Heaven is impregnable to vice, it will unavoidably happen that in proportion as they surmount the first difficulties of emigration, which bound them together in a common cause, they will begin to relax in their duty and attachment to each other: and this remissness will point out the necessity of establishing some form of government to supply the defect of moral virtue.

Some convenient tree will afford them a State House, under the branches of which the whole colony may assemble to deliberate on public matters. It is more than probable that their first laws will have the title only of regulations and be enforced by no other penalty than public disesteem. In this first parliament every man by natural right will have a seat.

But as the colony increases, the public concerns will increase likewise, and the distance at which the members may be separated, will render it too inconvenient for all of them to meet on every occasion as at first, when their number was small, their habitations near, and the public concerns few and trifling. This will point out the convenience of their consenting to leave the legislative part to be managed by a select number chosen from the whole body, who are supposed to have the same concerns at stake which those have who appointed them, and who will act in the same manner as the whole body would act were they present. If the colony continue increasing, it will become necessary to augment the number of representatives, and that the interest of every part of the colony may be attended to, it will be found best to divide the whole into convenient parts, each part sending its proper number: and that the *elected* might never form to themselves an interest separate from the *electors*, prudence will point out the propriety of having elections often: because as the *elected* might by that means return and mix again with the general body of the *electors* in a few months, their fidelity to the public will be secured by the prudent reflection of not making a rod for themselves. And as this frequent interchange will establish a common interest with every part of the community, they will mutually and naturally support each other, and on this, (not on the unmeaning name of king,) depends the *strength of government, and the happiness of the governed*.

Here then is the origin and rise of government; namely, a mode rendered necessary by the inability of moral virtue to govern the world; here too is the design and end of government, viz. freedom and security. And however our eyes may be dazzled with show, or our ears deceived by sound; however prejudice may warp our wills, or interest darken our understanding, the simple voice of nature and reason will say, 'tis right.

OF MONARCHY AND HEREDITARY SUCCESSION

Mankind being originally equals in the order of creation, the equality could only be destroyed by some subsequent circumstance: the distinctions of rich and poor may in a great measure be accounted for, and that without having recourse to the harsh ill-sounding names of oppression and avarice. Oppression is often the *consequence*, but seldom or never the *means* of riches; and though avarice will preserve a man from being necessitously poor, it generally makes him too timorous to be wealthy.

But there is another and greater distinction for which no truly natural or religious reason can be assigned, and that is the distinction of men into KINGS and SUBJECTS. Male and female are the distinctions of nature, good and bad the distinctions of heaven; but how a race of men came into the world so exalted above the rest, and distinguished like some new species, is worth inquiring into, and whether they are the means of happiness or of misery to mankind.

In the early ages of the world, according to the scripture chronology there were no kings; the consequence of which was, there were no wars; it is the pride of kings which throws mankind into confusion. Holland, without a king, hath enjoyed more peace for this last century than any of the monarchical governments of Europe. Antiquity favors the same remark; for the quiet and rural lives of the first Patriarchs have a happy something in them, which vanishes when we come to the history of Jewish royalty.

Government by kings was first introduced into the world by the heathens, from whom the children of Israel copied the custom. It was the most prosperous invention the devil ever set on foot for the promotion of idolatry. The heathens paid divine honors to their deceased kings, and the Christian world has improved on the plan by doing the same to their living ones. How impious is the title of sacred majesty applied to a worm, who in the midst of his splendor is crumbling into dust!

THOUGHTS ON THE PRESENT STATE
OF AMERICAN AFFAIRS

In the following pages I offer nothing more than simple facts, plain arguments, and common sense: and have no other preliminaries to settle with the reader, than that he will divest himself of prejudice and prepossession, and suffer his reason and his feelings to determine for themselves: that he will put on, or rather that he will not put off, the true character of a man, and generously enlarge his views beyond the present day.

Volumes have been written on the subject of the struggle between England and America. Men of all ranks have embarked in the controversy, from different motives, and with various designs; but all have been ineffectual, and the period of debate is closed. Arms as the last resource decide the contest; the appeal was the choice of the king, and the continent has accepted the challenge.

It hath been reported of the late Mr. Pelham (who though an able minister was not without his faults) that on his being attacked in the House of Commons on the score that his measures were only of a temporary kind, replied, *"they will last my time."* Should a thought so fatal and unmanly possess the colonies in the present contest, the name of ancestors will be remembered by future generations with detestation.

The sun never shone on a cause of greater worth. 'Tis not the affair of a city, a county, a province, or a kingdom; but of a continent—of at least one eighth part of the habitable globe. 'Tis not the concern of a day, a year, or an age; posterity are virtually involved in the contest, and will be more or less affected even to the end of time, by the proceedings now. Now is the seed-time of continental union, faith and honor. The least fracture now will be like a name engraved with the point of a pin on the tender rind of a young oak; the wound would enlarge with the tree, and posterity read it in full grown characters.

By referring the matter from argument to arms, a new era for politics is struck—a new method of thinkings has arisen. All plans, proposals, &c. prior to the nineteenth of April, *i.e.* to the commencement of hostilities, are like the almanacks of the last year; which though proper then, are superceded and useless now. Whatever was advanced by the advocates on either side of the question then, terminated in one and the same point, viz. a union with Great Britain; the only difference between the parties was the method of effecting it; the one proposing force, the other friendship; but it has so far happened that the first has failed, and the second has withdrawn her influence.

As much has been said of the advantages of reconciliation, which, like an agreeable dream, has passed away and left us as we were, it is but right that we should examine the contrary side of the argument, and inquire into some of the many material injuries which these colonies sustain, and always will sustain, by being connected with and dependant on Great Britain. To examine that connection and dependance, on the principles of nature and common sense, to see what we have to trust to, if separated, and what we are to expect, if dependant.

I have heard it asserted by some, that as America has flourished under her former connection with Great Britain, the same connection is necessary towards her future happiness, and will always have the same effect. Nothing can be more fallacious than this kind of argument. We may as well assert that because a child has thrived upon milk, that it is never to have meat, or that the first twenty years of our lives is to become a precedent for the next twenty. But even this is admitting more than is true; for I answer roundly, that America would have flourished as much, and probably much more, had no European power taken any notice of her. The commerce by which she hath enriched herself are the necessaries of life, and will always have a market while eating is the custom of Europe.

But she has protected us, say some. That she hath engrossed us is true, and defended the continent at our expense as well as her own, is admitted; and she would have defended Turkey from the same motive, *viz.* for the sake of trade and dominion.

Alas! we have been long led away by ancient prejudices and made large sacrifices to superstition. We have boasted the protection of Great Britain, without considering, that her motive was *interest* not *attachment*; and that she did not protect us from *our enemies* on *our account*; but from *her enemies* on *her own account*, from those who had no quarrel with us on any *other account*, and who will always be our enemies on the *same account*. Let Britain waive her pretensions to the continent, or the continent throw off the dependance, and we should be at peace with France and Spain, were they at war with Britain. The miseries of Hanover's last war ought to warn us against connections.

It hath lately been asserted in Parliament, that the colonies have no relation to each other but through the parent country, *i.e.* that Pennsylvania and the Jerseys, and so on for the rest, are sister colonies by the way of England; this is certainly a very roundabout way of proving relationship, but it is the nearest and only true way of proving enmity (or enemyship, if I may so call it.) France and Spain never were, nor perhaps ever will be, our enemies as *Americans*, but as our being the *subjects of Great Britain*.

But Britain is the parent country, say some. Then the more shame upon her conduct. Even brutes do not devour their young, nor savages make war upon their families; wherefore, the assertion, if true, turns to her reproach; but it happens not to be true, or only partly so, and the phrase *parent* or *mother country* hath been jesuitically adopted by the king and his parasites, with a low papistical design of gaining an unfair bias on the credulous weakness of our minds. Europe, and not England, is the parent country of America. This new world hath been the asylum for the persecuted lovers of civil and religious liberty from *every part* of Europe. Hither have they fled, not from the tender embraces of the mother, but from the cruelty of the monster; and it is so far true of England, that the same tyranny which drove the first emigrants from home, pursues their descendants still.

In this extensive quarter of the globe, we forget the narrow limits of three hundred and sixty miles (the extent of England) and carry our friendship on a larger scale; we claim brotherhood with every European Christian, and triumph in the generosity of the sentiment.

It is pleasant to observe by what regular gradations we surmount the force of local prejudices, as we enlarge our acquaintance with the world. A man born in any town in England divided into parishes, will naturally associate most with his fellow parishioners (because their interests in many cases will be common) and distinguish him by the name of *neighbor*; if he meet him but a few miles from home, he drops the narrow idea of a street, and salutes him by the name of *townsman*; if he travel out of the county and meet him in any other, he forgets the minor divisions of street and town, and calls him *countryman*, *i.e. countyman*; but if in their foreign excursions they should associate in France, or any other part of *Europe*, their local remembrance would be enlarged into that of *Englishman*. And by a just parity of reasoning, all Europeans meeting in America, or any other quarter of the globe, are *countrymen*; for England, Holland, Germany, or Sweden, when compared with the whole, stand in the same places on the larger scale, which the divisions of street, town, and county do on the smaller ones; distinctions too limited for continental minds. Not one third of the inhabitants, even of this province, [Pennsylvania], are of English descent. Wherefore, I reprobate the phrase of parent or mother country applied to England only, as being false, selfish, narrow and ungenerous.

But, admitting that we were all of English descent, what does it amount to? Nothing. Britain, being now an open enemy, extinguishes every other name and title: and to say that reconciliation is our duty, is truly farcical. The first king of England, of the present line (William the Conqueror) was a Frenchman, and half the peers of England are descendants from the same country; wherefore, by the same method of reasoning, England ought to be governed by France.

Much hath been said of the united strength of Britain and the colonies, that in conjunction they might bid defiance to the world. But this is mere presumption; the fate of war is uncertain, neither do the expressions mean any thing; for this continent would never suffer itself to be drained of inhabitants, to support the British arms in either Asia, Africa or Europe.

Besides, what have we to do with setting the world at defiance? Our plan is commerce, and that, well attended to, will secure us the peace and friendship of all Europe; because it is the interest of all Europe to have America a free port. Her trade will always be a protection, and her barrenness of gold and silver secure her from invaders.

I challenge the warmest advocate for reconciliation to show a single advantage that this continent can reap by being connected with Great Britain. I repeat the challenge; not a single advantage is derived. Our corn will fetch its price in any market in Europe, and our imported goods must be paid for, buy them where we will.

But the injuries and disadvantages which we sustain by that connection, are without number; and our duty to mankind at large, as well as to ourselves, instruct us to renounce the alliance: because, any submission to, or dependence on, Great Britain, tends directly to involve this continent in European wars and quarrels, and set us at variance with nations who would otherwise seek our friendship, and against whom we have neither anger nor complaint. As Europe is our market for trade, we ought to form no partial connection with any part of it. It is the true interest of America to steer clear of European contentions, which she never can do, while, by her dependence on Britain, she is made the make-weight in the scale of British politics.

Europe is too thickly planted with kingdoms to be long at peace, and whenever a war breaks out between England and any foreign power, the trade of America goes to ruin, *because of her connection with Britain*. The next war may not turn out like the last, and should it not, the advocates for reconciliation now will be wishing for separation then, because neutrality in that case would be a safer convoy than a man of war. Every thing that is right or reasonable pleads for separation. The blood of the slain, the weeping voice of nature cries, 'TIS TIME TO PART. Even the distance at which the Almighty hath placed England and America is a strong and natural proof that the authority of the one over the other, was never the design of heaven. The time likewise at which the continent was discovered, adds weight to the argument, and the manner in which it was peopled, encreases the force of it. The Reformation was preceded by the discovery of America: As if the Almighty graciously meant to open a sanctuary to the persecuted in future years, when home should afford neither friendship nor safety.

The authority of Great Britain over this continent, is a form of government, which sooner or later must have an end. And a serious mind can draw no true pleasure by looking forward, under the painful and positive conviction that what he calls "the present constitution" is merely temporary. As parents, we can have no joy, knowing that this government is not sufficiently lasting to insure any thing which we may bequeath to posterity. And by a plain method of argument, as we are running the next generation into debt, we ought to do the work of it, otherwise we use them meanly and pitifully. In order to discover the line of our duty rightly, we should take our children in our hand, and fix our station a few years farther into life; that eminence will present a prospect which a few present fears and prejudices conceal from our sight.

Though I would carefully avoid giving unnecessary offence, yet I am inclined to believe, that all those who espouse the doctrine of reconciliation, may be included within the following descriptions.

Interested men, who are not to be trusted, weak men who *cannot* see, prejudiced men who will not see, and a certain set of moderate men who think better of the European world than it deserves; and this last class, by an ill-judged deliberation, will be the cause of more calamities to this continent than all the other three.

It is the good fortune of many to live distant from the scene of present sorrow; the evil is not sufficiently brought to their doors to make them feel the precariousness with which all American property is possessed. But let our imaginations transport us a few moments to Boston; that seat of wretchedness will teach us wisdom, and instruct us for ever to renounce a power in whom we can have no trust. The inhabitants of that unfortunate city who but a few months ago were in ease and affluence, have now no other alternative than to stay and starve, or turn out to beg.* Endangered by the fire of their friends if they continue within the city, and plundered by the soldiery if they leave it, in their present situation they are prisoners without the hope of redemption, and in a general attack for their relief they would be exposed to the fury of both armies.

Men of passive tempers look somewhat lightly over the offences of Great Britain, and, still hoping for the best, are apt to call out, *Come, come, we shall be friends again for all this*. But examine the passions and feelings of mankind: bring the doctrine of reconciliation to the touchstone of nature, and then tell me whether you can hereafter love, honor, and faithfully serve the power that hath carried fire and sword into your land? If you cannot do all these, then are you only deceiving yourselves, and by your delay bringing ruin upon posterity. Your future connection with Britain, whom you can neither love nor honor, will be forced and unnatural, and being formed only on the plan of present convenience, will in a little time fall into a relapse more wretched than the first. But if you say, you can still pass the violations over, then I ask, hath your house been burnt? Hath your property been destroyed before your face? Are your wife and children destitute of a bed to lie on, or bread to live on? Have you lost a parent or a child by their hands, and yourself the ruined and wretched survivor? If you have not, then are you not a judge of those who have. But if you have, and can still shake hands with the murderers, then are you unworthy the name of husband, father, friend, or lover, and whatever may be your rank or title in life, you have the heart of a coward, and the spirit of a sycophant.

This is not inflaming or exaggerating matters, but trying them by those feelings and affections which nature justifies, and without which we should be incapable of discharging the social duties of

---

*Paine refers to the effects of the Coercive Acts, passed by Parliament in 1774 to retaliate for the Boston Tea Party. One of these acts, known as the Boston Port Bill, closed the Boston Harbor to all shipping until the East India Company, which transported the tea, was reimbursed. The act is reported to have caused widespread misery in Boston, putting some 15,000 people on the brink of starvation.—*Ed.*

life, or enjoying the felicities of it. I mean not to exhibit horror for the purpose of provoking revenge, but to awaken us from fatal and unmanly slumbers, that we may pursue determinately some fixed object. 'Tis not in the power of Britain or of Europe to conquer America, if she doth not conquer herself by delay and timidity. The present winter is worth an age if rightly employed, but if lost or neglected the whole continent will partake of the misfortune; and there is no punishment which that man doth not deserve, be he who, or what, or where he will, that may be the means of sacrificing a season so precious and useful.

'Tis repugnant to reason, to the universal order of things, to all examples from former ages, to suppose that this continent can long remain subject to any external power. The most sanguine in Britain doth not think so. The utmost stretch of human wisdom cannot, at this time, compass a plan, short of separation, which can promise the continent even a year's security. Reconciliation is *now* a fallacious dream. Nature has deserted the connection, and art cannot supply her place. For, as Milton wisely expresses, "never can true reconcilement grow where wounds of deadly hate have pierced so deep."

Every quiet method for peace hath been ineffectual. Our prayers have been rejected with disdain; and hath tended to convince us that nothing flatters vanity or confirms obstinacy in kings more than repeated petitioning—and nothing hath contributed more than that very measure to make the kings of Europe absolute. Witness Denmark and Sweden. Wherefore, since nothing but blows will do, for God's sake let us come to a final separation, and not leave the next generation to be cutting throats under the violated unmeaning names of parent and child.

To say they will never attempt it again is idle and visionary; we thought so at the repeal of the Stamp Act, yet a year or two undeceived us; as well may we suppose that nations which have been once defeated will never renew the quarrel.

As to government matters, 'tis not in the power of Britain to do this continent justice: the business of it will soon be too weighty and intricate to be managed with any tolerable degree of convenience, by a power so distant from us, and so very ignorant of us; for if they cannot conquer us, they cannot govern us. To be always running three or four thousand miles with a tale or a petition, waiting four or five months for an answer, which, when obtained, requires five or six more to explain it in, will in a few years be looked upon as folly and childishness. There was a time when it was proper, and there is a proper time for it to cease. Small islands not capable of protecting themselves are the proper objects for government to take under their care; but there is something absurd, in supposing a Continent to be perpetually governed by an island. In no instance hath nature made the satellite larger than its primary planet; and as England and America, with respect to each other, reverse the common order of nature, it is evident that they belong to different systems. England to Europe: America to itself.

I am not induced by motives of pride, party or resentment to espouse the doctrine of separation and independence; I am clearly, positively, and conscientiously persuaded that it is the true interest of this continent to be so; that everything short of *that* is mere patchwork, that it can afford no lasting felicity,—that it is leaving the sword to our children, and shrinking back at a time when a little more, a little further, would have rendered this continent the glory of the earth.

As Britain hath not manifested the least inclination towards a compromise, we may be assured that no terms can be obtained worthy the acceptance of the continent, or any ways equal to the expense of blood and treasure we have been already put to.

The object contended for, ought always to bear some just proportion to the expense. The removal of North, or the whole detestable junto, is a matter unworthy the millions we have expended. A temporary stoppage of trade was an inconvenience, which would have sufficiently balanced the repeal of all the acts complained of, had such repeals been obtained; but if the whole continent must take up arms, if every man must be a soldier, 'tis scarcely worth our while to fight against a contemptible ministry only. Dearly, dearly do we pay for the repeal of the acts, if that is all we fight for; for, in a just estimation 'tis as great a folly to pay a Bunker Hill price for law as for land. As I have always considered the independency of this continent, as an event which sooner or later must arrive, so from the late rapid progress of the continent to maturity, the event cannot be far off. Wherefore, on the breaking out of hostilities, it was not worth the while to have disputed a matter which time would have finally redressed, unless we meant to be in earnest: otherwise it is like wasting an estate on a suit at law, to regulate the trespasses of a tenant whose lease is just expiring. No man was a warmer wisher for a reconciliation than myself, before the fatal nineteenth of April, 1775, but the moment the event of that day was made known, I rejected the hardened, sullen-tempered Pharaoh of England for ever; and disdain the wretch, that with the pretended title of FATHER OF HIS PEOPLE can unfeelingly hear of their slaughter, and composedly sleep with their blood upon his soul.

But admitting that matters were now made up, what would be the event? I answer, the ruin of the continent. And that for several reasons.

First. The powers of governing still remaining in the hands of the king, he will have a negative over the whole legislation of this continent. And as he hath shown himself such an inveterate enemy to liberty, and discovered such a thirst for arbitrary power, is he, or is he not, a proper person to say to these colonies, *You shall make no laws but what I please!?* And is there any inhabitant of America so ignorant as not to know, that according to what is called the *present Constitution*, this continent can make no laws but what the king gives leave to; and is there any man so unwise as not to see, that (considering what has happened) he will suffer no law to be made here but such as suits *his* purpose? We may be as effectually enslaved by the want of laws in America, as by submitting to laws made for us in England. After matters are made up (as it is called) can there be any doubt, but the whole power of the crown will be exerted to keep this continent as low and humble as possible? Instead of going forward we shall go backward, or be perpetually quarrelling, or ridiculously petitioning. We are already greater than the king wishes us to be, and will he not hereafter endeavor to make us less? To bring the matter to one point, Is the power who is jealous of our prosperity, a proper power to govern us? Whoever says *No*, to this question, is an independent for independency means no more than this, whether we shall make our own laws, or, whether the king, the greatest enemy this continent hath, or can have, shall tell us *there shall be no laws but such as I like*.

But the king, you will say, has a negative in England; the people there can make no laws without his consent. In point of right and good order, it is something very ridiculous that a youth of twenty-

one (which hath often happened) shall say to several millions of
people older and wiser than himself, "I forbid this or that act of
yours to be law." But in this place I decline this sort of reply,
though I will never cease to expose the absurdity of it, and only
answer that England being the king's residence, and America not
so, makes quite another case. The king's negative here is ten times
more dangerous and fatal than it can be in England; for there he
will scarcely refuse his consent to a bill for putting England into as
strong a state of defense as possible, and in America he would
never suffer such a bill to be passed.

America is only a secondary object in the system of British
politics. England consults the good of this country no further than
it answers her own purpose. Wherefore, her own interest leads her
to suppress the growth of ours in every case which doth not
promote her advantage, or in the least interferes with it. A pretty
state we should soon be in under such a second hand government,
considering what has happened! Men do not change from enemies
to friends by the alteration of a name: And in order to show that
reconciliation now is a dangerous doctrine, I affirm, *that it would
be policy in the king at this time to repeal the acts, for the sake of
reinstating himself in the government of the provinces*; In order
that HE MAY ACCOMPLISH BY CRAFT AND SUBTLETY, IN THE LONG
RUN, WHAT HE CANNOT DO BY FORCE AND VIOLENCE IN THE
SHORT ONE. Reconciliation and ruin are nearly related.

Secondly. That as even the best terms which we can expect to
obtain can amount to no more than a temporary expedient, or a
kind of government by guardianship, which can last no longer than
till the colonies come of age, so the general face and state of things
in the interim will be unsettled and unpromising. Emigrants of
property will not choose to come to a country whose form of
government hangs but by a thread, and who is every day tottering
on the brink of commotion and disturbance; and numbers of the
present inhabitants would lay hold of the interval to dispose of their
effects, and quit the continent.

But the most powerful of all arguments is, that nothing but
independence, *i.e.* a continental form of government, can keep the
peace of the continent and preserve it inviolate from civil wars. I
dread the event of a reconciliation with Britain now, as it is more
than probable that it will be followed by a revolt some where or

other, the consequences of which may be far more fatal than all the malice of Britain. . . .

If there is any true cause of fear respecting independence, it is because no plan is yet laid down. Men do not see their way out. Wherefore, as an opening into that business I offer the following hints; at the same time modestly affirming, that I have no other opinion of them myself, than that they may be the means of giving rise to something better. Could the straggling thoughts of individuals be collected, they would frequently form materials for wise and able men to improve into useful matter.

Let the assemblies be annual, with a president only. The representation more equal, their business wholly domestic, and subject to the authority of a Continental Congress.

Let each colony be divided into six, eight, or ten, convenient districts, each district to send a proper number of delegates to Congress, so that each colony send at least thirty. The whole number in Congress will be at least 390. Each Congress to sit and to choose a President by the following method. When the delegates are met, let a colony be taken from the whole thirteen colonies by lot, after which let the Congress choose (by ballot) a President from out of the delegates of that province. In the next Congress, let a colony be taken by lot from twelve only, omitting that colony from which the President was taken in the former Congress, and so proceeding on till the whole thirteen shall have had their proper rotation. And in order that nothing may pass into a law but what is satisfactorily just, not less than three-fifths of the Congress to be called a majority. He that will promote discord, under a government so equally formed as this, would have joined Lucifer in his revolt.

But as there is a peculiar delicacy from whom, or in what manner, this business must first arise, and as it seems most agreeable and consistent that it should come from some intermediate body between the governed and the governors, that is, between the Congress and the people, let a continental conference be held in the following manner, and for the following purpose.

A committee of twenty-six members of Congress, *viz*. Two for each colony. Two members from each House of Assembly, or Provincial Convention; and five representatives of the people at large, to be chosen in the capital city or town of each province, for, and in behalf of the whole province, by as many qualified voters as shall think proper to attend from all parts of the province for that purpose; or, if more convenient, the representatives may be chosen in two or three of the most populous parts thereof. In this conference, thus assembled, will be united the two grand principles of business, *knowledge* and *power*. The Members of Congress, Assemblies, or Conventions, by having had experience in national concerns, will be able and useful counsellors, and the whole, being impowered by the people, will have a truly legal authority.

The conferring members being met, let their business be to frame a Continental Charter, or Charter of the United Colonies; (answering to what is called the Magna Charta of England) fixing the number and manner of choosing Members of Congress, Members of Assembly, with their date of sitting; and drawing the line of business and jurisdiction between them: Always remembering, that our strength is continental, not provincial. Securing freedom and property to all men, and above all things, the free exercise of religion, according to the dictates of conscience; with such other matter as it is necessary for a charter to contain. Immediately after which, the said conference to dissolve, and the bodies which shall be chosen conformable to the said charter, to be the legislators and governors of this continent for the time being: Whose peace and happiness, may GOD preserve. AMEN.

Should any body of men be hereafter delegated for this or some similar purpose, I offer them the following extracts from that wise observer on governments, Dragonetti. "The science," says he, "of the politician consists in fixing the true point of happiness and freedom. Those men would deserve the gratitude of ages, who should discover a mode of government that contained the greatest sum of individual happiness, with the least national expense." (Dragonetti on "Virtues and Reward.")

But where, say some, is the king of America? I'll tell you, friend, he reigns above, and doth not make havoc of mankind like the royal brute of Great Britain. Yet that we may not appear to be defective even in earthly honors, let a day be solemnly set apart for proclaiming the charter; let it be brought forth placed on the divine law, the Word of God; let a crown be placed thereon, by which the world may know, that so far as we approve of monarchy, that in

America the law is king. For as in absolute governments the king is law, so in free countries the law ought to be king; and there ought to be no other. But lest any ill use should afterwards arise, let the crown at the conclusion of the ceremony be demolished, and scattered among the people whose right it is.

A government of our own is our natural right: and when a man seriously reflects on the precariousness of human affairs, he will become convinced, that it is infinitely wiser and safer, to form a Constitution of our own in a cool deliberate manner, while we have it in our power, than to trust such an interesting event to time and chance. If we omit it now, some Massanello* may hereafter arise, who, laying hold of popular disquietudes, may collect together the desperate and the discontented, and by assuming to themselves the powers of government, finally sweep away the liberties of the continent like a deluge. Should the government of America return again into the hands of Britain, the tottering situation of things will be a temptation for some desperate adventurer to try his fortune; and in such a case, what relief can Britain give? Ere she could hear the news, the fatal business might be done; and ourselves suffering like the wretched Britons under the oppression of the conqueror. Ye that oppose independence now, ye know not what ye do: ye are opening a door to eternal tyranny, by keeping vacant the seat of government. There are thousands and tens of thousands, who would think it glorious to expel from the continent, that barbarous and hellish power, which hath stirred up the Indians and the Negroes to destroy us; the cruelty hath a double guilt, it is dealing brutally by us, and treacherously by them.

To talk of friendship with those in whom our reason forbids us to have faith, and our affections wounded through a thousand pores instruct us to detest, is madness and folly. Every day wears out the little remains of kindred between us and them; and can there be any reason to hope, that as the relationship expires, the affection will increase, or that we shall agree better when we have ten times more and greater concerns to quarrel over than ever?

Ye that tell us of harmony and reconciliation, can ye restore to

*Thomas Anello, otherwise Massanello, a fisherman of Naples, who after spiriting up his countrymen in the public market place, against the oppression of the Spaniards, to whom the place was then subject, prompted them to revolt, and in the space of a day became king.—*Author*.

us the time that is past? Can ye give to prostitution its former innocence? neither can ye reconcile Britain and America. The last cord now is broken, the people of England are presenting addresses against us. There are injuries which nature cannot forgive; she would cease to be nature if she did. As well can the lover forgive the ravisher of his mistress, as the continent forgive the murders of Britain. The Almighty hath implanted in us these unextinguishable feelings for good and wise purposes. They are the guardians of his image in our hearts. They distinguish us from the herd of common animals. The social compact would dissolve, and justice be extirpated from the earth, or have only a casual existence were we callous to the touches of affection. The robber and the murderer would often escape unpunished, did not the injuries which our tempers sustain, provoke us into justice.

O! ye that love mankind! Ye that dare oppose not only the tyranny but the tyrant, stand forth! Every spot of the old world is overrun with oppression. Freedom hath been hunted round the globe. Asia and Africa have long expelled her. Europe regards her like a stranger, and England hath given her warning to depart. O! receive the fugitive, and prepare in time an asylum for mankind.

C. *Richard Henry Lee:*
A Populist Critique of the Constitution

Richard Henry Lee (1732-1794), a member of the famous Virginia family, was an early advocate of American independence, a member of the Continental Congress and the first to make the motion that "these united colonies are, and of right ought to be, Free and Independent states." Like many signers of the Declaration of Independence, Lee was to have strong reservations about the Constitution drafted in Philadelphia eleven years later.

Lee was neither a debtor nor a leveler, and in his *Letters from the Federal Farmer,** (1787) from which the selection is taken, he distinguishes himself from the "Shaysites." Far more dangerous,

*Reprinted from Paul Leicester Ford, ed., *Pamphlets on the Constitution of the United States* (Brooklyn, N.Y.: 1888).

in Lee's opinion, were those who "avariciously grasp at all power and property; you may discover in all the actions of these men, an evident dislike to free and equal government . . . these are called aristocrats, moneyites, etc." Conceding that the proposed Constitution had many excellent features, Lee expressed his concern that it was being pressed upon the American people in too great a haste, with the result that an instrument might be adopted which would give undue power to these "aristocrats" and "moneyites."

The chief defect of the Constitution, as Lee saw it, was its "want of that one important factor in a free government, a representation of the people." In his analysis of the Constitution he argued that it would have the effect of placing the majority under control of the minority. The analysis, unlike most others produced by opponents of the Constitution, is calm, fair-minded, and almost detached—the perfect rejoinder to the *Federalist* papers. Lee is obviously not a populist of the "Shaysite" variety—he is moderate both in opinion and income—but he belongs in the best tradition of Enlightenment populism by his grand contempt for those aiming at "immense fortunes, offices and power," and his unshakable faith in the majority of his countrymen.

The confederation was formed when great confidence was placed in the voluntary exertions of individuals, and of the respective states; and the framers of it, to guard against usurpation, so limited, and checked the powers, that, in many respects, they are inadequate to the exigencies of the union. We find, therefore, members of congress urging alterations in the federal system almost as soon as it was adopted. It was early proposed to vest congress with powers to levy an impost, to regulate trade, &c. but such was known to be the caution of the states in parting with power, that the vestment even of these, was proposed to be under several checks and limitations. During the war, the general confusion, and the introduction of paper money, infused in the minds of people vague ideas respecting government and credit. We expected too much from the return of peace, and of course we have been disappointed. Our governments have been new and unsettled; and several legislatures, by making tender, suspension, and paper money laws, have given just cause of uneasiness to creditors. By these and other causes, several orders of men in the community have been prepared, by degrees, for a change of government; and this very abuse of power in the legislatures, which in some cases has been charged upon the democratic part of the community, has furnished aristocratical men with those very weapons, and those very means, with which, in great measure, they are rapidly effecting their favourite object. And should an oppressive government be the consequence of the proposed change, prosperity may reproach not only a few overbearing, unprincipled men, but those parties in the states which have misused their powers.

The conduct of several legislatures, touching paper money, and tender laws, has prepared many honest men for changes in government, which otherwise they would not have thought of—when by the evils, on the one hand, and by the secret instigations of artful men, on the other, the minds of men were become sufficiently uneasy, a bold step was taken, which is usually followed by a revolution, or a civil war. A general convention for mere commercial purposes was moved for—the authors of this measure saw that the people's attention was turned solely to the amendment of the federal system; and that, had the idea of a total change been started, probably no state would have appointed members to the convention. The idea of destroying, ultimately, the state government, and forming one consolidated system, could not have been admitted—a convention, therefore, merely for vesting in congress power to regulate trade was proposed. This was pleasing to the commercial towns; and the landed people had little or no concern about it. September, 1786, a few men from the middle states met at Annapolis, and hastily proposed a convention to be held in May, 1787, for the purpose, generally, of amending the confederation—this was done before the delegates of Massachusetts, and of the other states arrived—still not a word was said about destroying the old constitution, and making a new one—The states still unsuspecting, and not aware that they were passing the Rubicon, appointed members to the new convention, for the sole and express purpose of revising and amending the confederation—and, probably, not one man in ten thousand in the United States, till within these ten or twelve days, had an idea that the old ship was to be destroyed, and he put to the alternative of embarking in the new ship presented, or of being left in danger of sinking—The States, I believe, universally supposed the convention would report alterations in the confederation, which would pass an examination in congress, and after being agreed to there, would be confirmed by all the legislatures, or be rejected. Virginia made a very respectable appointment, and placed at the head of it the first man in America. In this appointment there was a mixture of political characters; but Pennsylvania appointed principally those men who are esteemed aristocratical. Here the favourite moment for changing the government was evidently discerned by a few men, who seized it with address. Ten other states appointed, and tho' they chose men principally connected with commerce and the judicial department yet they appointed many good republican characters—had they all attended we should now see, I am persuaded, a better system presented. The non-attendance of eight or nine men, who were appointed members of the convention, I shall ever consider as a very unfortunate event to the United States.—Had they attended, I am pretty clear that the result of the convention would not have had that strong tendency to aristocracy now discernible in every part of the plan. There would not have been so great an accumulation of powers, especially as to the internal police of this country in a few hands as the constitution reported proposes to vest in them—the young visionary men, and the consolidating aristocracy, would have been more restrained than they have been. Eleven states met in the convention, and after four months close attention presented the new constitution, to be adopted or rejected by the people. The uneasy and fickle part of the community may be prepared to receive any form of government; but I presume the enlightened and substantial part will give any constitution presented for their adoption a candid and thorough examination; and silence those designing or empty men, who weakly and rashly attempt to precipitate the adoption of a system of so much importance—We shall view the convention with proper respect—and, at the same time, that we reflect there were men of abilities and integrity in it, we must recollect how disproportionately the democratic and aristocratic parts of the community were represented—Perhaps the judicious friends and opposers of the new constitution will agree, that it is best to let it rely solely on its own merits, or be condemned for its own defects. . . .

They propose to lodge in the general government very extensive powers—*powers* nearly, if not altogether, complete and unlimited, over the purse and the sword. But, in its organization, they furnish the strongest proof that the proper limbs, or parts of a government, to support and execute those powers on proper principles (or in which they can be safely lodged) cannot be formed. These powers must be lodged somewhere in every society; but then they should be lodged where the strength and guardians of the people are collected. They can be wielded, or safely used, in a free country only by an able executive and judiciary, a respectable senate, and a secure, full, and equal representation of the people. I think the principles I have premised or brought into view, are well founded—I think they will not be denied by any fair reasoner. It is in connection with these, and other solid principles, we are to examine the constitution. It is not a few democratic phrases, or a few well formed features, that will prove its merits; or a few small omissions that will produce its rejection among men of sense; they will enquire what are the essential powers in a community, and what are nominal ones; where and how the essential powers shall be lodged to secure government, and to secure true liberty.

In examining the proposed constitution carefully, we must clearly perceive an unnatural separation of these powers from the substantial representation of the people. The state government will exist, with all their governors, senators, representatives, officers and expences; in these will be nineteen twentieths of the representatives of the people; they will have a near connection, and their members an immediate intercourse with the people; and the probability is, that the state governments will possess the confidence of the people, and be considered generally as their immediate guardians.

The general government will consist of a new species of executive, a small senate, and a very small house of representatives. As many citizens will be more than three hundred miles from the seat of this government as will be nearer to it, its judges and officers cannot be very numerous, without making our governments very expensive. Thus will stand the state and the general governments, should the constitution be adopted without any alterations in their organization; but as to powers, the general government will possess all essential ones, at least on paper, and those of the states a mere shadow of power. And therefore, unless the people shall make some great exertions to restore to the state governments their powers in matters of internal police; as the powers to lay and collect, exclusively, internal taxes, to govern the militia, and to hold the decisions of their own judicial courts upon their own laws final, the balance cannot possibly continue long; but the state governments must be annihilated, or continue to exist for no purpose.

It is however to be observed, that many of the essential powers given the national government are not exclusively given; and the general government may have prudence enough to forbear the exercise of those which may still be exercised by the respective states. But this cannot justify the impropriety of giving powers, the exercise of which prudent men will not attempt, and imprudent men will, or probably can, exercise only in a manner destructive of free government. The general government, organized as it is, may be adequate to many valuable objects, and be able to carry its laws into execution on proper principles in several cases; but I think its warmest friends will not contend, that it can carry all the powers proposed to be lodged in it into effect, without calling to its aid a military force, which must very soon destroy all elective governments in the country, produce anarchy, or establish despotism. Though we cannot have now a complete idea of what will be the operations of the proposed system, we may, allowing things to have their common course, have a very tolerable one. The powers lodged in the general government, if exercised by it, must intimately effect the internal police of the states, as well as external concerns; and there is no reason to expect the numerous state governments, and their connections, will be very friendly to the execution of federal laws in those internal affairs, which hitherto have been under their own immediate management. There is more reason to believe, that the general government, far removed from the people, and none of its members elected oftener than once in two years, will be forgot or neglected, and its laws in many cases disregarded, unless a multitude of officers and military force be continually kept in view, and employed to enforce the execution of the laws, and to make the government feared and respected. No position can be truer than this. That in this country either neglected laws, or a military execution of them, must lead to a revolution, and to the destruction of freedom. Neglected laws must first lead to anarchy and confusion; and a military execution of laws is only a shorter way to the same point—despotic government. . . .

The vice president is not a very important, if not an unnecessary part of the system—he may be a part of the senate at one period, and act as the supreme executive magistrate at another—The election of this officer, as well as of the president of the United States seems to be properly secured; but when we examine the powers of the president, and the forms of the executive, we shall perceive that the general government, in this part, will have a strong tendency to aristocracy, or the government of the few. The executive is, in fact, the president and senate in all transactions of any importance; the president is connected with, or tied to the senate; he may always act with the senate, but never can effectually counteract its views: The president can appoint no officer, civil or military, who shall not be agreeable to the senate; and the presumption is, that the will of so important a body will not be very easily controuled, and that it will exercise its powers with great address.

In the judicial department, powers ever kept distinct in well balanced governments, are no less improperly blended in the hands of the same men—in the judges of the supreme court is lodged the law, the equity and the fact. It is not necessary to pursue the minute organical parts of the general government proposed.—There were various interests in the convention, to be reconciled, especially of large and small states; of carrying and non-carrying states; and of states more and states less democratic—vast labour and attention were by the convention bestowed on the organization of the parts of the constitution offered; still it is acknowledged there are many things radically wrong in the essential parts of this constitution—but it is said that these are the result of our situation: On a full examination of the subject, I believe it; but what do the laborious inquiries and determination of the convention prove? If they prove any thing, they prove that we cannot consolidate the states rights on proper principles: The organization of the government presented proves, that we cannot form a general government in which all power can be safely lodged; and a little attention to the parts of the one proposed will make it appear very evident, that all the powers proposed to be lodged in it, will not be then well deposited, either for the purposes of government, or the preservation of liberty. I will suppose no abuse of power in those cases, in which the abuse of it is not well guarded against—I will suppose the words authorizing the general government to regulate the elections of its own members struck out of the plan, or free district elections, in each state, amply secured.—That the small representation provided for shall be as fair and equal as it is capable of being made—I will suppose the judicial department regulated on pure principles, by future laws, as far as it can be by the constitution, and consist with the situation of the country—still there will be an unreasonable accumulation of powers in the general government if all be granted, enumerated in the plan proposed. The plan does not present a well-balanced government: The senatorial branch of the legislative and the executive are substantially united, and the president, or the state executive magistrate, may aid the senatorial interest when weakest, but never can effectually support the democratic, however it may be opposed;—the excellency, in my mind, of a well-balanced government is that it consists of distinct branches, each sufficiently strong and independent to keep its own station, and to aid either of the other branches which may occasionally want aid.

The convention found that any but a small house of representatives would be expensive, and that it would be impracticable to assemble a large number of representatives. Not only the determination of the convention in this case, but the situation of the states, proves the impracticability of collecting, in any one point, a proper representation.

The formation of the senate, and the smallness of the house, being, therefore, the result of our situation, and the actual state of things, the evils which may attend the exercise of many powers in this national government may be considered as without a remedy.

All officers are impeachable before the senate only—before the men by whom they are appointed, or who are consenting to the appointment of these officers. No judgment of conviction, on an impeachment, can be given unless two thirds of the senators agree. Under these circumstances the right of impeachment, in the house, can be of but little importance; the house cannot expect often to convict the offender; and, therefore, probably, will but seldom or never exercise the right. In addition to the insecurity and inconveniences attending this organization beforementioned, it may be observed, that it is extremely difficult to secure the people against the fatal effects of corruption and influence. The power of making any law will be in the president, eight senators, and seventeen representatives, relative to the important objects enumerated in the constitution. Where there is a small representation a sufficient number to carry any measure, may, with ease, be influenced by bribes, offices and civilities; they easily form private juntoes, and out-door meetings, agree on measures, and carry them by silent votes.

Impressed, as I am, with a sense of the difficulties there are in the way of forming the parts of a federal government on proper principles, and seeing a government so unsubstantially organized, after so arduous an attempt has been made, I am led to believe, that powers ought to be given to it with great care and caution.

In the second place it is necessary, therefore, to examine the extent, and the probable operations of some of those extensive powers proposed to be vested in this government. These powers, legislative, executive, and judicial, respect internal as well as external objects. Those respecting external objects, as all foreign concerns, commerce, imposts, all causes arising on the seas, peace and war, and Indian affairs, can be lodged no where else, with any propriety, but in this government. Many powers that respect internal objects ought clearly to be lodged in it; as those to regulate trade between the states, weights and measures, the coin or current monies, post-offices, naturalization, &c. These powers may be exercised without essentially effecting the internal police of the respective states: But powers to lay and collect internal taxes, to form the militia, to make bankrupt laws, and to decide on appeals, questions arising on the internal laws of the respective states, are of a very serious nature, and carry with them almost all other powers. These taken in connection with the others, and powers to raise armies and build navies, proposed to be lodged in this government, appear to me to comprehend all the essential powers in this community, and those which will be left to the states will be of no great importance. . : .

The power in the general government to lay and collect internal taxes, will render its powers respecting armies, navies and the militia, the more exceptionable. By the constitution it is proposed that congress shall have power "to raise and support armies, but no appropriation of money to that use shall be for a longer term than two years; to provide and maintain a navy; to provide for calling forth the militia to execute the laws of the union; suppress insurrections, and repel invasions: to provide for organizing, arming, and disciplining the militia;" reserving to the states the right to appoint the officers, and to train the militia according to the discipline prescribed by congress; congress will have unlimited power to raise armies, and to engage officers and men for any number of years; but a legislative act applying money for their support can have operation for no longer term that two years, and if a subsequent congress do not within the two years renew the appropriation, or further appropriate monies for the use of the army, the army will be left to take care of itself. When an army shall once be raised for a number of years, it is not probable that it will find much difficulty in getting congress to pass laws for applying monies to its support. I see so many men in America fond of a standing army, and especially among those who probably will have a large share in administering the federal system; it is very evident to me, that we shall have a large standing army as soon as the monies to support them can be possibly found. An army is not a very agreeable place of employment for the young gentlemen of many families. A power to raise armies must be lodged some where; still this will not justify the lodging this power in a bare majority of so few men without any checks; or in the government in which the great body of the people, in the nature of things, will be only nominally represented. In the state governments the great body of the people, the yeomanry, &c. of the country, are represented: It is true they will chuse the members of congress, and may now and then chuse a man of their own way of thinking; but it is not impossible for forty, or thirty thousand people in this country, one time in ten to find a man who can possess similar feelings, views, and interests with themselves: Powers to lay and collect taxes and to raise armies are of the greatest moment; for carrying them into effect, laws need not be frequently made, and the yeomanry, &c. of the country ought substantially to have a check upon the passing of these laws; this check ought to be placed in the legislatures, or at least, in the few men the common people of the country, will, probably, have

in congress, in the true sense of the word, "from among themselves." It is true, the yeomanry of the country possess the lands,
the weight of property, possess arms, and are too strong a body of
men to be openly offended—and, therefore, it is urged, they will
take care of themselves, that men who shall govern will not dare
pay any disrespect to their opinions. It is easily perceived, that if
they have not their proper negative upon passing laws in congress,
or on the passage of laws relative to taxes and armies, they may in
twenty or thirty years be by means imperceptible to them, totally
deprived of that boasted weight and strength: This may be done in a
great measure by congress, if disposed to do it, by modelling the
militia. Should one-fifth or one-eighth part of the men capable of
bearing arms, be made a select militia, as has been proposed, and
those the young and ardent part of the community, possessed of but
little or no property, and all the others put upon a plan that will
render them of no importance, the former will answer all the
purposes of an army, while the latter will be defenceless. The state
must train the militia in such form and according to such systems
and rules as congress shall prescribe: and the only actual influence
the respective states will have respecting the militia will be in
appointing the officers. I see no provision made for calling out the
posse comitatus for executing the laws of the union, but provision
is made for congress to call forth the militia for the execution of
them—and the militia in general, or any select part of it, may be
called out under military officers, instead of the sheriff to enforce
an execution of federal laws, in the first instance, and thereby
introduce an entire military execution of the laws. I know that
powers to raise taxes, to regulate the military strength of the
community on some uniform plan, to provide for its defence and
internal order, and for duly executing the laws, must be lodged
somewhere; but still we ought not so to lodge them, as evidently to
give one order of men in the community, undue advantages over
others; or commit the many to the mercy, prudence, and moderation of the few. And so far as it may be necessary to lodge any of
the peculiar powers in the general government, a more safe exercise of them ought to be secured, by requiring the consent of
two-thirds or three-fourths of congress thereto—until the federal
representation can be increased, so that the democratic members in
congress may stand some tolerable chance of a reasonable nega-

tive, in behalf of the numerous, important, and democratic part of the community. . . .

It may also be worthy our examination, how far the provision for amending this plan, when it shall be adopted, is of any importance. No measures can be taken towards amendments, unless two-thirds of the congress, or two-thirds of the legislature of the several states shall agree.—While power is in the hands of the people, or democratic part of the community, more especially as at present, it is easy, according to the general course of human affairs, for the few influential men in the community, to obtain conventions, alterations in government, and to persuade the common people that they may change for the better, and to get from them a part of the power: But when power is once transferred from the many to the few, all changes become extremely difficult; the government, in this case, being beneficial to the few, they will be exceedingly artful and adroit in preventing any measures which may lead to a change; and nothing will produce it, but great exertions and severe struggles on the part of the common people. Every man of reflection must see, that the change now proposed, is a transfer of power from the many to the few, and the probability is, the artful and ever active aristocracy, will prevent all peaceful measures for changes, unless when they shall discover some favorable moment to increase their own influence. I am sensible, thousands of men in the United States, are disposed to adopt the proposed constitution, though they perceive it be be essentially defective, under an idea that amendments of it, may be obtained when necessary. This is a pernicious idea, it argues a servility of character totally unfit for the support of free government; it is very repugnant to that perpetual jealousy respecting liberty, so absolutely necessary in all free states, spoken of by Mr. Dickinson.—However, if our countrymen are so soon changed, and the language of 1774, is become odious to them, it will be in vain to use the language of freedom, or to attempt to rouse them to free enquiries: But I shall never believe this is the case with them, whatever present appearances may be, till I shall have very strong evidence indeed of it. . . .

Thus I have examined the federal constitution as far as a few days leisure would permit. It opens to my mind a new scene; instead of seeing powers cautiously lodged in the hands of numerous legislators, and many magistrates, we see all important powers collecting in one centre, where a few men will possess them almost at discretion. And instead of checks in the formation of the government, to secure the rights of the people against the usurpations of those they appoint to govern, we are to understand the equal division of lands among our people, and the strong arm furnished them by nature and situation, are to secure them against those usurpations. If there are advantages in the equal division of our lands, and the strong and manly habits of our people, we ought to establish governments calculated to give duration to them, and not governments which never can work naturally, till that equality of property, and those free and manly habits shall be destroyed; these evidently are not the natural basis of the proposed constitution. No man of reflection, and skilled in the science of government, can suppose these will move on harmoniously together for ages, or even for fifty years. As to the little circumstances commented upon, by some writers, with applause—as the age of a representative, of the president, &c.—they have, in my mind, no weight in the general tendency of the system.

There are, however, in my opinion, many good things in the proposed system. It is founded on elective principles, and the deposits of powers in different hands, is essentially right. The guards against those evils we have experienced in some states in legislation are valuable indeed; but the value of every feature in this system is vastly lessened for the want of that one important feature in a free government, a representation of the people. Because we have sometimes abused democracy, I am not among those men who think a democratic branch a nuisance; which branch shall be sufficiently numerous to admit some of the best informed men of each order in the community into the administration of government.

While the radical defects in the proposed system are not so soon discovered, some temptations to each state, and to many classes of men to adopt it, are very visible. It uses the democratic language of several of the state constitutions, particularly that of Massachusetts; the eastern states will receive advantages so far as the regulation of trade, by a bare majority, is committed to it: Connecticut and New Jersey will receive their share of a general impost: The middle states will receive the advantages surrounding the seat of government: The southern states will receive protection, and have their negroes represented in the legislature, and large back countries will soon have a majority in it. This system promises a large field of employment to military gentlemen, and gentlemen of the law; and in case the government shall be executed without convulsions, it will afford security to creditors, to the clergy, salary-men and others depending on money payments. So far as the system promises justice and reasonable advantages, in these respects, it ought to be supported by all honest men; but whenever it promises unequal and improper advantages to any particular states, or orders of men, it ought to be opposed.

I have, in the course of these letters, observed that there are many good things in the proposed constitution, and I have endeavored to point out many important defects in it. I have admitted that we want a federal system—that we have a system presented, which, with several alterations may be made a tolerable good one—I have admitted there is a well founded uneasiness among creditors and mercantile men. In this situation of things, you ask me what I think ought to be done? My opinion in this case is only the opinion of an individual, and so far only as it corresponds with the opinions of the honest and substantial part of the community, is it entitled to consideration. Though I am fully satisfied that the state conventions ought most seriously to direct their exertions to altering and amending the system proposed before they shall adopt it—yet I have not sufficiently examined the subject, or formed an opinion, how far it will be practicable for those conventions to carry their amendments. As to the idea, that it will be in vain for those conventions to attempt amendments, it cannot be admitted; it is impossible to say whether they can or not until the attempt shall be made; and when it shall be determined, by experience, that the conventions cannot agree in amendments, it will then be an important question before the people of the United States, whether they will adopt or not the system proposed in its present form. This subject of consolidating the states is new: and because forty or fifty men have agreed in a system, to suppose the good sense of this country, an enlightened nation, must adopt it without examination, and though in a state of profound peace, without endeavouring to amend those parts they perceive are defective, dangerous to freedom, and destructive of the valuable principles of republican government—is truly humiliating. It is true there may be danger in delay; but there is danger in adopting the system in its present form; and I see the danger in either case will arise principally from the conduct and views of two very unprincipled parties in the United States—two fires, between which the honest and substantial people have long found themselves situated. One party is composed of little insurgents, men in debt, who want no law, and who want a share of the property of others; these are called levellers, Shaysites, &c. The other party is composed of a few, but more dangerous men, with their servile dependents; these avariciously grasp at all power and property; you may discover in all the actions of these men, an evident dislike to free and equal government, and they will go systematically to work to change, essentially, the forms of government in this country; these are called aristocrats, m——ites, &c., &c. Between these two parties is the weight of the community; the men of middling property, men not in debt on the one hand, and men, on the other, content with republican governments, and not aiming at immense fortunes, offices, and power. In 1786, the little insurgents, the levellers, came forth, invaded the rights of others, and attempted to establish governments according to their wills. Their movements evidently gave encouragement to the other party, which, in 1787, has taken the political field, and with its fashionable dependents, and the tongue and the pen, is endeavoring to establish in a great haste, a politer kind of government. These two parties, which will probably be opposed or united as it may suit their interests and views, are really insignificant, compared with the solid, free, and independent part of the community. It is not my intention to suggest, that either of these parties, and the real friends of the proposed constitution, are the same men. The fact is, these aristocrats support and hasten the adoption of the proposed constitution, merely because they think it is a stepping stone to their favorite object. I think I am well founded in this idea; I think the general politics of these men support it, as well as the common observation among them, That the proffered plan is the best that can be got at present, it will do for a few years, and lead to something better. The sensible and judicious part of the community will carefully weigh all these circumstances; they will view the late convention as a respectable body of men—America probably never will see an assembly of men, of a like number, more respectable. But the members of the convention met without knowing the sentiments of one man in ten thousand in these states respecting the new ground taken. Their doings are but the first attempts in the most important scene ever opened. Though each individual in the state conventions will not, probably, be so respectable as each individual in the federal convention, yet as the state conventions will probably consist of fifteen hundred or two thousand men of abilities, and versed in the science of government, collected from all parts of the community and from all orders of men, it must be acknowledged that the weight of respectability will be in them—In them will be collected the solid sense and the real political character of the country. Being revisers of the subject, they will possess peculiar advantages. To say that these conventions ought not to attempt, coolly and deliberately, the revision of the system, or that they cannot amend it, is very foolish or very assuming. If these conventions, after examining the system, adopt it, I shall be perfectly satisfied, and wish to see men make the administration of the government an equal blessing to all orders of men. I believe the great body of our people to be virtuous and friendly to good government, to the protection of liberty and property; and it is the duty of all good men, especially of those who are placed as sentinels to guard their rights—it is their duty to examine into the prevailing politics of parties, and to disclose them—while they avoid exciting undue suspicions, to lay facts before the people, which will enable them to form a proper judgment. Men who wish the people of this country to determine for themselves, and deliberately to fit the government to their situation, must feel some degree of indignation at those attempts to hurry the adoption of a system, and to shut the door against examination. The very attempts create suspicions, that those who make them have secret views, or see some defects in the system, which, in the hurry of affairs, they expect will escape the eye of a free people.

What can be the views of those gentlemen in Pennsylvania, who precipitated decisions on this subject? What can be the views of those gentlemen in Boston, who countenanced the Printers in shutting up the press against a fair and free investigation of this important system in the usual way. The members of the convention have done their duty—why should some of them fly to their states—almost forget a propriety of behaviour, and precipitate measures for the adoption of a system of their own making? I confess candidly, when I consider these circumstances in connection with the unguarded parts of the system I have mentioned, I feel disposed to proceed with very great caution, and to pay more attention than usual to the conduct of particular characters. If the constitution presented be a good one, it will stand the test with a well informed people: all are agreed that there shall be state conventions to examine it; and we must believe it will be adopted, unless we suppose it is a bad one, or that those conventions will make false divisions respecting it. I admit improper measures are taken against the adoption of the system as well for it—all who object to the plan proposed ought to point out the defects objected to, and to propose those amendments with which they can accept it, or to propose some other system of government, that the public mind may be known, and that we may be brought to agree in some system of government, to strengthen and execute the present, or to provide a substitute. I consider the field of enquiry just opened, and that we are to look to the state conventions for ultimate decisions on the subject before us; it is not to be presumed, that they will differ about small amendments, and lose a system when they shall have made it substantially good; but touching the essential amendments, it is to be presumed the several conventions will pursue the most rational measures to agree in and obtain them; and such defects as they shall discover and not remove, they will probably notice, keep them in view as the ground work of future amendments, and in the firm and manly language which every free people ought to use, will suggest to those who may hereafter administer the government, that it is their expectation, that the system will be so organized by legislative acts, and the government so administered, as to render those defects as little injurious as possible. Our countrymen are entitled to an honest and faithful government; to a government of laws and not of men; and also to one of their chusing—as a citizen of the country, I wish to see these objects secured, and licentious, assuming, and overbearing men restrained; if the constitution or social compact be vague and unguarded, then we depend wholly upon the prudence, wisdom and moderation of those who manage the affairs of government; or on what, probably, is equally uncertain and precarious, the success of the people oppressed by the abuse of government, in receiving it from the hands of those who abuse it, and placing it in the hands of those who will use it well.

In every point of view, therefore, in which I have been able, as yet, to contemplate this subject, I can discern but one rational mode of proceeding relative to it: and that is to examine it with freedom and candour, to have state conventions some months hence, which shall examine coolly every article, clause, and word in the system proposed, and to adopt it with such amendments as they shall think fit. How far the state conventions ought to pursue the mode prescribed by the federal convention of adopting or rejecting the plan in toto, I leave it to them to determine. Our examination of the subject hitherto has been rather of a general nature. The republican characters in the several states, who wish to make this plan more adequate to security of liberty and property, and to the duration of the principles of a free government, will, no doubt, collect their opinions to certain points, and accurately define those alterations and amendments they wish; if it shall be found they essentially disagree in them, the conventions will then be able to determine whether to adopt the plan as it is, or what will be proper to be done.

Under these impressions, and keeping in view the improper and unadvisable lodgment of powers in the general government, organized as it at present is, touching internal taxes, armies and militia, the elections of its own members, causes between citizens of different states, &c. and the want of a more perfect bill of rights, &c. I drop the subject for the present, and when I shall have leisure to revise and correct my ideas respecting it, and to collect into points the opinions of those who wish to make the system more secure and safe, perhaps I may proceed to point out particularly for your consideration, the amendments which ought to be ingrafted into this system, not only in conformity to my own, but the deliberate opinions of others—you will with me perceive, that the objections to the plan proposed may, by a more leisure examination, be set in a stronger point of view, especially the important one, that there is no substantial representation of the people provided for in a government in which the most essential powers, even as to the internal police of the country, is proposed to be lodged.

I think the honest and substantial part of the community will wish to see this system altered, permanency and consistency given to the constitution we shall adopt; and therefore they will be anxious to apportion the powers to the features and organizations of the government, and to see abuse in the exercise of power more effectually guarded against. It is suggested, that state officers, from interested motives will oppose the constitution presented—I see no reason for this, their places in general will not be affected, but new openings to offices and places of profit must evidently be made by the adoption of the constitution in its present form.

Your's, &c.
THE FEDERAL FARMER.

D. *Early Agrarian Protests:*
Shays' Rebellion:
An Interview with Some Rebels*

Scarcely had the new American nation broken with the mother country than some of its citizens began to apply the principles of the Declaration of Independence to their own economic situation. During the years of 1785-86, farmers, small retailers, laboring men, and debtors in general frequently found themselves unable to meet their obligations; as a result their possessions were handed over to tax gatherers and creditors by means of foreclosure and seizure, and they themselves were sometimes confined to debtors' prisons.

The Declaration had insisted that all men are created equal. Yet these classes saw themselves as victims of an unequal system of taxation. The Declaration had extolled the rights of life, liberty, and the pursuit of happiness. Yet here they were, many in prison, staggering under debts and taxes, their happiness, their property, and their very lives jeopardized by creditors, banks, and courts. If America could declare its independence of foreign tyranny, why

---

*From "The Spirit of the Times: Addressing the People of Massachusetts," *Massachusetts Centinal*, October 25, 1786. Unsigned.

could not they declare their independence of this new domestic tyranny?

Sometimes the farmers acted through the legislatures. Stay laws, impairment of contracts, legal tender acts, and increased issues of paper money were not uncommon in those states where forces friendly to Western farmers had taken control of the legislatures. In other states, property qualifications for voting kept the legislatures in the hands of the affluent classes. Massachusetts was one of these states, and when, in 1786, the legislature enacted a new tax which fell more heavily on farmers than on merchants and moneylenders, the farmers rebelled. A group of insurgents seized the courthouse in Northampton, forcibly preventing the court from sitting. Another group, led by Captain Daniel Shays—who had fought at Lexington, Bunker Hill, Saratoga, and Stony Point —forced an adjournment of the court at Springfield. The rebellion was quashed in 1787, but its memory served as a symbol, dividing populists from elitists on the eve of the Constitutional Convention. Hamilton invoked it as a reminder of what happens when power passes into the hands of the rabble, while Jefferson welcomed it as a sign of democratic vitality. Shays' Rebellion prefigured other battles that would be fought again and again in the populist tradition: soft versus hard currency, creditors versus debtors, laymen versus lawyers and judges, country versus city.

The Whiskey Rebellion occurred eight years later in the state of Pennsylvania, but it ultimately involved the same *dramatis personae*—frontier farmers against Eastern capitalists. Alexander Hamilton, seeking revenues by which he hoped to encourage the support of manufacturing, proposed an excise tax on spirituous liquors, and a Federalist Congress obliged by passing the tax in 1791. This came as a blow to Western farmers, who had been converting much of their grain crops into whiskey. Meetings, protests, resolutions, and petitions eventually gave way to outright noncompliance, and finally to armed insurrection in western Pennsylvania. It was easily put down by federal troops, but the climate out of which it arose helped to identify Hamilton's party as the enemy of the common people, paving the way for Jefferson's victory in 1800.

The selections present contemporary newspaper comments on Shays' Rebellion and on the Whiskey Rebellion (see Selection E).

I speak to a people who glory in their knowledge—Trust, therefore, that I can explain to you who I am, and that you will understand what I say. Your philosophers will tell you that there is a vital and active spirit contained in every living thing; and don't your own good sense tell you that when that living thing, which contains the spirit, is cut, maimed or broken, so as to be deprived of life, then the active spirit contained in it, is set at liberty?—Such a spirit am I; and the people of Massachusetts will find me benevolent to them.

I find it to be a general inquiry wherefore were the late risings of the people [Text is blurred here.—Ed.] in rebelling against the commonwealth, what influenced them thus to rise and oppose government? What did they aim at thereby? Some are apt to think these hard questions; and a general answer, that the people were uneasy and did this to manifest their uneasiness, don't satisfy the minds of the inquisitive.—As therefore I was present with them at the late rising, went through all their ranks, conversed with almost every one, and penetrated to the secret recesses of their souls, benevolence induces me to answer the foregoing enquiries of the people, and to open the minds of the insurgents as they were opened to me as I penetrated into them. In the general ferment, when one cried one thing, and another another thing, it would have puzzled a wiser spirit than I am, even to have guessed wherefore they came together, or what they aimed at. I therefore took the stillest time in the profoundest silence of the night—I inquired of an old ploughjogger the confessed aim of the people of that assembly? He said to get redress of grievances. I asked what grievances? He said we have all grievances enough, I can tell you mine. I have laboured hard all my days, and fared hard; I have been greatly abused; been obliged to do more than my part in the war; been loaded with class-rates, town-rates, province-rates, continental-rates, and all rates, lawsuits, and have been pulled and hauled by sheriffs, constables and collectors, and had my cattle sold for less than they were worth. I have been obliged to pay and no body will pay me: I have lost a great deal by this man, and that man, and t'other man; and the great men are going to get all we have; and I think it is time for us to rise and put a stop to it, and have no more courts, nor sheriffs, nor collectors, nor lawyers; I design to pay no more and I know we have the biggest party, let them say what they will. I smiled at his laconick answers, and being for inquiry.

I next asked a pert lad, who was hard by him, the cause of his rising. The lad (who fancied himself a deep politician) made a long harrangue upon governors, and jobbers, and lawyers, and judges, and sherriffs, and counsellors, and deputies, and senators, and justices, and constables, and deputies, and senators, and justices, and constables, and treasurers, and sallaries, and fees, and pensions, and such as one has ten times too much, and such five times too much, and the continent owes so much, and the state so much, and the town so much, and the great men pocket up all the money and live easy, and we work hard, and we can't pay it, and we won't pay it. I found many youths among them equally versed in political knowledge.—Thus I went from rank to rank, through all the mobility—I founded their leaders, and (whether willing or unwilling) I got the secrets of their hearts. It would tire your patience to hear the whole conversations and all the discoveries I made. I found that they were influenced by various motives to assemble, and had various aims to pursue.

E. *Early Agrarian Protests:*
   The Whiskey Rebellion:
   An Appeal for Understanding*

To the PRESIDENT of the UNITED STATES.

. . . As the first executive officer of the United States you have made a requisition of a certain proportion of militia from four States to act against the citizens of the western country, who are in a state of hostile opposition to the excise law should they not return to their duty before the short time given to the 1st of September. It is certainly the duty of the first magistrate to see the laws which are entrusted to him faithfully executed, but the means by which they shall be put in operation depend in some measure upon his wisdom

*From *General Advertiser* (Aurora), August 12, 1794, in Rebecca Gruver, ed., *American Nationalism, 1793-1830: A Self-Portrait* (New York: Capricorn Books, 1970). For headnote, see Selection D.

and discretion. It can hardly be supposed that the strong arm of power is immediately to be raised before lenient means are employed; for as freemen are more under the guidance of reason than the lash, the milder mode ought to be the first resort. When men enter into a social compact to secure their happiness and their rights every violation of them begets uneasiness, and when to this is added other causes of discontent, more than a common portion of forbearance is necessary to subdue the spirit of revolt. The citizens, Sir, of the western country consider an excise law as repugnant to liberty, they consider it as an invasion of those privileges which the revolution bestowed upon them, hence their opposition to the law. But it is not probable that this opposition would have appeared in military terror had not recent circumstances produced great irritation. It is a fact too well known to be disputed that the frontier people have not enjoyed that security and protection which the citizens of other parts of the states have experienced; their country has been ravaged by a barbarous foe, and their women and children have been exposed to the cruelties of the murdering savage. To protect its citizens, the State of Pennsylvania determined on an establishment at Presque Isle, and in the moment of the execution of a law of the State to give security to its frontier citizens, you, Sir, interposed, and a suspension took place. If this interposition was caused by a desire to negotiate with savages, and stop the effusion of blood, would not the same humanity which dictated it have led to pacific rather than military means to bring our own citizens to a sense of right? This act of suspension must have added to the discontents of those people, and a recourse to the rigor of the law in this moment of inflammation will explain the unfortunate state of the western country. Now, Sir, permit me to appeal to those feelings of humanity which led to an appointment of a special envoy to the court of Great Britain, after every aggression which a nation could suffer. This appointment was dictated by a desire of peace, a benevolent wish to spare the effusion of blood. It surely cannot be contended that Great Britain had not been guilty of outrages great enough to excite us to resistance, whence then so great a concern for the lives of our citizens when a foreign foe was concerned, and such an immediate reference to arms when our own citizens are implicated? Negotiation ought to be tried before hostilities are entered into, was the language when Great Britain was concerned, and why ought not the same temper to govern on the present occasion? Shall citizen be armed against citizen, shall a brother imbrue his hands in the blood of his brother before imperious necessity calls for it? Shall Pennsylvania be converted into a human slaughter house because the dignity of the United States will not admit of conciliatory measures? Shall torrents of blood be spil'd to support an odious excise system, producing a pitiful revenue, and millions be sacrificed rather than maintain our national sovereignty? Shall savages be entitled to conciliatory measures and our own citizens have less consideration than savages? Forbid it Heaven.

Sir, the fate of the United States, like the tyrant's sword, is suspended by a thread, and in your hands is the event. Coercion will destroy the slight web by which it is suspended, and a melancholy scene will ensue—a scene at which imagination starts appal'd, and every humane heart views with horror. I mean not to justify any outrage against the laws—I mean not to justify the conduct of the western people—it cannot be justified. Such hostility has my most decided disapprobation, and must be disapproved by every friend to order; but no more can an immediate appeal to arms meet with approbation than can their conduct be supported; for if war is the ultima ratio of monarchies, how much more ought it to be the dernier resort of republics. War in any shape is a real evil, but this evil comes armed with every horror when the swords of citizens are turned against each other. To avoid this, I trust, will be your first care, for it ought to be the care of every friend to humanity.

Consider, sir, the consequences of proceeding to extremity in this case. The heat of the western people will lead them to a violent resistance; they will, perhaps, find proselytes to their cause, and a flame may be kindled which will consume the fair fabric of freedom, and spread desolation thro' our happy country. Let me conjure you to avert, if possible, such a calamity, and as a desire to prevent the shedding of human blood has in one case determined your conduct, let it not be said, that there is a want of consistency in your humanity, and that there was less anxiety to shed blood of American citizens than that of *ferocious Britons* or *inhuman savages*.

*   *   *

F. *Andrew Jackson:*
Vetoing the Bank of "The Rich and Powerful"*

Andrew Jackson (1767-1845) was born in the backcountry of South Carolina and fought in the American Revolution when he was little more than a boy. At twenty he began practicing law on the North Carolina frontier; a year later he moved to Nashville, Tennessee, where he served first as prosecutor, then as U.S. Senator, then as a judge of the state Supreme Court. During this period he also fought Indians in Tennessee and Florida, and the British at New Orleans. Here, already, were some of the ingredients that were later to make him a populist folk hero: He was a self-made man, a frontiersman, an Indian fighter, an Anglophobe, a rugged individualist, and a man of action.

Although he was something of an economic royalist in his early years, his fortunes were nearly wiped out in the panic of the early 1790's. He turned to cotton-planting and gradually acquired the viewpoint of an agrarian. It was then that he wholeheartedly adopted the political philosophy of Jefferson and came to hate all sorts of monopolies, especially bank monopolies like the Bank of the United States.

Jackson did not initiate the movement toward political and social democracy that brought him to power, but he exploited it and built his reputation upon it. The undemocratic caucus system for Presidential nominations was replaced by the convention system, but it was the anti-Masons, not the Jacksonians, who brought about that change. The popular election of Presidential electors, along with an expanded suffrage, were instituted by the individual states and not by Jackson's administration. These political developments, coupled with the opening of the West, trebled the number of voters between 1838 and 1848.

Jackson welcomed these developments. He had learned to speak the language of the yeoman farmer—he was considered uncouth by his Eastern opponents—and he forged an alliance with small

*From "Veto Message, Washington, July 10, 1832," in James B. Richardson, *Messages and Papers of the Presidents*, Vol. II (1817-1833), Washington: Bureau of National Literature, 1904.

businessmen and the newly enfranchised mechanics and factory workers of the cities. What this unstructured majority wanted above all was freedom—freedom from the burden of taxes and responsibilities, freedom from government interference, freedom to expand and advance. Jacksonian populism thus gave strong reinforcement to the *laissez-faire* tendencies in Jeffersonianism. The egalitarianism in Jackson's ideology did not anticipate equality of condition, only equality of opportunity. Jackson did not attack the Bank of the United States because he was opposed to financial transactions—far from it—but because he saw the Bank as a privileged financial institution standing in the way of economic individualism.

The selection presents excerpts from Jackson's famous message in 1832 vetoing the bill for the Second Bank of the United States.

To the Senate:

The bill "to modify and continue" the act entitled "An act to incorporate the subscribers to the Bank of the United States" was presented to me on the 4th July instant. Having considered it with that solemn regard to the principles of the Constitution which the day was calculated to inspire, and come to the conclusion that it ought not to become a law, I herewith return it to the Senate, in which it originated, with my objections.

A bank of the United States is in many respects convenient for the Government and useful to the people. Entertaining this opinion, and deeply impressed with the belief that some of the powers and privileges possessed by the existing bank are unauthorized by the Constitution, subversive of the rights of the States, and dangerous to the liberties of the people, I felt it my duty at an early period of my Administration to call the attention of Congress to the practicability of organizing an institution combining all its advantages and obviating these objections. I sincerely regret that in the act before me I can perceive none of those modifications of the bank charter which are necessary, in my opinion, to make it compatible with justice, with sound policy, or with the Constitution of our country.

The present corporate body, denominated the president, directors, and company of the Bank of the United States, will have existed at the time this act is intended to take effect twenty years. It enjoys an exclusive privilege of banking under the authority of the General Government, a monopoly of its favor and support, and, as a necessary consequence, almost a monopoly of the foreign and domestic exchange. The powers, privileges, and favors bestowed upon it in the original charter, by increasing the value of the stock far above its par value, operated as a gratuity of many millions to the stockholders.

An apology may be found for the failure to guard against this result in the consideration that the effect of the original act of incorporation could not be certainly foreseen at the time of its passage. The act before me proposes another gratuity to the holders of the same stock, and in many cases to the same men, of at least seven millions more. This donation finds no apology in any uncertainty as to the effect of the act. On all hands it is conceded that its passage will increase at least 20 or 30 per cent more the market price of the stock, subject to the payment of the annuity of $200,000 per year secured by the act, thus adding in a moment one-fourth to its par value. It is not our own citizens only who are to receive the bounty of our Government. More than eight millions of the stock of this bank are held by foreigners. By this act the American Republic proposes virtually to make them a present of some millions of dollars. For these gratuities to foreigners and to some of our own opulent citizens the act secures no equivalent whatever. They are the certain gains of the present stockholders under the operation of this act, after making full allowance for the payment of the bonus.

Every monopoly and all exclusive privileges are granted at the expense of the public, which ought to receive a fair equivalent. The many millions which this act proposes to bestow on the stockholders of the existing bank must come directly or indirectly out of the earnings of the American people. It is due to them, therefore, if their Government sell monopolies and exclusive privileges, that they should at least exact for them as much as they are worth in open market. The value of the monopoly in this case may be correctly ascertained. The twenty-eight millions of stock would probably be at an advance of 50 per cent, and command in market at least $42,000,000, subject to the payment of the present bonus. The present value of the monopoly, therefore, is $17,000,000, and this the act proposes to sell for three millions, payable in fifteen annual installments of $200,000 each.

It is not conceivable how the present stockholders can have any claim to the special favor of the Government. The present corporation has enjoyed its monopoly during the period stipulated in the original contract. If we must have such a corporation, why should not the Government sell out the whole stock and thus secure to the people the full market value of the privileges granted? Why should not Congress create and sell twenty-eight millions of stock, incorporating the purchasers with all the powers and privileges secured in this act and putting the premium upon the sales into the Treasury?

But this act does not permit competition in the purchase of this monopoly. It seems to be predicated on the erroneous idea that the present stockholders have a prescriptive right not only to the favor but to the bounty of Government. It appears that more than a fourth part of the stock is held by foreigners and the residue is held by a few hundred of our own citizens, chiefly of the richest class. For their benefit does this act exclude the whole American people from competition in the purchase of this monopoly and dispose of it for many millions less than it is worth. This seems the less excusable because some of our citizens not now stockholders petitioned that the door of competition might be opened, and offered to take a charter on terms much more favorable to the Government and country.

But this proposition, although made by men whose aggregate wealth is believed to be equal to all the private stock in the existing bank, has been set aside, and the bounty of our Government is proposed to be again bestowed on the few who have been fortunate enough to secure the stock and at this moment wield the power of the existing institution. I can not perceive the justice or policy of this course. If our Government must sell monopolies, it would seem to be its duty to take nothing less than their full value, and if gratuities must be made once in fifteen or twenty years let them not be bestowed on the subjects of a foreign government nor upon a designated and favored class of men in our own country. It is but justice and good policy, as far as the nature of the case will admit, to confine our favors to our own fellow citizens, and let each in his turn enjoy an opportunity to profit by our bounty. In the bearings of the act before me upon these points I find ample reasons why it should not become a law.

It has been urged as an argument in favor of rechartering the present bank that the calling in its loans will produce great embarrassment and distress. The time allowed to close its concerns is ample, and if it has been well managed its pressure will be light, and heavy only in case its management has been bad. If, therefore, it shall produce distress, the fault will be its own, and it would furnish a reason against renewing a power which has been so obviously abused. But will there ever be a time when this reason will be less powerful? To acknowledge its force is to admit that the bank ought to be perpetual, and as a consequence the present stockholders and those inheriting their rights as successors be established a privileged order, clothed both with great political power and enjoying immense pecuniary advantages from their connection with the Government.

The modifications of the existing charter proposed by this act are not such, in my view, as make it consistent with the rights of the States or the liberties of the people. The qualification of the right of the bank to hold real estate, the limitation of its power to establish branches, and the power reserved to Congress to forbid the circulation of small notes are restrictions comparatively of little value or importance. All the objectionable principles of the existing corporation, and most of its odious features, are retained without alleviation.

The fourth section provides "that the notes or bills of the said corporation, although the same be, on the faces thereof, respectively made payable at one place only, shall nevertheless be received by the said corporation at the bank or at any of the offices of discount and deposit thereof if tendered in liquidation or payment of any balance or balances due to said corporation or to such office of discount and deposit from any other incorporated bank." This provision secures to the State banks a legal privilege in the Bank of the United States which is withheld from all private citizens. If a State bank in Philadelphia owe the Bank of the United States and have notes issued by the St. Louis branch, it can pay the debt with those notes, but if a merchant, mechanic, or other private citizen be in like circumstances he can not by law pay his debt with those notes, but must sell them at a discount or send them to St. Louis to be cashed. This boon conceded to the State banks, though not unjust in itself, is most odious because it does not measure out equal justice to the high and the low; the rich and the poor. To the extent of its practical effect it is a bond of union among the banking establishments of the nation, erecting them into an interest separate from that of the people, and its necessary tendency is to unite the Bank of the United States and the State banks in any measure which may be thought conducive to their common interest.

The ninth section of the act recognizes principles of worse tendency than any provision of the present charter.

It enacts that "the cashier of the bank shall annually report to the Secretary of the Treasury the names of all stockholders who are not resident citizens of the United States, and on the application of the treasurer of any State shall make out and transmit to such treasurer a list of stockholders residing in or citizens of such State, with the amount of stock owned by each." Although this provision, taken in connection with a decision of the Supreme Court, surrenders, by its silence, the right of the States to tax the banking institutions created by this corporation under the name of branches throughout the Union, it is evidently intended to be construed as a concession of their right to tax that portion of the stock which may be held by their own citizens and residents. In this light, if the act becomes a law, it will be understood by the States, who will probably proceed to levy a tax equal to that paid upon the stock of banks incorporated by themselves. In some States that tax is now 1 per cent, either on the capital or on the shares, and that may be assumed as the amount which all citizen or resident stockholders would be taxed under the operation of this act. As it is only the stock *held* in the States and not that *employed* within them which would be subject to taxation, and as the names of foreign stockholders are not to be reported to the treasurers of the States, it is obvious that the stock held by them will be exempt from this burden. Their annual profits will therefore be 1 per cent more than the citizen stockholders, and as the annual dividends of the bank may be safely estimated at 7 per cent, the stock will be worth 10 or 15 per cent more to foreigners than to citizens of the United States. To appreciate the effects which this state of things will produce, we must take a brief review of the operations and present condition of the Bank of the United States.

By documents submitted to Congress at the present session it appears that on the 1st of January, 1832, of the twenty-eight millions of private stock in the corporation, $8,405,000 were held by foreigners, mostly of Great Britain. The amount of stock held in the nine Western and Southwestern States is $140,200, and in the four Southern States is $5,623,100, and in the Middle and Eastern States is about $13,522,000. The profits of the bank in 1831, as shown in a statement to Congress, were about $3,455,598; of this there accrued in the nine Western States about $1,640,048; in the four Southern States about $352,507, and in the Middle and Eastern States about $1,463,041. As little stock is held in the West, it is obvious that the debt of the people in that section to the bank is principally a debt to the Eastern and foreign stockholders; that the interest they pay upon it is carried into the Eastern States and into Europe, and that it is a burden upon their industry and a drain of their currency, which no country can bear without inconvenience and occasional distress. To meet this burden and equalize the exchange operations of the bank, the amount of specie drawn from those States through its branches within the last two years, as shown by its official reports, was about $6,000,000. More than half a million of this amount does not stop in the Eastern States, but passes on to Europe to pay the dividends of the foreign stockholders. In the principle of taxation recognized by this act the Western States find no adequate compensation for this perpetual burden on their industry and drain of their currency. The branch bank at Mobile made last year $95,140, yet under the provisions of this act the State of Alabama can raise no revenue from these profitable operations, because not a share of the stock is held by any of her citizens. Mississippi and Missouri are in the same condition in relation to the branches at Nachez and St. Louis, and such, in a greater or less degree, is the condition of every Western State. The tendency of the plan of taxation which this act proposes will be to place the whole United States in the same relation to foreign countries which the Western States now bear to the Eastern. When by a tax on resident stockholders the stock of this bank is made worth 10 or 15 per cent more to foreigners than to residents, most of it will inevitably leave the country.

Thus will this provision in its practical effect deprive the Eastern as well as the Southern and Western States of the means of raising a revenue from the extension of business and great profits of this institution. It will make the American people debtors to aliens in nearly the whole amount due to this bank, and send across the Atlantic from two to five millions of specie every year to pay the bank dividends.

In another of its bearings this provision is fraught with danger. Of the twenty-five directors of this bank five are chosen by the Government and twenty by the citizen stockholders. From all voice in these elections the foreign stockholders are excluded by the charter. In proportion, therefore, as the stock is transferred to foreign holders the extent of suffrage in the choice of directors is curtailed. Already is almost a third of the stock in foreign hands and not represented in elections. It is constantly passing out of the country, and this act will accelerate its departure. The entire control of the institution would necessarily fall into the hands of a few citizen stockholders, and the ease with which the object would be accomplished would be a temptation to designing men to secure that control in their own hands by monopolizing the remaining stock. There is danger that a president and directors would then be able to elect themselves from year to year, and without responsibility or control manage the whole concerns of the bank during the existence of its charter. It is easy to conceive that great evils to our country and its institutions might flow from such a concentration of power in the hands of a few men irresponsible to the people.

Is there no danger to our liberty and independence in a bank that in its nature has so little to bind it to our country? The president of the bank has told us that most of the State banks exist by its forbearance. Should its influence become concentered, as it may under the operation of such an act as this, in the hands of a self-elected directory whose interests are identified with those of the foreign stockholders, will there not be cause to tremble for the purity of our elections in peace and for the independence of our country in war? Their power would be great whenever they might choose to exert it; but if this monopoly were regularly renewed every fifteen or twenty years on terms proposed by themselves, they might seldom in peace put forth their strength to influence elections or control the affairs of the nation. But if any private citizen or public functionary should interpose to curtail its powers or prevent a renewal of its privileges, it can not be doubted that he would be made to feel its influence.

Should the stock of the bank principally pass into the hands of the subjects of a foreign country, and we should unfortunately become involved in a war with that country, what would be our condition? Of the course which would be pursued by a bank almost wholly owned by the subjects of a foreign power, and managed by those whose interests, if not affections, would run in the same direction there can be no doubt. All its operations within would be in aid of the hostile fleets and armies without. Controlling our currency, receiving our public moneys, and holding thousands of our citizens in dependence, it would be more formidable and dangerous than the naval and military power of the enemy.

If we must have a bank with private stockholders, every consideration of sound policy and every impulse of American feeling admonishes that it should be *purely American*. Its stockholders should be composed exclusively of our own citizens, who at least ought to be friendly to our Government and willing to support it in times of difficulty and danger. So abundant is domestic capital that competition in subscribing for the stock of local banks has recently led almost to riots. To a bank exclusively of American stockholders, possessing the powers and privileges granted by this act, subscriptions for $200,000,000 could be readily obtained. Instead of sending abroad the stock of the bank in which the Government must deposit its funds and on which it must rely to sustain its credit in times of emergency, it would rather seem to be expedient to prohibit its sale to aliens under penalty of absolute forfeiture.

It is maintained by the advocates of the bank that its constitutionality in all its features ought to be considered as settled by precedent and by the decision of the Supreme Court. To this conclusion I can not assent. Mere precedent is a dangerous source of authority, and should not be regarded as deciding questions of constitutional power except where the acquiescence of the people and the States can be considered as well settled. So far from this being the case on this subject, an argument against the bank might be based on precedent. One Congress, in 1791, decided in favor of a bank; another, in 1811, decided against it. One Congress, in 1815, decided against a bank; another, in 1816, decided in its favor. Prior to the present Congress, therefore, the precedents drawn from that source were equal. If we resort to the States, the expressions of legislative, judicial, and executive opinions against the bank have been probably to those in its favor as 4 to 1. There is nothing in precedent, therefore, which, if its authority were admitted, ought to weigh in favor of the act before me.

If the opinion of the Supreme Court covered the whole ground of this act, it ought not to control the coordinate authorities of this Government. The Congress, the Executive, and the Court must each for itself be guided by its own opinion of the Constitution. Each public officer who takes an oath to support the Constitution swears that he will support it as he understands it, and not as it is understood by others. It is as much the duty of the House of Representatives, of the Senate, and of the President to decide upon the constitutionality of any bill or resolution which may be presented to them for passage or approval as it is of the supreme judges when it may be brought before them for judicial decision. The opinion of the judges has no more authority over Congress than the opinion of Congress has over the judges, and on that point the President is independent of both. The authority of the Supreme Court must not, therefore, be permitted to control the Congress or the Executive when acting in their legislative capacities, but to have only such influence as the force of their reasoning may deserve. . . .

It is to be regretted that the rich and powerful too often bend the acts of government to their selfish purposes. Distinctions in society will always exist under every just government. Equality of talents, of education, or of wealth can not be produced by human institutions. In the full enjoyment of the gifts of Heaven and the fruits of superior industry, economy, and virtue, every man is equally entitled to protection by law; but when the laws undertake to add to these natural and just advantages artificial distinctions, to grant titles, gratuities, and exclusive privileges, to make the rich richer and the potent more powerful, the humble members of society—the farmers, mechanics, and laborers—who have neither the time nor the means of securing like favors to themselves, have a right to complain of the injustice of their Government. There are no necessary evils in government. Its evils exist only in its abuses.

If it would confine itself to equal protection, and, as Heaven does its rains, shower its favors alike on the high and the low, the rich and the poor, it would be an unqualified blessing. In the act before me there seems to be a wide and unnecessary departure from these just principles.

Nor is our Government to be maintained or our Union preserved by invasions of the rights and powers of the several States. In thus attempting to make our General Government strong we make it weak. Its true strength consists in leaving individuals and States as much as possible to themselves—in making itself felt, not in its power, but in its beneficence; not in its control, but in its protection; not in binding the States more closely to the center, but leaving each to move unobstructed in its proper orbit.

Experience should teach us wisdom. Most of the difficulties our Government now encounters and most of the dangers which impend over our Union have sprung from an abandonment of the legitimate objects of Government by our national legislation, and the adoption of such principles as are embodied in this act. Many of our rich men have not been content with equal protection and equal benefits, but have besought us to make them richer by act of Congress. By attempting to gratify their desires we have in the results of our legislation arrayed section against section, interest against interest, and man against man, in a fearful commotion which threatens to shake the foundations of our Union. It is time to pause in our career to review our principles, and if possible revive that devoted patriotism and spirit of compromise which distinguished the sages of the Revolution and the fathers of our Union. If we can not at once, in justice to interests vested under improvident legislation, make our Government what it ought to be, we can at least take a stand against all new grants of monopolies and exclusive privileges, against any prostitution of our Government to the advancement of the few at the expense of the many, and in favor of compromise and gradual reform in our code of laws and system of political economy.

I have now done my duty to my country. If sustained by my fellow-citizens, I shall be grateful and happy; if not, I shall find in the motives which impel me ample grounds for contentment and peace. In the difficulties which surround us and the dangers which

threaten our institutions there is cause for neither dismay nor
alarm. For relief and deliverance let us firmly rely on that kind
Providence which I am sure watches with peculiar care over the
destinies of our Republic, and on the intelligence and wisdom of
our countrymen. Through *His* abundant goodness and *their* patriotic devotion our liberty and Union will be preserved.

ANDREW JACKSON.

II. THE PEOPLE'S PARTY:
RISE AND DECLINE

Agrarian protest, we have seen, is as old as America. But the movement that was to culminate in the "People's Party" was greatly accelerated after the Civil War. The railroads facilitated the opening of the trans-Mississippi West. Generous bounties were granted to the railroads by the federal and state governments, and they in turn lured settlers to the Western regions with grandiose promises of land for farming. Eastern financial interests, seeking promising outlets for the surplus capital made possible by war prosperity, offered loans to settlers, and these were eagerly seized. Vast expanses of prairie land, easily cleared and containing some excellent soil, seemed to promise abundance. But the drought years and consequent crop failures of the late 1880's finally caused the bubble to burst. Speculators ran for cover, and farmers, unable to keep up mortgage payments, saw their farms taken away by banks and courts. Even those who did manage to hold on to their lands and grow a good crop found their profits squeezed by what seemed to be exorbitant freight rates and other "middlemen" fees, and small farmers found that railroads discriminated on behalf of the big shippers.

Farmers also looked around and saw what seemed to them an unhealthy growth of big business, monopolistic industries brought into existence by the demands of Civil War technology, saw a scandal-ridden Grant Administration and numerous cases of bribery in their own state legislatures, saw changing mores and class alignments, saw a breakneck pace of national life that seemed to be leaving the farmer and his ways behind.

So the farmers and their champions turned back to the vast

literature of rural romanticism, the eulogies of decentralized government, the myths of Andrew Jackson and Thomas Jefferson —turned to them not for solace but for strength, which they then mixed with their own evangelical Protestantism to create a powerful fighting faith.

By 1890 the Farmer's Alliance, a pre-Populist organization, had brought this amalgamation of gospel singing and radical politics to a fever-pitch throughout the Plains states. John D. Hicks in his standard work, *The Populist Revolt*, quotes a contemporary newspaper account.

> In vain the reports of the meetings were suppressed by a partisan press. In vain the Republican and Democratic leaders sneered at and ridiculed this new gospel, while they talked tariff and war issues to small audiences. . . . The excitement and enthusiasm were contagious, and the Alliance men deserted their former parties by thousands.
>
> Women who never dreamed of becoming public speakers, grew eloquent in their zeal and fervor. Farmers' wives and daughters rose earlier and worked later to gain time to cook picnic dinners, to paint the mottos on the banners, to practice with the glee clubs, to march in procession. Josh Billings' saying that "wimmin is everywhere" was literally true in that wonderful picnicking, speech-making Alliance summer of 1890.*

After some preliminary conventions in 1889, 1890, and 1891, the People's Party held its first national convention in Omaha, Nebraska, on the Fourth of July, 1892. Its platform supported free silver, public ownership of railroads, a graduated income tax, the initiative and referendum, along with other reforms intended to increase the power and benefits of the "plain people." Hicks quotes another contemporary newspaper source as describing the reaction to these planks as a "regular Baptist camp meeting chorus."*

*John D. Hicks, *The Populist Revolt* (Lincoln, Nebraska: The University of Nebraska Press, 1961), p. 114.
*John D. Hicks, *op. cit.*, p. 232.

The Populists seemed off to a good start. They nominated General James B. Weaver, a respected Civil War veteran with a background in reform causes, as Presidential candidate, and won a million popular votes and twenty-two electoral votes in their first Presidential bid. In 1894 the People's Party votes in the various state elections had increased the party's strength by 42 percent.

In 1896, however, the Populists made a fatal mistake—fusion with the Democrats. In endorsing the Presidential candidacy of William Jennings Bryan, the Democratic nominee, the People's Party reduced itself to a helpless appendage of the Democrats, destroying its reputation for independence without acquiring any decisive influence over the Democratic policymakers. Indeed, the opposite occurred: In order not to offend some of the more conservative elements of the Democratic Party, the Populists finessed and glossed over the full spectrum of reform they had advocated in 1892, concentrating most of their religious fervor on the panacea of "free silver."

The Populist-Democratic coalition did well in 1896—Bryan's total in popular votes came within 600,000 of the victorious McKinley's—but not well enough. Bryan's strength was overwhelmingly in the rural areas west of the Mississippi. He lost the industrial states and was devastated in New England. In subsequent bids for the Presidency he did even worse, dragging down with him the parties that had staked so much on his charisma.

The Populists were defeated by other factors than their own mistakes. The reemergence of white supremacy as the central issue in Southern politics crushed the Populists in that region, and in the nation generally the return of farm prosperity after 1896 undermined the party's economic *raison d'être*. But would the People's Party have collapsed so completely if it were not for its doctrinal fluidity? It hardly seems likely. The Populists, after all, were concerned about more than the restoration of prosperity; they had set out to redress the economic and political imbalances in American society. Yet the means they adopted to attain this great aim remained continually elusive. On one day it might be "free silver"; on another it might be a patchwork of "solutions," from public ownership of railroads to the keeping out of foreign labor. This platform ambiguity reflected a deeper problem in the People's

Party, which was a lack of conceptual clarity. If an "out" party, lacking the power of patronage, is to have cohesion, it must be held together by some doctrine or ideology that can be articulated and defended. The Populists, in the final analysis, were held together by lofty feelings and good intentions. When their party dissolved some went back to the Democrats and Republicans, some to the Progressive Party of Robert La Follette, others to the "left" and "right" fringes of America—to the Socialists and Communists, to the Prohibitionists and the Klan. And all could trace their lineage back to the People's Party, to its "elevating" spirit, its social pietism, and its protean mixture of reforms.

A. *People's Party Platform:*
Restoring the "Plain People"*

In 1892, with General Weaver as its candidate, the People's Party made its first bid for the Presidency. Its platform contained a wide panoply of reforms, reforms which we now take for granted but which were certainly considered radical in their time: the initiative and referendum, direct election of Senators, limited terms of office for President and Vice President, the secret ballot and the progressive income tax. Some, like public ownership of railroads and a cutoff of government subsidies to big business, are still beyond the range of politics-as-usual in America.

This courageous and prophetic platform was emasculated in 1896. The Democrats, with whom the Populists had fused, would not abide public ownership of railroads, so the proposal was finessed into a mere regulation of the railroads. The rest of the platform was also largely forgotten as the Populists became fanatically preoccupied with the "free silver" panacea. Henry Demarest Lloyd, who watched the degeneration with amazement and disgust, likened the free silver issue to a cowbird, a predator who waits for other birds to lay eggs, then steals them. All of the fervor

---

*From "The National People's Party Platform of 1892," *The World Almanac* (New York: Press Publishing Co., 1893), pp. 83-85.

generated by early Populism, a fervor growing out of its hope of real reforms—such as those in the 1892 platform—was stolen away by the free silverites and squandered on a single plank, and a dubious one at that.

This selection, then, can be seen as an official, authorized summary of the Populist outlook at its boldest.

Assembled upon the 116th anniversary of the Declaration of Independence, the People's Party of America, in their first national convention, invoking upon their action the blessing of Almighty God, put forth in the name and on behalf of the people of this country, the following preamble and declaration of principles:

PREAMBLE

The conditions which surround us best justify our co-operation; we meet in the midst of a nation brought to the verge of moral, political, and material ruin. Corruption dominates the ballot-box, the Legislatures, the Congress, and touches even the ermine of the bench. The people are demoralized; most of the States have been compelled to isolate the voters at the polling places to prevent universal intimidation and bribery. The newspapers are largely subsidized or muzzled, public opinion silenced, business prostrated, homes covered with mortgages, labor impoverished, and the land concentrating in the hands of capitalists. The urban workman are denied the right to organize for self-protection, imported pauperized labor beats down their wages, a hireling standing army, unrecognized by our laws, is established to shoot them down, and they are rapidly degenerating into European conditions. The fruits of the toil of millions are boldly stolen to build up colossal fortunes for a few, unprecedented in the history of mankind; and the possessors of those, in turn, despise the Republic and endanger liberty. From the same prolific womb of governmental injustice we breed the two great classes—tramps and millionaires.

The national power to create money is appropriated to enrich bondholders; a vast public debt payable in legal tender currency has been funded into gold-bearing bonds, thereby adding millions to the burdens of the people.

Silver, which has been accepted as coin since the dawn of history, has been demonetized to add to the purchasing power of gold by decreasing the value of all forms of property as well as human labor, and the supply of currency is purposely abridged to fatten usurers, bankrupt enterprise, and enslave industry. A vast conspiracy against mankind has been organized on two continents, and it is rapidly taking possession of the world. If not met and overthrown at once it forebodes terrible social convulsions, the destruction of civilization, or the establishment of an absolute despotism.

We have witnessed for more than a quarter of a century the struggles of the two great political parties for power and plunder, while grievous wrongs have been inflicted upon the suffering people. We charge that the controlling influences dominating both these parties have permitted the existing dreadful conditions to develop without serious effort to prevent or restrain them. Neither do they now promise us any substantial reform. They have agreed together to ignore, in the coming campaign, every issue but one. They propose to drown the outcries of a plundered people with the uproar of a sham battle over the tariff, so that capitalists, corporations, national banks, rings, trusts, watered stock, the demonetization of silver and the oppressions of the usurers may all be lost sight of. They propose to sacrifice our homes, lives, and children on the altar of mammon; to destroy the multitude in order to secure corruption funds from the millionaires.

Assembled on the anniversary of the birthday of the nation, and filled with the spirit of the grand general and chief who established our independence, we seek to restore the government of the Republic to the hands of "the plain people," with which class it originated. We assert our purposes to be identical with the purposes of the National Constitution; to form a more perfect union and establish justice, insure domestic tranquillity, provide for the common defence; promote the general welfare, and secure the blessings of liberty for ourselves and our posterity.

We declare that this Republic can only endure as a free government while built upon the love of the whole people for each other and for the nation; that it cannot be pinned together by bayonets; that the civil war is over, and that every passion and resentment which grew out of it must die with it, and that we must be in fact, as we are in name, one united brotherhood of free men.

Our country finds itself confronted by conditions for which there is no precedent in the history of the world; our annual agricultural productions amount to billions of dollars in value, which must, within a few weeks or months, be exchanged for billions of dollars' worth of commodities consumed in their production; the existing currency supply is wholly inadequate to make this exchange; the results are falling prices, the formation of combines and rings, the impoverishment of the producing class. We pledge ourselves that if given power we will labor to correct these evils by wise and reasonable legislation, in accordance with the terms of our platform.

We believe that the power of government—in other words, of the people—should be expanded (as in the case of the postal service) as rapidly and as far as the good sense of an intelligent people and the teachings of experience shall justify, to the end that oppression, injustice, and poverty shall eventually cease in the land.

While our sympathies as a party of reform are naturally upon the side of every proposition which will tend to make men intelligent, virtuous, and temperate, we nevertheless regard these questions, important as they are, as secondary to the great issues now pressing for solution, and upon which not only our individual prosperity but the very existence of free institutions depend; and we ask all men to first help us to determine whether we are to have a Republic to administer before we differ as to the conditions upon which it is to be administered, believing that the forces of reform this day organized will never cease to move forward until every wrong is remedied and equal rights and equal privileges securely established for all the men and women of this country.

PLATFORM

We declare, therefore—
 First.—That the union of the labor forces of the United States

this day consummated shall be permanent and perpetual; may its spirit enter into all hearts for the salvation of the Republic and the uplifting of mankind.

Second.—Wealth belongs to him who creates it, and every dollar taken from industry without an equivalent is robbery. "If any will not work, neither shall he eat." The interests of rural and civic labor are the same; their enemies are identical.

Third.—We believe that the time has come when the railroad corporations will either own the people or the people must own the railroads, and should the government enter upon the work of owning and managing all railroads, we should favor an amendment to the Constitution by which all persons engaged in the government service shall be placed under a civil-service regulation of the most rigid character, so as to prevent the increase of the power of the national administration by the use of such additional government employees.

Finance.—We demand a national currency, safe, sound, and flexible, issued by the general government only, a full legal tender for all debts, public and private, and that without the use of banking corporations, a just, equitable, and efficient means of distribution direct to the people, at a tax not to exceed 2 per cent per annum, to be provided, as set forth in the sub-treasury plan of the Farmers' Alliance, or a better system; also by payments in discharge of its obligations for public improvements.

1. We demand free and unlimited coinage of silver and gold at the present legal ratio of 16 to 1.

2. We demand that the amount of circulating medium be speedily increased to not less than $50 per capita.

3. We demand a graduated income tax.

4. We believe that the money of the country should be kept as much as possible in the hands of the people, and hence we demand that all State and national revenues shall be limited to the necessary expenses of the government, economically and honestly administered.

5. We demand that postal savings banks be established by the government for the safe deposit of the earnings of the people and to facilitate exchange.

Transportation.—Transportation being a means of exchange and a public necessity, the government should own and operate the railroads in the interest of the people. The telegraph, telephone, like the post-office system, being a necessity for the transmission of news, should be owned and operated by the government in the interest of the people.

Land.—The land, including all the natural sources of wealth, is the heritage of the people, and should not be monopolized for speculative purposes, and alien ownership of land should be prohibited. All land now held by railroads and other corporations in excess of their actual needs, and all lands now owned by aliens should be reclaimed by the government and held for actual settlers only.

EXPRESSION OF SENTIMENTS

Your Committee on Platform and Resolutions beg leave unanimously to report the following:

WHEREAS, Other questions have been presented for our consideration, we hereby submit the following, not as a part of the Platform of the People's Party, but as resolutions expressive of the sentiment of this Convention:

1. *Resolved*, That we demand a free ballot and a fair count in all elections, and pledge ourselves to secure it to every legal voter without Federal intervention, through the adoption by the States of the unperverted Australian or secret ballot system.

2. *Resolved*, That the revenue derived from a graduated income tax should be applied to the reduction of the burden of taxation now levied upon the domestic industries of this country.

3. *Resolved*, That we pledge our support to fair and liberal pensions to ex-Union soldiers and sailors.

4. *Resolved*, That we condemn the fallacy of protecting American labor under the present system, which opens our ports to the pauper and criminal classes of the world and crowds out our wage-earners; and we denounce the present ineffective laws against contract labor, and demand the further restriction of undesirable emigration.

5. *Resolved*, That we cordially sympathize with the efforts of organized workingmen to shorten the hours of labor, and demand a rigid enforcement of the existing eight-hour law on Government

work, and ask that a penalty clause be added to the said law.

6. *Resolved*, That we regard the maintenance of a large standing army of mercenaries, known as the Pinkerton system, as a menace to our liberties, and we demand its abolition; and we condemn the recent invasion of the Territory of Wyoming by the hired assassins of plutocracy, assisted by Federal officers.

7. *Resolved*, That we commend to the favorable consideration of the people and the reform press the legislative system known as the initiative and referendum.

8. *Resolved*, That we favor a constitutional provision limiting the office of President and Vice-President to one term, and providing for the election of Senators of the United States by a direct vote of the people.

9. *Resolved*, That we oppose any subsidy or national aid to any private corporation for any purpose.

10. *Resolved*, That this convention sympathizes with the Knights of Labor and their righteous contest with the tyrannical combine of clothing manufacturers of Rochester, and declare it to be the duty of all who hate tyranny and oppression to refuse to purchase the goods made by the said manufacturers, or to patronize any merchants who sell such goods.

B. *James B. Weaver:*
"A Call to Action"*

The most widely respected figure in the People's Party was James B. Weaver (1833-1912), Populist Presidential candidate in 1892. Born in Ohio and graduated from Cincinnati law school in 1854, Weaver emigrated soon afterward to Iowa, where he practiced law until the outbreak of the Civil War. He enlisted on the Union side, was promoted through the ranks to brigadier general, and honored for "gallantry in the field." An active Republican until 1877, he broke with the party that year and won election to Congress a year later as a Greenbacker with Democratic support.

*James B. Weaver, *A Call to Action* (Des Moines: Iowa Printing Co., 1892).

In 1880 he was the Greenback nominee for President, and from 1883 to 1887 he was back in Congress as a Greenback-Democrat. By 1890 he had cut even his hyphenated tie with the major parties and was ready to join the "Union Labor Industrial Party of Iowa," a pre-Populist organization.

By this time Weaver's fame as an advocate of economic justice, with his added appeal to veterans of the Union army, had spread far beyond the bounds of Iowa. He was thus the logical, and the overwhelming, choice of the newly formed Populist Party as Presidential candidate. He then embarked upon a strenuous and courageous campaign, braving everything from verbal heckling to thrown eggs in some areas (according to Mary Lease, another prominent Populist, who toured the South with him, General Weaver "was made a regular walking omelet by the Southern chivalry of Georgia"). At its end he made a good showing for the candidate of a new party, receiving over a million popular and twenty-two electoral votes, the first new party to break into the electoral college since the Civil War. It was a brave beginning, or so it seemed at the time, and much of it had to do with Weaver's reputation as a man of balance and moderation.

Yet, ironically, Weaver's penchant for practicality may have had much to do with the decline of his party after 1896. He was the strongest advocate of fusion with the Democrats in 1896, and this proved to be a fatal embrace.

Whatever his tactical errors, Weaver was no moral sellout. His sensitive conscience, his high ideals, his deep indignation at the "piracy" of the corporate magnates, all are evident in these brief selections from a 445-page book he published in 1892, entitled *A Call to Action*.

PREFACE

The author's object in publishing this book is to call attention to some of the more serious evils which now disturb the repose of American society and threaten the overthrow of free institutions.

We are nearing a serious crisis. If the present strained relations between wealth owners and wealth producers continue much longer they will ripen into frightful disaster. This universal discontent must be quickly interpreted and its causes removed. It is the country's imperative Call to Action, and can not be longer disregarded with impunity.

The sovereign right to regulate commerce among our magnificent union of States, and to control the instruments of commerce, the right to issue the currency and to determine the money supply for sixty-three million people and their posterity, have been leased to associated speculators. The brightest lights of the legal profession have been lured from their honorable relation to the people in the administration of justice, and through evolution in crime the corporation has taken the place of the pirate; and finally a bold and aggressive plutocracy has usurped the Government and is using it as a policeman to enforce its insolent decrees. It has filled the Senate with its adherents, it controls the popular branch of the National Legislature by cunningly filling the Speaker's chair with its representatives, and it has not hesitated to tamper with our Court of last resort. The public domain has been squandered, our coal fields bartered away, our forests denuded, our people impoverished, and we are attempting to build a prosperous commonwealth among people who are being robbed of their homes—a task as futile and impossible as it would be to attempt to cultivate a thrifty forest without soil to sustain it. The corporation has been placed above the individual and an armed body of cruel mercenaries permitted, in times of public peril, to discharge police duties which clearly belong to the State. Wall Street has become the Western extension of Threadneedle and Lombard streets, and the wealthy classes of England and America have been brought into touch. They are no longer twain, but one, and have restored to Great Britain all the dominion she desires over her long lost colonies. We have in late years become an important prop to the British throne and the hope of her dominant classes. We are careful not to act in monetary affairs without her consent; and if not in monetary affairs, then in none other, for money has become the Alpha and Omega of modern life.

The aristocratic classes in the old country constantly point their turbulent starving masses to the United States, in proof that republics afford no refuge or hope to the oppressed millions of mankind.

But the present stupendous uprising among the industrial people of the new world confounds them. It is the second revolt of the colonies. It required seven years for our fathers to overthrow the outward manifestations of tyranny in colonial days. But our weapons now are not carnal, but mighty to the pulling down of strongholds. Their children can vanquish the American and British plutocracy combined in a single day—at the ballot-box. They have resolved to do it. If this book can in the least aid in the mighty work, we shall be content.

The few haughty millionaires who are gathering up the riches of the new world, make use of certain instruments to accomplish their selfish purposes. The people are beginning to understand what these instrumentalities are, and are preparing to resist their destructive force. The purpose of this book is to make clear the great work which lies before us. It must be thorough and complete in order to be permanent. The magnitude of our task will appear as we advance in the struggle.

We have made no attack upon individuals, but have confined our criticisms to evil systems and baleful legislation. We have endeavored to be accurate, but claim no literary merit for our effort. We submit the work to the criticism of our contemporaries and the candid consideration of patriotic people.

THE AUTHOR.

"LET US ALONE."

. . . The corporations and special interests of every class created during the past twenty-five years by various species of class legislation and favoritism, have grown rich and powerful. They are now pleading to be let alone. They cry out, "You will disturb the peace, unsettle business and violate our vested constitutional rights." The world has heard similar lamentations before. The same spirit has lurked in the pathway of progress and hissed its sinister protests from behind the Constitution and from beneath the very altars of our holy religion, from the beginning until now. The same argument was urged against the introduction of the gospel in the early days of Christianity.

. . . This old plea is now urged, however, in behalf of corporation usurpers and tyrants. They have nothing to gain by change. On

the contrary everything to lose. Their Juggernaut must move and
the car of progress stand still. They would not have the situation
otherwise than it is, and as the most effectual method of enforcing
this policy they have quietly filled the Senate with their friends.
The punishment meted out by the corporations to Judge Thurman,
of Ohio, for the faithful discharge of his duty concerning the
Pacific railroads, while a member of the Senate, and the defeat of
General Van Wyck, in Nebraska, after the people had expressed a
desire for his re-election—these and a score of similar
instances—attest only too accurately the extent and the deadly
character of corporate influence in this body. . . .

The Senate, as we have seen, was incorporated into our legislative system as a check upon the rashness and apprehended extremes of the popular branch of Congress. But it was not contem-
plated, even by Dickinson and Hamilton, that it should become the
stronghold of monopoly, nor that it should hedge up the way to all
reform and make impossible the peaceful overthrow of conceded
abuses. In fact no tendency in this direction was observable until
within the past thirty years. But of late this body has come to
represent both the evil and the inertia of government. When you
visit the Senate chamber you are at once reminded of antiquity.
You feel that you are not far removed from that period when the
changeless laws of the Medes and Persians were in force. If,
without diverting your attention, you could be suddenly transported to an Egyptian charnel-house filled with mummies, you
would be likely to mistake it for a Senate cloak-room. The very
foot-falls of the Senators, as they walk across the tessellated
floors, sound like a constant iteration of statu quo! statu quo! statu
quo! . . .

THE DECLINE OF THE SENATE.

There is not a single great leader in the Senate of to-day, not one
who is abreast of the times, or who can be truthfully said to be the
exponent of American civilization or the active champion of the
reforms made necessary by the growth and changed relations of a
century, and which are now struggling for recognition.
. . . They are stifled by their surroundings and dwarfed by their

parties. One and all, they stand dumb and aimless in the presence of the mighty problems of the age. The situation reminds one of the era in the history of our planet mentioned in the book of Genesis, when it is said: "There was not a man to till the ground."

This august body is literally filled with splendid specimens of a by-gone epoch—men whose only mission is to preserve the old order of things—to guard the embalmed corpse of the past from the touch of the profane reformer. They are the lineal descendents of the fellows who skulked in the camp of Israel when Joshua insisted on crossing the Jordan into the promised land. They are as much out of place in this pulsating age of reform as a mastodon or a megatherium would be among a herd of our modern well-bred domestic animals. They are fit only to adorn museums and musty cabinets. If their commissions could be recalled to-day and the question of their return referred to an open vote of their constituents, there is not one in ten who would stand a ghost of a show for re-election. They are not in touch with the people. Their strength lies in their entrenched position—not in their achievements nor the principles which they represent. If dislodged, they would be powerless to make another stand. We, of course, do not include in this criticism the two or three prophets of the new order of things, who have but recently been commissioned to go unto Ninevah, that great city, and to preach unto it the preaching whereunto they have been called. It will be time enough to speak of them when they shall have had opportunity to obey those who sent them.

Every great movement and struggle of the race develops its own leaders, who are forced to assault fortified positions and fight against great odds. Some positions have to be carried by storm, while others can only be taken by regular approaches which sorely try the endurance and resources of the besieging columns. Such were the characteristics of the great struggle of the 60's. Their storming parties were hurled forward with dash and power, and their sieges were stubborn and successful. To change the figure, the pioneers in the movement doubtless had a clear vision of the land to be ultimately possessed, but they quickly passed away and were succeeded by an inferior order of leaders who felt that they had done their whole duty when they had driven out the wild beasts, cleared away the forest and prepared the ground for the reception of good seed. They then rested upon their laurels and allowed the enemy to sow the field with taxes. The seed has grown, the harvest has ripened, and the reapers are under orders to burn the tares.

The moral, intellectual and political leaders during the twenty years immediately following the war, with the single exception of Wendell Phillips, failed to comprehend the problems which confronted them. They stopped with the overthrow of the outward form of slavery. Through the strength and suffering of the great army of the people they succeeded in breaking the chains of chattel slavery and prepared the way for the complete triumph of man over those who lived by the enslavement of labor. All that was necessary was one more forward movement of the column, and the victory would have been complete. But they failed to make it and surrendered to a handful of task masters of another type, whose triumphs in the slave trade have never, in all the ages, been limited by distinctions of race or complexions of skin. This class of slave drivers have never yet been routed or permanently crippled. They have plied their cruel vocation among all the families of men. To overthrow them is the grand work of the new crusade. Confederated labor has proclaimed the new emancipation. Now let the great army of toilers move on the enemy's works and enforce the decree. . . .

THE SUPREME COURT

Why should the American judiciary of to-day be exempted from elective control or hold their position for life? The idea was adopted in the old world, not because it was free from objection, but because it was less objectionable than any other under the peculiar circumstances by which they were environed. The conditions which called for these so-called safeguards have vanished even there; but the evils inherent in the system still remain both here and abroad to curse mankind and imperil the safety of society. It is not probable that any representative body of men, chosen by the people of the United States to-day, would seriously entertain a proposition to grant to our Supreme Court the powers now claimed by that tribunal. Nor would they for a moment think of appointing the judges for life. The growth of plutocratic spirit, the rapid rise of corporate influence, and the varied experiences of a Century under our Constitution, would imperatively forbid it. Power must of course be confided to human hands, but it is constantly subject to abuse. Those who exercise it should always be under the restraint of those from whom it was derived. Elective control is the only safeguard of liberty. If the history of the republics of the earth has in store for our race a single lesson of value, it is this.

The learned Chancellor Kent, in his great work on American law, attempts to justify the mode by which we select our Federal Judiciary and the tenure by which they hold their seats, by resorting to the following bit of casuistry: "But all plans of Government which suppose the people will always act with wisdom and integrity are plainly eutopian and contrary to uniform experience. Governments must be formed for man as he is, and not as he would be if he were free from vice!" It does not seem to have occurred to the learned jurist that it is equally contrary to experience and fully as eutopian to suppose that our judges appointed for life will always act with wisdom and prudence. It is quite as important that Government should be formed for the judge as he is and not for the judge as he would be if he were free from the vices and passions incident to human nature. Besides, the people must touch their Government at some point; and is it not probable that they would act with as much wisdom and prudence in selecting their Judiciary, were they permitted to do so, as they now do in selecting those with whom the appointing power is to reside?

Our Federal Judicial system is remarkable and anomalous. It is lifted above both State and Federal governments, and is not responsible to either except in matters of personal misbehavior, or malfeasance in office, to an extent that would render the individual judges liable to impeachment. Their method of appointment, freedom from responsibility, life tenure of office, exemption from the ordinary struggles common to human nature in the battle for bread, their arbitrary and extraordinary power, tend, in this day and age, to separate them entirely from the great body of the people and to impart growth and vigor to all the dangerous elements of human nature.

The Executive never consults popular sentiment in making his nominations. In practice it is rarely ever known who is to be chosen until the official notification is sent in to the Senate. When that body and the Executive are in political accord, confirmation, as a rule, follows quickly. When once confirmed, the wisdom of the appointment can never be reviewed. A member of this Court, appointed at the age of forty-five and serving until he is seventy, will witness twelve complete changes in the House of Representatives, four in the Senate, and six in the Executive. A whole generation may live, suffer and pass from the stage of action before the wrong inflicted by a bad appointment can be corrected, unless the legislative arm shall interpose. How strange that just at the point where we lodge the greatest power we should sever all connection with the people, who are the embodiment of Sovereignty and the fountain of all authority. We shall learn before we reach the close of this chapter that it is quite as important that popular liberty and the peace of society shall be protected from the inconsiderate, incompetent, rash and tyrannical tendencies inherent in our Court of Last resort, as it is that we should establish safeguards against the encroachments and infidelity of any other class of public servants.

The Government of the United States is composed of three co-ordinate branches, Legislative, Executive and Judicial. But the Legislative is sub-divided into two independent bodies—the Senate and the House of Representatives. To speak accurately then, Sovereignty with us has been divided into four parts, represented by the House, the Senate, and Executive and the Judiciary. It is a startling fact that the people are only permitted to directly elect one out of the four, the House, while the other three-fourths are exempt from elective control and popular supervision. Should the reader insist that the Executive is chosen in fact, though not in form, by the people, the following figures will serve to fully dispel that illusion: In 1844 Polk received less than fifty per cent of the popular vote, but 62 per cent of the Electoral vote. In 1848 Gen. Taylor received 47 per cent of the popular vote and 56 per cent of the Electoral vote. In 1852 Mr. Pierce received a small majority on the popular vote and 85 per cent of the Electoral vote. Mr. Buchanan in 1856 received but 45 per cent of the popular vote and 59 per cent of the Electoral vote. Mr. Lincoln received in 1860, 40 per cent of the popular vote and 59 per cent of the Electoral vote. In 1864 he received 55 per cent of the popular vote and 91 per cent of the Electoral vote. Gen. Grant in 1868, had 57 per cent, and in 1872, 55 per cent; while in his first election he had 73 per cent and in his second 81 per cent of the Electoral vote. In 1876 Hayes had 49 per cent of the popular vote and 50-1/2 per cent of the Electoral vote. Gen. Garfield had barely a majority of the popular vote but 60 per cent of the Electoral vote. Mr. Cleveland had 48-3/4 per cent of the popular vote and 54-3/4 per cent of the Electoral vote. President Harrison had a fraction over 48 per cent of the popular vote and 58-1/4 per cent of the Electoral vote. Prior to the year 1824 the Presidential electors were not chosen by the people but were selected by the State Legislatures, and since that time, as the reader is well aware, in a large majority of instances, the candidates selected for the Chief Magistracy by the National conventions of the old established parties, are generally designated by a few skillful manipulators, after an understanding has been reached that the selection of the particular candidate will inure to the special benefit of the combination, and not because of the fitness of the candidate for the high duties of the office. So the fact remains beyond dispute that under our present system, three out of the four subdivisions of Government are practically placed beyond the control of the multitude. It is creditable to the corporations, that at every election for Members of the House of Representatives, they show some willingness to run an even race to see whether they or the people shall control the remaining one-fourth.

Let us now proceed to inquire closely into the practical operation of our Judicial system and see if any dangerous tendencies have manifested themselves during the Century in which it has been upon trial.

DANGEROUS ASSUMPTION OF POWER.

Under the kingly prerogatives of our Supreme Court, which will never willingly be surrendered, Congress may enact a law and, after the fullest consultation with his Constitutional advisers, the Executive may give it his approval, and yet a majority of the Judges of the Supreme Court may, and often do, assume to declare the joint and solemn act of the National Legislature and of the Executive to be null and void. The fact that both branches of Congress acting separately, the Executive and his Cabinet and the great body of the people before whom it may have been discussed, have reached a different conclusion, does not in the least deter the court from the exercise of this power. It was the boast of our fathers, as it has been the pride of their children, that we had gotten rid of that cruel fallacy of kingcraft—"the King can do no wrong." But it seems that we have incarnated it, clothed it with the Ermine and given it an abiding place in our Federal Judiciary.

The first term of the Supreme Court was held in New York, then the seat of the Federal Government, in the month of February, 1790. As early as 1792, some of the Circuit judges had refused to comply with an early act of Congress, directing the Secretary of War to place upon the pension list the names of such disabled officers and soldiers as should be reported to him by the Circuit courts. The judges deemed the act unconstitutional and refused to certify the names of the soldiers. But in 1803, in the case of *Marbury vs. Jas. Madison*, the whole question of the authority of the court to declare an Act of Congress unconstitutional was elaborately reviewed by Chief Justice Marshall, who pronounced the unanimous opinion of the court. The question was with regard to a provision of the Act of Congress establishing the judicial system of the United States, which clothed the Supreme Court with authority to issue writs of mandamus to public officers. The object sought to be accomplished in this particular case was to compel James Madison, then Secretary of State, to deliver to Marbury his commission as justice of the peace, which had been signed by Thomas Jefferson, President of the United States, and placed in Mr. Madison's hands for delivery to Marbury, delivery having been refused for some reason. The learned Chief Justice declared that it was the prerogative and the duty of the Court to pass upon the constitutionality of the Acts of Congress, when properly raised, and then held that the act in question was repugnant to the Constitution and therefore void. This early decision has been followed uniformly through subsequent years in a great variety of cases, until at present the power of the Court in this respect seems to be no longer questioned. It is now *imperium in imperio*. The better doctrine, that the co-ordinate branches of the government are independent, possessing the right to interpret the Constitution for themselves, seems to have lost favor with both bar and bench. The safety of our modern progressive civilization calls aloud for a return to this construction of our fundamental law, or at least for some modification of present judicial pretensions.

The Federal Judiciary is co-ordinate, but should not be regarded as superior in authority to the other departments of Government. This is the only safe cannon of interpretation.

Mr. Jefferson, as late as September 28, 1820, in a letter written to Mr. Jarvis, denies in the most emphatic manner that the framers of the Constitution ever intended or ever did clothe the Supreme Court with any such power, and claimed that the exercise of such authority was a gross usurpation. He says:

> "You seem to consider the judges the ultimate arbiters of all constitutional questions; a very dangerous doctrine indeed, and one which would place us under the despotism of an oligarchy. Our judges are as honest as other men and not more so. They have, with others, the same passion for party, for power and the privilege of their corps. Their maxim is "*boni judicis est ampliare jurisdictionem,*" and their power the more dangerous as they are in office for life, and not responsible, as the other functionaries are, to the elective control. The Constitution has enacted no such single tribunal, knowing that to whatever hands confided, with the corruption of time and party its members would become despots."
> (Vol. 7, page 177, of Jefferson's Correspondence.)

This distinguished statesman and philosopher further declares that the people themselves are the only safe depository of the ultimate powers of society, and that in case either the Legislative or Executive functionaries act unconstitutionally, the people can rectify the abuse through the force of public opinion and at the ballot box.

President Jackson vigorously asserted the same doctrine in his message vetoing the bill to re-charter the United States Bank. The friends of the Bank claimed that the constitutionality of the measure had been settled in their favor by a decision of the Supreme Court; that the question of expediency alone remained, concerning which the judgment of Congress must be held to be conclusive. The bill passed both branches of Congress by very decided majorities, but met with a prompt veto from the Executive and failed to become a law. Among the reasons given by President Jackson to justify the Executive action was the unconstitutionality of the proposed legislation. As to the conclusiveness of the decision of the Supreme Court upon the question, the President says: "The Congress, the Executive and the Court, must each for itself be guided by its own opinion of the Constitution. . . . It is as much the duty of the House of Representatives, of the Senate and of the President, to decide upon the constitutionality of any bill or resolution which may be presented to them for passage or approval as it is of the Supreme Judges when it may be brought before them for judicial decision. The opinion of the Judges has no more authority over Congress than the opinion of Congress has over the Judges; and on that point the President is independent of both. The authority of the Supreme Court, must not, therefore, be permitted to control the Congress or the Executive, when acting in their legislative capacity, but to have only such influence as the force of their reasoning may deserve."

We believe that Jefferson and Jackson were sound in their contention, and this was the verdict of the people when they again elevated General Jackson to the Presidency at the succeeding election. The rugged utterances of these statesmen ring out to-day like a startling impeachment of our time. They comport with the dictates of enlightened judgment. There is enough in them to completely transform and re-invigorate our present suppliant and helpless state of public opinion. These declarations were uttered in the purer days of the republic and before the various departments of Government had seriously felt the baleful and seductive influence of corporate wealth and power. . . .

It is the plain duty of the Governors of the various States to forbid the presence of private police within their States and especially at points where trouble is anticipated. And if they make their appearance they should be dealt with like all disturbers of the peace and be punished for their unlawful assumption of power. Where the laws wink at the use of such police force, the Governor, as the law is not mandatory, should refuse to appoint and commission them. There is ample power in the various States to preserve the peace and to protect life and property without the assistance of these modern bravos.

State Legislatures should at once pass stringent laws forbidding the employment of this disturbing force within their borders. They are only calculated to precipitate riots and bloodshed, and they endanger both life and property. It is solemn duty of the State to protect the lives and property of its citizens, and regularly constituted officials should always be in command in times of public danger. . . .

TRUSTS

A Trust is defined to be a combination of many competing concerns under one management. The object is to increase profits through reduction of cost, limitation of product and increase of the price to the consumer. The term is now applied, and very properly, to all kinds of combinations in trade which relate to prices, and without regard to whether all or only part of the objects named are had in view.

Combinations which we now call trusts have existed in this country for a considerable period, but they have only attracted general attention for about ten years. We have in our possession copies of the agreements of the Standard Oil and Sugar Trusts. The former is dated January 2, 1882, and the latter August 6, 1887.

Trusts vary somewhat in their forms of organization. This is caused by the character of the property involved and the variety of objects to be attained. The great trusts of the country consist of an association or consolidation of a number of associations engaged in the same line of business—each company in the trust being first separately incorporated. The stock of these companies is then turned over to a board of trustees who issue back trust certificates in payment for the stock transferred. The trust selects its own board of directors and henceforth has complete control of the entire business and can regulate prices, limit or stimulate production as they may deem best for the parties concerned in the venture. The trust itself is not necessarily incorporated. Many of the strongest, such as the "Standard Oil Trust," the "Sugar Trust," and "The American Cotton Seed Oil Trust" and others are not. They are the invisible agents of associated artificial intangible beings. They are difficult to find, still harder to restrain and so far as present experience has gone they are practically a law unto themselves.

The power of these institutions has grown to be almost incalculable. Trustees of the Standard Oil Trust have issued certificates to the amount of $90,000,000, and each certificate is worth to-day $165 in the market, which makes their real capital at least $148,500,000, to say nothing of the added strength of their recent European associations. They have paid quarterly dividends since their organization in 1882. The profits amount to $20,000,000 per year. The Trust is managed by a Board of Trustees all of whom reside in New York. The combine really began in 1869, but the present agreement dates no further back than January, 1882. The only record kept of the meetings of these Trustees is a note stating that the minutes of the previous meeting were read and approved. The minutes themselves are then destroyed. These facts were brought to light by an investigation before the New York Senate, February, 1888. Col. George Bliss and Gen. Roger A. Pryor acted as council for the people and a great many things were brought out concerning the Standard, and a multitude of other combines, which had not before been well understood. John D. Rockefeller, Charles Pratt, Henry M. Rogers, H. M. Flagler, Benjamin Brewster, J. N. Archibald, William Rockefeller and W. H. Tilford are the trustees and they personally own a majority of the stock. Seven hundred other persons own the remainder. This trust holds the stock of forty-two corporations, extending into thirteen States. The Cotton Seed Oil Trust holds the stock of eighty-five corporations extending into fifteen States.

Trust combinations now dominate the following products and divisions of trade: Kerosene Oil, Cotton Seed Oil, Sugar, Oat Meal, Starch, White Corn Meal, Straw Paper, Pearled Barley, Coal, Straw Board, Lumber, Castor Oil, Cement, Linseed Oil, Lard, School Slate, Oil Cloth, Salt, Cattle, Meat Products, Gas, Street Railways, Whisky, Paints, Rubber, Steel, Steel Rails, Steel and Iron Beams, Cars, Nails, Wrought Iron Pipes, Iron Nuts, Stoves, Lead, Copper, Envelopes, Wall Paper, Paper Bags, Paving Pitch, Cordage, Coke, Reaping, Binding and Mowing Machines, Threshing Machines, Plows, Glass, Water Works, Warehouses, Sand Stone, Granite, Upholsterers' Felt, Lead Pencils, Watches and Watch Cases, Clothes Wringers, Carpets, Undertakers' Goods and Coffins, Planes, Breweries, Milling, Flour, Silver Plate, Plated Ware and a vast variety of other lines of trade.

The Standard Oil and its complement, the American Cotton Oil Trust, were the advance guard of the vast army of like associations which have overrun and now occupy every section of the country and nearly all departments of trade. The Standard has developed into an international combine and has brought the world under its yoke. In 1890 the largest German and Dutch petroleum houses fell under the control of the Standard Oil Company, and the oil importing companies of Bremen, Hamburg and Stettin were united by the Standard into a German-American Petroleum Company, with its seat at Bremen. In 1891 the Paris Rothschilds, who control the Russian oil fields, effected a combination with the Standard Oil Trust, which makes the combine world wide; and so far as this important article of consumption is concerned, it places all mankind at their mercy. Our information concerning this international oil trust is derived from the report concerning the Petroleum Monopoly of Europe by Consul-General Edwards, of Berlin, made to the Secretary of State, June 25, 1891, and published in Consular Reports No. 131.

Now that the Petroleum Combine has accomplished the conquest of the world, what is to hinder every other branch of business from accomplishing the same end? The Standard has led the way and demonstrated the feasibility of such gigantic enterprises and others will doubtless be quick to follow. Already, indeed, the Anthracite coal barons have followed their example so far as this country is concerned, and the "Big Four," who control the meat products of this country, have reached out and subsidized the ship room and other facilities for international trade in that line. We hear also well authenticated rumors that other combinations, looking to the complete control of every branch of mercantile business, are already in existence and making what they regard as very satisfactory progress.

The Sugar Trust, which now fixes the price of 3,000,000,000 pounds of sugar annually consumed in the United States, is managed upon substantially the same plan as the Standard Oil Trust, and so, in fact, are all of the great combines. They rule the whole realm of commerce with a rod of iron and levy tribute upon the country amounting to hundreds of millions of dollars annually—an imposition which the people would not think for a moment of submitting to if exacted by their Government.

ARE TRUSTS LEGAL?

It is clear that trusts are contrary to public policy and hence in conflict with the Common law. They are monopolies organized to destroy competition and restrain trade. Enlightened public policy favors competition in the present condition of organized society. . . .

It is contended by those interested in Trusts that they tend to cheapen production and diminish the price of the article to the consumer. It is conceded that these results may follow temporarily and even permanently in some instances. But it is not the rule. When such effects ensue they are merely incidental to the controlling object of the association. Trusts are speculative in their purposes and formed to make money. Once they secure control of a given line of business they are masters of the situation and can dictate to the two great classes with which they deal—the producer of the raw material and the consumer of the finished product. They limit the price of the raw material so as to impoverish the producer, drive him to a single market, reduce the price of every class of labor connected with the trade, throw out of employment large numbers of persons who had before been engaged in a meritorious calling and finally, prompted by insatiable avarice, they increase the price to the consumer and thus complete the circle of their depredations. Diminished prices is the bribe which they throw into the market to propitiate the public. They will take it back when it suits them to do so.

The Trust is organized commerce with the Golden Rule excluded and the trustees exempted from the restraints of conscience.

They argue that competition means war and is therefore destructive. The Trust is eminently docile and hence seeks to destroy competition in order that we may have peace. But the peace which they give us is like that which exists after the leopard has devoured the kid. This professed desire for peace is a false pretense. They dread the war of competition because the people share in the spoils. When rid of that they always turn their guns upon the masses and depredate without limit or mercy. The main weapons of the trust are threats, intimidation, bribery, fraud, wreck and pillage. Take one well authenticated instance in the history of the Oat Meal Trust as an example. In 1887 this Trust decided that part of their mills should stand idle. They were accordingly closed. This resulted in the discharge of a large number of laborers who had to suffer in consequence. The mills which were continued in operation would produce seven million barrels of meal during the year. Shortly after shutting down the Trust advanced the price of meal one dollar per barrel and the public was forced to stand the assessment. The mills were more profitable when idle than when in operation.

The Sugar Trust has it within its power to levy a tribute of $30,000,000 upon the people of the United States by simply advancing the price of sugar one cent per pound for one year.

If popular tumult breaks out and legislation in restraint of these depredations is threatened, they can advance prices, extort campaign expenses and corruption funds from the people and force the disgruntled multitude to furnish the sinews of war for their own destruction. They not only have the power to do these things, but it is their known mode of warfare and they actually practice it from year to year.

The most distressing feature of this war of the Trusts is the fact that they control the articles which the plain people consume in their daily life. It cuts off their accumulations and deprives them of the staff upon which they fain would lean in their old age.

THE REMEDY.

For nearly three hundred years the Anglo-Saxon race has been trying to arrest the encroachments of monopoly and yet the evil has flourished and gained in strength from age to age. The courts have come to the aid of enlightened sentiment, pronounced all such combinations contrary to public policy, illegal and their contracts void; and still they have continued to thrive. Thus far repressive and prohibitory legislation have proved unavailing. Experience has shown that when men, for the sake of gain, will openly violate the moral law and infringe upon the plain rights of their neighbors, they will not be restrained by ordinary prohibitory measures. It is the application of force to the situation and force must be met with force. The States should pass stringent penal statutes which will visit personal responsibility upon all agents and representatives of the trust who aid or assist in the transaction of its business within the State. The General Government, through its power to lay and collect taxes, should place an excise or internal revenue tax of from 25 to 40 per cent on all manufacturing plants, goods, wares or merchandise of whatever kind and wherever found when owned by or controlled in the interest of such combines or associations, and this tax should be a first lien upon such property until the tax is paid. The details of such a bill would not be difficult to frame. Such a law would destroy the Trust root and branch. Whenever the American people really try to overthrow these institutions they will be able to do so and to further postpone action is a crime.

WHAT OF THE FUTURE?

One of the main charges against Charles the First, was that he had fostered and created monopolies. His head went to the block. Nearly every great struggle of the English race has been caused by the unjust exactions of tribute—against the extortions of greed. Our own war for Independence was a war against taxes. Our late internal struggle was for the freedom of labor and the right of the laborer to possess and enjoy his own. That struggle is still on and it is now thundering at our gates with renewed energy. It will not down, though the Trust heap Ossa upon Pelion. The people will rise and overturn the despoilers though they shake the earth by the displacement.

These vast struggles are great teachers and the world is learning rapidly. We are coming to know that great combinations reduce the cost of production and soon the world will grasp the idea that the people can combine and protect themselves. In this combine, in this co-operation of all, there will be no discrimination and the bounties of Heaven will be open alike to the weak and the powerful. We welcome the conflict. There is no time to lose nor can the battle begin too soon. . . .

*   *   *

THE GREAT UPRISING.

The financial storm which opened upon this country in the autumn of 1873, quickly expanded into a tempest which swept with fury every section of the Union. It was accompanied by strange phenomena which temporarily baffled the wisest heads in the land. Unlike former catastrophes of the kind the confidence of the people in their currency remained unshaken from first to last. If a man could command either form of our currency he felt secure from disaster. The paper money was the mountain summit which bid defiance to the floods, while the productive industries were the low-lands submerged and swept by the raging torrent. In all former panics the currency was first to give way—the first reed that was broken.

The prolonged stay of this calamity led to wide-spread investigation as to its causes, which happily resulted in a general revival of economic learning. Men began to inquire anew into systems and to dig down to the very bedrock of democratic institutions. Fortunately, they had the lamp of their own personal experience to guide them, and a whole generation of living men and women as their witnesses. Upon examination they ascertained exactly where the black plague had started and who were responsible for its inoculation.

A protracted period of educational effort followed and for years it ebbed and flowed like the tides. It was an expensive school but it graduated strong men and sent them forth by the hundred equipped for the controversy destined to follow.

Truth is a marvelous weapon; it transforms itself into a thousand shapes, but it is always the truth.

Sometimes it is keen and lithe like a Damascus blade and again heavy, blunt and jagged like a savage battle-ax of the medieval age. This wonderful agency has done its work during the nineteen years just passed. The farmers through their Grange movement led the way. Then followed the Peter Cooper movement led by the purest philanthropist of the times, and represented upon the hustings by one of the most brilliant, powerful and persuasive orators which this country has ever produced, Gen. Samuel F. Cary, of Ohio. Succeeding this came the Union Labor party, and now the united movement of all the industrial forces of the continent. Through all this period those who have administered public affairs—presidents and cabinets, law-makers and parties—have unwittingly wrought in unison with the patient efforts of self-sacrificing philanthropists to unerringly demonstrate, in a variety of ways, that all of the accusations which had been made against them and against existing leadership, were absolutely true and that no good thing could be expected of them.

We have also had the contrasts of bountiful harvests accompanied by ever-existing destitution; of penury following close upon the track of industry; of vast armies of homeless tramps ever wandering alongside of vacant land held for speculation; of employers building palaces in foreign lands out of profits filched from toil, and labor forced into the maelstrom of strikes, riots and lock-outs; of armed mercenaries usurping the place of regular police; of corporations crowding the individual to the wall and trampling the poor into the dust; of one-half of every city set apart for the abode of Lazzaroni and the other for the sumptuous palaces of the rich and powerful. Such things—such aggravating contrasts have aided to convince the judgment and ripen the convictions of millions of honest men and women dwelling in every section of the Union. Of one accord they have risen up, pledged fidelity to one another and sworn that these things shall cease. Nor is this the result of the hasty ebullition of passion. It is the outcome of sober conviction based upon thorough investigation and verified by personal experience. It is sanctified by the convictions of justice and the promptings of charity. It has passed the point of experimental endeavor and reached the plane of lofty resolve where the Golden Rule becomes the law of the conscience and where personal sacrifice is welcomed as a boon.

Such is the character—such the interpretation of this mighty movement. It bodes no ill to our country or to mankind. Its mission is one of justice and peace. It is the religion of the Master in motion among men and is prompted by charity for all and malice toward none. It is the eagle tempered with the dove—the paw of the Lion of the tribe of Judah interposed to raise our prostrate industries from the dust. It proposes to hail and salute the advent of the twentieth century with the glad songs of emancipated labor and to present the world with an illuminated copy of our glorious

Declaration of Independence enacted into law and reduced to practice in the daily life of the Republic. . . .

DANGER AND DUTY.

The American people have entered upon the mightiest civic struggle known to their history. Many of the giant wrongs which they are seeking to overthrow are as old as the race of man and are rock-rooted in the ignorant prejudices and controlling customs of every nation in christendom. We must expect to be confronted by a vast and splendidly equipped army of extortionists, usurers and oppressors marshalled from every nation under heaven. Every instrumentality known to man,—the state with its civic authority, learning with its lighted torch, armies with their commissions to take life, instruments of commerce essential to commercial intercourse, and the very soil upon which we live, move and have our being—all these things and more, are being perverted and used to enslave and impoverish the people. The Golden Rule is rejected by the heads of all the great departments of trade, and the law of Cain, which repudiates the obligations that we are mutually under to one another, is fostered and made the rule of action throughout the world. Corporate feudality has taken the place of chattel slavery and vaunts its power in every state.

The light of past civilization is shining full upon us all, and knowing that cause and effect follow closely upon each other, we believe that we fairly discern the outlines of the main events which the near future has in store for the American people. We do not claim to see clearly all the concomitant phenomena destined to follow the social earthquake just at hand. Such prevision is not accorded to man. But of this much we are certain: In their flight from their task masters the people have about reached the Red Sea. We can not retreat. Either the floods will be parted for us and close, as of old, upon our pursuers, or a life and death struggle will ensue between oppressors and oppressed—between those who would destroy and enslave and those who are seeking to enter into the inheritance prepared for them by a beneficent Father. Our danger lurks in the alternative stated. It behooves every man who desires a peaceful solution of our ever increasing complications to do all in his power to make the deliverance peaceful and humane. To further postpone the controversy is to invite chaos and challenge the arbitrament of the sword. Our past experience should be sufficient to warn us to steer clear of this abyss of peril and the hell of war.

All the Nations of antiquity were scourged exactly as our people are now being scourged. They were afflicted, they complained, rebelled and perished—oppressors and oppressed together. Their innate sense of justice enabled them to discern clearly between right and wrong, but their passion for revenge and thirst for blood made it impossible for the people to retain power even when the fortunes of war had placed it in their hands.

But thanks to the all-conquering strength of Christian enlightenment we are at the dawn of the golden age of popular power. We have unshaken faith in the integrity and final triumph of the people. But their march to power will not be unobstructed. The universal uprising of the industrial forces will result in unifying the monopolistic and plutocratic elements also, and through the business and social influences of these potential and awakened forces, thousands of well-meaning professional and business men of all classes will be induced, for a time, to make common cause against us. This makes it necessary for the friends of reform to put forth herculean efforts to disabuse the minds of well-meaning people concerning the underlying objects of the movement, and this calls for systematic, energetic, and constant educational work, covering the whole range of the reforms proposed. It is also the surest method of overcoming the obstacle of indifference among the people.

We must also be prepared to see the two well-organized and equipped political parties march to the assistance of each other at critical points along the line. The leaders will spare no effort to accomplish this end. Two influences, now at work, are ample to at least partially precipitate this result—the use of money and the community of danger inspired by the appearance of the new political force. The great mass of voters should be faithfully warned of this danger before designing leaders have made the attempt to mislead them. In this manner the evil consequences of their efforts can be largely averted.

THE GREAT DANGER.

If the economic revolution now in progress in the United States is not speedily successful, the industrial people will have no one to blame but themselves. Through suffering and research they have learned the causes of their distress. They have organized, decided upon remedies and made known their demands. They have the numbers to make their wishes effective. The Constitution and laws of the country place the whole matter within their hands. The great initial battles have been fought in the Courts and this constitutes their Gibraltar and impregnable vantage ground. Nothing is now needed but a proper use of the ballot.

If the friends of reform will make one united and fearless effort the victory will be won. Fidelity to truth, to home, to family and to the brotherhood of purpose is all that is required. Capital possesses one thing which labor does not—ready cash. They will not hesitate to make the best possible use of it. But labor possesses that which capital does not—numbers. They should be made effective. Will they longer refuse to make use of the peaceful weapon which their fathers placed in their hands? If we will not with courage and conscience choose the methods of peace, the sword is inevitable. Persistent oppression on the one hand and neglect to make proper use of the ballot on the other, in the very nature of things, call for the application of force as the only solution. Avenging armies always follow close upon the heels of legalized injustice. If we would escape the sword we must at once conquer through the power of truth and through knowledge incarnated and set in motion.

STRIKE NOW!

We have challenged the adversary to battle and our bugles have sounded the march. If we now seek to evade or shrink from the conflict it will amount to a confession of cowardice and a renunciation of the faith. Let us make the year 1892 memorable for all time to come as the period when the great battle for industrial emancipation was fought and won in the United States. It is glorious to live in this age, and to be permitted to take part in this heroic combat is the greatest honor that can be conferred upon mortals. It is an opportunity for every man, however humble, to strike a blow that will permanently benefit his race and make the world better for his having lived. Throughout all history we have had ample evidence that the new world is the theater upon which the great struggle for the rights of man is to be made, and the righteous movement now in progress should again forcibly remind us of our enviable mission, under Providence, among the nations of the earth.

C. *Henry Demarest Lloyd:* "Wealth Against Commonwealth"*

Henry Demarest Lloyd (1847-1903) departed from the archetype of vintage populism in two important ways. First of all, as we might expect from the son of a Greenwich Village bookseller, he was an intellectual, a lover of ideas. And since ideas have a way of crossing national boundaries, Lloyd's "Americanism" was qualified by a larger cosmopolitanism. He acknowledged a large intellectual debt to Giuseppe Mazzini, the Italian reformer, and regularly corresponded with other social thinkers in England and on the Continent. Lloyd's intellectual sophistication also placed him above the religious fundamentalism and cultural isolation usually associated with vintage populism. Lloyd's religion, which he embraced as fervently as any revivalist, was a thoroughly secularized "religion of humanity." His cosmopolitanism permitted him a broader understanding of all classes, not merely farmers; he was one of the few populists who truly understood the plight of the urban masses.

A second atypical feature of Lloyd's populism is that it comes close to being socialist. Lloyd belongs on the "left" fringe of vintage populism because he saw the task of the reformer as being more than the restoration of free competition or the abolition of the gold standard. Instead of turning back to a Jeffersonian past, he

*From Henry Demarest Lloyd, *Wealth Against Commonwealth* (New York: Harper Brothers, 1894).

would move forward to a new order in which competition might be replaced by a cooperative economic system.

Both these features of Lloyd's approach—his cosmopolitanism and his belief in comprehensive reform—were affronted in 1896 when the Populists endorsed Bryan as their candidate and free silver as their major plank. Both these choices seemed trivial and opportunist to him. He was thus driven to desert the Populists that year and vote for the Socialist Party, which he did again in 1900. In 1903, at the end of his life, he finally joined the Socialists.

Yet even his final conversion to socialism did not change his fundamentally populist outlook. What bothered him most about socialism was its class consciousness. In her biography of her brother Caro Lloyd describes his outlook on classes in these terms:

> He put himself outside of his own class, of every class, and surveyed the entire field. His heart beat closer to the working class, but never lost the sympathetic realisation of the thraldom of the whole people. . . .
>
> "I have little confidence in a class movement," he wrote, "even tho it be so good a class as labor." He urged business men and the middle class, generally, to make common cause with the working men. For many years it had been one of his conscious aims to make men of property see that they, too, belonged with the exploited.*

Even as he joined the Socialists, which was virtually on his deathbed, he confessed that all their talk "about the everlasting 'proletariat' and 'class conscious' slang . . . makes me squirm." Lloyd may have been a strange populist, but he would have made a much stranger socialist. Found among his notes after his death was an emendation of Marx: "Working men of the world, unite," should be, he wrote, "People of the world, unite."

The selection consists of some excerpts from *Wealth Against Commonwealth*, Lloyd's most famous work which was published in 1894.

---

*Caro Lloyd, *Henery Demarest Lloyd, 1847-1903: A Biography*, Vol. II (New York: G. P. Putnam's Sons, 1912), pp. 263-64.

"THERE ARE NONE"—"THEY ARE LEGION"

Nature is rich; but everywhere man, the heir of nature, is poor. Never in this happy country or elsewhere—except in the Land of Miracle, where "they did all eat and were filled"—has there been enough of anything for the people. Never since time began have all the sons and daughters of men been all warm, and all filled, and all shod and roofed. Never yet have all the virgins, wise or foolish, been able to fill their lamps with oil.

The world, enriched by thousands of generations of toilers and thinkers, has reached a fertility which can give every human being a plenty undreamed of even in the Utopias. But between this plenty ripening on the boughs of our civilization and the people hungering for it step the "cornerers," the syndicates, trusts, combinations, with the cry of "over-production"—too much of everything. Holding back the riches of earth, sea, and sky from their fellows who famish and freeze in the dark, they declare to them that there is too much light and warmth and food. They assert the right, for their private profit, to regulate the consumption by the people of the necessaries of life, and to control production, not by the needs of humanity, but by the desires of a few for dividends. The coal syndicate thinks there is too much coal. There is too much iron, too much lumber, too much flour—for this or that syndicate.

The majority have never been able to buy enough of anything; but this minority have too much of everything to sell.

Liberty produces wealth and wealth destroys liberty. "The splendid empire of Charles V," says Motley, "was erected upon the grave of liberty." Our bignesses—cities, factories, monopolies, fortunes, which are our empires, are the obesities of an age gluttonous beyond its powers of digestion. Mankind are crowding upon each other in the centres, and struggling to keep each other out of the feast set by the new sciences and the new fellowships. Our size has got beyond both our science and our conscience. The vision of the railroad stockholder is not far-sighted enough to see into the office of the General Manager; the people cannot reach across even a ward of a city to rule their rulers; Captains of Industry "do not know" whether the men in the ranks are dying from lack of food and shelter; we cannot clean our cities nor our politics; the locomotive has more man-power than all the ballot-boxes, the mill-wheels wear out the hearts of workers unable to keep up beating time to their whirl. If mankind had gone on pursuing the ideals of the fighter, the time would necessarily have come when there would have been only a few, then only one, and then none left. This is what we are witnessing in the world of livelihoods. Our ideals of livelihood are ideals of mutual deglutition. We are rapidly reaching the stage where in each province only a few are left; that is the key to our times. Beyond the deep is another deep. This era is but a passing phase in the evolution of industrial Caesars, and these Caesars will be of a new type —corporate Caesars.

THE OLD SELF-INTEREST

The corn of the coming harvest is growing so fast that, like the farmer standing at night in his fields, we can hear it snap and crackle. We have been fighting fire on the well-worn lines of old-fashioned politics and political economy, regulating corporations, and leaving competition to regulate itself. But the flames of a new economic evolution run around us, and when we turn to find that competition has killed competition, that corporations are grown greater than the State and have bred individuals greater than themselves, and that the naked issue of our time is with property becoming master instead of servant, property in many necessaries of life becoming monopoly of the necessaries of life.

We are still, in part, as Emerson says, in the quadruped state. Our industry is a fight of every man for himself. The prize we give the fittest is monopoly of the necessaries of life, and we leave these winners of the powers of life and death to wield them over us by the same ''self-interest'' with which they took them from us. In all this we see at work a ''principle'' which will go into the records as one of the historic mistakes of humanity. Institutions stand or fall by their philosophy, and the main doctrine of industry since Adam Smith has been the fallacy that the self-interest of the individual was a sufficient guide to the welfare of the individual and society. Heralded as a final truth of ''science'' this proves to have been nothing higher than a temporary formula for a passing problem. It was a reflection in words of the policy of the day.

"It is a law of business for each proprietor to pursue his own interest," said the committee of Congress which in 1893 investigated the coal combinations. "There is no hope for any of us, but the weakest must go first," is the golden rule of business. There is no other field of human associations in which any such rule of action is allowed. The man who should apply in his family or his citizenship this "survival of the fittest" theory as it is practically professed and operated in business would be a monster, and would be speedily made extinct, as we do with monsters. To divide the supply of food between himself and his children according to their relative powers of calculation, to follow his conception of his own self-interest in any matter which the self-interest of all has taken charge of, to deal as he thinks best for himself with foreigners with whom his country is at war, would be a short road to the penitentiary or the gallows. In trade men have not yet risen to the level of the family life of the animals. The true law of business is that all must pursue the interest of all. In the law, the highest product of civilization, this has long been a commonplace. The safety of the people is the supreme law. We are in travail to bring industry up to this. Our century of the caprice of the individual as the law-giver of the common toil, to employ or disemploy, to start or stop, to open or close, to compete or combine, has been the disorder of the school while the master slept. The happiness, self-interest, or individuality of the whole is not more sacred than that of each, but it is greater. They are equal in quality, but in quantity they are greater. In the ultimate which the mathematician, the poet, the reformer projects the two will coincide.

Our world, operated by individual motive, is the country of the Chinese fable, in which the inhabitants went on one leg. Yes, but an "enlightened self-interest"? The perfect self-interest of the perfect individual is an admirable conception, but it is still individual, and the world is social. The music of the spheres is not to be played on one string. Nature does nothing individually. All forces are paired like the sexes, and every particle of matter in the universe has to obey every other particle. When the individual has progressed to a perfect self-interest, there will be over against it, acting and reacting with it, a correspondingly perfect self-interest of the community. Meanwhile, we who are the creators of society have got the times out of joint, because, less experienced than the

Creator of the balanced matter of earth, we have given the precedence to the powers on one side. As gods we are but half-grown. For a hundred years or so our economic theory has been one of industrial government by the self-interest of the individual. Political government by the self-interest of the individual we call anarchy. It is one of the paradoxes of public opinion that the people of America, least tolerant of this theory of anarchy in political government, lead in practising it in industry. Politically, we are civilized; industrially, not yet. Our century, given to this *laissez-faire*—"leave the individual alone; he will do what is best for himself and what is best for him is best for all"—has done one good: it has put society at the mercy of its own ideals, and has produced an actual anarchy in industry which is horrifying us into a change of doctrines.

History is condensed in the catchwords of the people. In the phrases of individual self-interest which have been the shibboleths of the main activities of our last hundred years were prophesied: the filling up of the Mississippi by the forest-destroying, self-seeking lumber companies of the North; the disintegration of the American family—among the rich by too little poverty, and among the poor by too much; the embezzlement of public highways and public franchises into private property; the devolution of the American merchants and manufacturers into the business dependants—and social and political dependants, therefore—of a few men in each great department of trade, from dry-goods to whiskey; the devolution of the free farmer into a tenant, and of the working-man into a fixture of the locomotive or the factory, forbidden to leave except by permission of his employer or the public; and that melee of injunctions, bayonets, idle men and idle machinery, rich man's fear of poor man and poor man's fear of starvation, we call trade and industry.

Where the self-interest of the individual is allowed to be the rule both of social and personal action, the level of all is forced down to that of the lowest. Business excuses itself for the things it does —cuts in wages, exactions in hours, tricks of competition—on the plea that the merciful are compelled to follow the cruel. "It is pleaded as an excuse by those [common carriers] who desire to obey the [Interstate Commerce] law that self-preservation drives them to violate it because other carriers persist in doing so,'' says Senator Cullom. When the self-interest of society is made the standard the lowest must rise to the average. The one pulls down, the other up. That men's hearts are bad and that bad men will do bad things has a truth in it. But whatever the general average of morals, the anarchy which gives such individuals their head and leaves them to set the pace for all will produce infinitely worse results than a policy which applies mutual checks and inspirations. Bad kings make bad reigns, but monarchy is bad because it is arbitrary power, and that, whether it be political or industrial, makes even good men bad.

A partial truth universally applied as this of self-interest has been is a universal error. Everything goes to defeat. Highways are used to prevent travel and traffic. Ownership of the means of production is sought in order to ''shut down'' production, and the means of plenty make famine. All follow self-interest to find that though they have created marvellous wealth it is not theirs. We pledge ''our lives, our fortunes, and our sacred honor'' to establish the rule of the majority, and end by finding that the minority—a minority in morals, money, and men—are our masters whichever way we turn. We agonize over ''economy,'' but sell all our grain and pork and oil and cotton at exchanges where we pay brokerage on a hundred or a thousand barrels or bushels or bales of wind to get one real one sold. These intolerabilities—sweat-shops where model merchants buy and sell the cast-off scarlet-fever skins of the poor, factory and mine where childhood is forbidden to become manhood and manhood is forbidden to die a natural death, mausoleums in which we bury the dead rich, slums in which we bury the living poor, coal pools with their manufacture of artificial winter—all these are the rule of private self-interest arrived at its destination.

A really human life is impossible in our cities, but they cannot be reconstructed under the old self-interest. Chicago was rebuilt wrong after the fire. Able men pointed out the avenues to a wider and better municipal life, but they could not be opened through the private interpositions that blocked the way. The slaughter of railway men coupling cars was shown, in a debate in the United States Senate, to be twice as great as it would be if the men were in active service in war. But under the scramble for private gain our society on its railway side cannot develop the energy to introduce the improved appliances ready to hand which would save these lives, all young and vigorous. The cost of the change would be repaid in 100-per-cent dividends every year by the money value alone to us of the men now killed and wounded. But we shall have to wait for a nobler arithmetic to give us investments so good as that. . . .

If all will sacrifice themselves, none need be sacrificed. But if one may sacrifice another, all are sacrificed. That is the difference between self-interest and other-self-interest. In industry we have been substituting all the mean passions that can set man against man in place of the irresistible power of brotherhood. To tell us of the progressive sway of brotherhood in all human affairs is the sole message of history. "Love thy neighbor as thyself" is not the phrase of a ritual of sentiment for the unapplied emotion of pious hours; it is the exact formula of the force to-day operating the greatest institutions man has established. It is as secular as sacred. Only by each neighbor giving the other every right of free thought, free movement, free representation which he demands for himself; only by calling every neighbor a friend, and literally laying down his life for his friend against foreign invasion or domestic tumult; only by the equalization which gives the vote to all and denies kingship to all, however strong or "fittest"—only thus is man establishing the community, the republic, which, with all its failings, is the highest because the realest application of the spirit of human brotherhood. Wonderful are the dividends of this investment. You are but one, and can give only yourself to America. You give free speech, and 65,000,000 of your countrymen will guard the freedom of your lips. Your single offer of your right arm puts 65,000,000 of sheltering arms about you. Does "business" pay such profits? Wealth will remain a secret unguessed by business until it has reincorporated itself under the law which reckons as the property of each one the total of all the possessions of all his neighbors.

. . . Business colors the modern world as war reddened the ancient world. Out of such delirium monsters are bred, and their excesses destroy the system that brought them forth. . . . Eras show their last stages by producing men who sum up individually the morbid characteristics of the mass. When the crisis comes in which the gathering tendencies of generations shoot forward in the avalanche, there is born some group of men perfect for their function—good be it or bad. They need to take time for no second thought, and will not delay the unhalting reparations of nature by so much as the time given to one tear over the battle-field or the bargain. . . . The righteous indignation that other men feel against sin these men feel against that which withstands them. Sincere as rattlesnakes, they are selfish with the unconsciousness possible to only the entirely commonplace, without the curiosity to question their times or the imagination to conceive the pain they inflict, and their every ideal is satisfied by the conventionalities of church, parlor, and counting-room. These men are the touchstones to wither the cant of an age.

Poor thinking means poor doing. In casting about for the cause of our industrial evils, public opinion has successively found it in "competition," "combination," the "corporations," "conspiracies," "trusts." But competition has ended in combination and our new wealth takes as it chooses the form of corporation or trust, or corporation again, and with every change grows greater and worse. Under these kaleidoscopic masks we begin at last to see progressing to its terminus a steady consolidation, the end of which is one-man power. The conspiracy ends in one, and one cannot conspire with himself. When this solidification of many into one has been reached, we shall be at last face to face with the naked truth that it is not only the form but the fact of arbitrary power, of control without consent, of rule without representation that concerns us.

Business motived by the self-interest of the individual runs into monopoly at every point it touches the social life—land monopoly, transportation monopoly, trade monopoly, political monopoly in all its forms, from contraction of the currency to corruption in office. The society in which in half a lifetime a man without a penny can become a hundred times a millionaire is as over-ripe, industrially, as was, politically, the Rome in which the most popular bully could lift himself from the ranks of the legion on to the throne of the Caesars. Our rising issue is with business. Monopoly is business at the end of its journey. It has got there. The irrepressible conflict is now as distinctly with business as the issue so lately met was with slavery. Slavery went first only because it was the cruder form of business.

AND THE NEW

The question is not whether monopoly is to continue. The sun sets every night on a greater majority against it. We are face to face with the practical issue: Is it to go through ruin or reform? Can we forestall ruin by reform? If we wait to be forced by events we shall be astounded to find how much more radical they are than our utopias. Louis XVI waited until 1793, and gave his head and all his investitures to the people who in 1789 asked only to sit at his feet and speak their mind. Unless we reform of our own free will, nature will reform us by force, as nature does. Our evil courses have already gone too far in producing misery, plagues, hatreds, national enervation. Already the leader is unable to lead, and has begun to drive with judges armed with bayonets and Gatling guns. History is the serial obituary of the men who thought they could drive men.

Reform is the science and conscience with which mankind in its manhood overcomes temptations and escapes consequences by killing the germs. Ruin is already hard at work among us. Our libraries are full of the official inquiries and scientific interpretations which show how our master-motive is working decay in all our parts. The family crumbles into a competition between the father and the children whom he breeds to take his place in the factory, to unfit themselves to be fathers in their turn. A thorough, stalwart resimplification, a life governed by simple needs and loves, is the imperative want of the world. It will be accomplished, either self-conscious volition does it, or the slow wreck and decay of superfluous and unwholesome men and matters. The latter is the method of brutes and brute civilizations. The other is the method of man, so far as he is divine. Has not man, who has in personal reform risen above the brute method, come to the height at which he can achieve social reform in masses and by nations? We must learn; we can learn by reason. Why wait for the crueler teacher?

* * *

''Regenerate the individual'' is a half-truth; the reorganization of the society which he makes and which makes him is the other half. . . .

History has taught us nothing if not that men can continue to associate only by the laws of association. The golden rule is the first and last of these, but the first and last of the golden rule is that it can be operated only through laws, habits, forms, and institutions. The Constitution and laws of the United States are, however imperfectly, the translation into the language of politics of doing as you would be done by—the essence of equal rights and government by consent. To ask individuals to-day to lead by their single sacrifices the life of the brother in the world of business is as if the American colonist had been asked to lead by his individual enterprise the life of the citizen of a republic. That was made possible to him only by union with others. The business world is full of men who yearn to abandon its methods and live the love they feel; but to attempt to do so by themselves would be martyrdom, and that is ''caviare to the general.'' ''We admire martyrdom,'' Mazzini, the martyr, said, ''but we do not recommend it.'' The change must be social, and its martyrdoms have already begun.

New freedoms cannot be operated through the old forms of slavery. The ideals of Washington and Hamilton and Adams could not breathe under kingly rule. Idle to say they might. Under the mutual dependence of the inside and outside of things their change has all through history always been dual. Change of heart is no more redemption than hunger is dinner. We must have honesty, love, justice in the heart of the business world, but for these we must also have the forms which will fit them. These will be very different from those through which the intercourse of man with man in the exchange of services now moves to such ungracious ends. Forms of Asiatic and American government, of early institutions and to-day's, are not more different. The cardinal virtues cannot be established and kept at work in trade and on the highways with the old apparatus. In order that the spirit that gave rebates may go to stay, the rebate itself must go. If the private use of private ownership of highways is to go, the private ownership must go. There must be no private use of public power or public property. These are created by the common sacrifices of all, and can be rightfully used only for the common good of all—from all, by all, for all. All the grants and franchises that have been given to private hands for private profit are void in morals and void in that higher law which sets the copy for the laggard pens of legislatures and judges. "No private use of public powers" is but a threshold truth. The universe, says Emerson, is the property of every creature in it. . . .

There is to be a people in industry, as in government. The same rising genius of democracy, which discovered that mankind did not cooperate in the State to provide a few with palaces and king's evil, is disclosing that men do not cooperate in trade for any other purpose than to mobilize the labor of all for the benefit of all, and that the only true guidance comes from those who are led, and the only valid titles from those who create. Very wide must be the emancipation of their new self-interest. If we free America we shall still be not free, for the financial, commercial, possessory powers of modern industrial life are organized internationally. If we rose to the full execution of the first, simplest, and most pressing need of our times and put an end to all private use of public powers, we should still be confronted by monopolies existing simply as private property, as in coal mines, oil lands.

It is not a verbal accident that science is the substance of the word conscience. We must know the right before we can do the right. When it comes to know the facts the human heart can no more endure monopoly than American slavery or Roman empire. The first step to a remedy is that the people care. If they know, they will care. To help them to know and care, to stimulate new hatred of evil, new love of the good, new sympathy for the victims of power, and, by enlarging its science, to quicken the old into a new conscience, this compilation of fact has been made. Democracy is not a lie. There live in the body of the commonality the unexhausted virtue and the ever-refreshened strength which can rise equal to any problems of progress. In the hope of tapping some reserve of their powers of self-help this story is told to the people.

D. *William Jennings Bryan:*
"The Cross of Gold"*

"Heave an egg out of a Pullman window," said H. L. Mencken in 1926, "and you will hit a Fundamentalist almost everywhere in the United States today." In this cruel "Memoriam" to William Jennings Bryan (1860-1925), Mencken portrayed him as the spokesman of the rural "yokel": the crude Fundamentalist, the know-nothing, the opponent of progress and enlightenment.

Yet this same Bryan, who ended his career—and his life —prosecuting a young teacher of evolution, began it as a spellbinding "boy orator" who stirred audiences with talk of a progressive income tax, popular election of Senators, flexible currency, and economic justice for the workingman. It was the same Bryan who during his long career had fought for women's suffrage, Philippine independence, and against imperialistic wars and corporate conglomerates.

The seeming paradox of the progressive-reactionary is easily enough explained. Bryan was the all-too-faithful voice of rural and small-town America. When, during the 1890's, it supplied the cutting edge of reform, he was a reformer. When, during the 1920's, it felt threatened by urbanization and changing mores and turned for comfort to its old-time religion, so did he.

Bryan's way of thinking puts Jeffersonianism to its sorest test. If we are really to believe in the sovereignty of the people, it would seem to follow that "teachers in public schools must teach what the taxpayers desire taught." Even if the taxpayers desire that nonsense be taught? Bryan could answer by observing that the questioner seems to think he knows what nonsense is. And how does he know? Because he is educated? That is a circular answer because we first must know what he has learned, who set the standards for what he learned, and how *they* derived the authority to set them.

But all this has the ring of sophistry. Jefferson, despite occasional lapses, was committed to free inquiry. He did not believe

---

*William Jennings Bryan, "Speech Before Democratic National Convention, Chicago, 1896," in J. S. Ogilvie, ed., *Life and Speeches of William J. Bryan* (New York: J. S. Ogilvie Publishing Company, 1896).

that the function of education was to bolster popular prejudice. Yet Bryan came close to suggesting this by his words and his actions throughout his career. When asked about the issue of free silver in 1892, Bryan replied, "I don't know anything about free silver. The people of Nebraska are for free silver and I am for free silver. I will look up the arguments later." This is pushing democratic faith to the brink of nihilism. Jefferson believed in the people, but he also believed in the distinction between truth and error. Jefferson opposed "artificial" aristocracies, but he favored a "natural" aristocracy of "virtue and talents." Bryan's tendency was to sweep everything aside in favor of head counts. And if later commentators were unfair in making him out as a kind of sweaty ignoramus, the *primus inter pares* of the yokels, the fact remains that he lacked the depth, the ability to get beyond pretty words and into tough analysis, the willingness to lead public opinion rather than merely trumpet it, that depth that marks greatness in politics.

The selection, "The Cross of Gold" speech, is a case in point. The occasion was the debate at the Democratic Convention of 1886 on the question of whether to support unlimited coinage of silver as currency. Bryan had by this time looked up the arguments for free silver. What we see, however, is not a mundane discourse on fiscal policy but a revivalist harangue in which the theme of "gold" is used to evoke all the predictable reactions from his audience. At its end Bryan had everything he could have wanted: roars of approval during the speech, an hour's ovation—and the Democratic nomination.

Mr. Chairman and Gentlemen of the Convention:—

I would be presumptuous, indeed, to present myself against the distinguished gentlemen to whom you have listened if this were a mere measuring of abilities; but this is not a contest between persons. The humblest citizen in all the land, when clad in the armor of a righteous cause, is stronger than all the hosts of error. I come to speak to you in defense of a cause as holy as the cause of liberty—the cause of humanity.

When this debate is concluded, a motion will be made to lay upon the table the resolution offered in commendation of the administration, and also the resolution offered in condemnation of the administration. We object to bringing this question down to the level of persons. The individual is but an atom; he is born, he acts, he dies; but principles are eternal; and this has been a contest over a principle.

Never before in the history of this country has there been witnessed such a contest as that through which we have just passed. Never before in the history of American politics has a great issue been fought out as this issue has been, by the voters of a great party. On the fourth of March, 1895, a few Democrats, most of them Members of Congress, issued an address to the Democrats of the nation, asserting that the money question was the paramount issue of the hour; declaring that a majority of the Democratic party had the right to control the action of the party on this paramount issue; and concluding with the request that the believers in the free coinage of silver in the Democratic party should organize, take charge of, and control the policy of the Democratic party. Three months later, at Memphis, an organization was perfected, and the silver Democrats went forth openly and courageously proclaiming their belief, and declaring that, if successful, they would crystallize into a platform the declaration which they had made. Then began the conflict. With a zeal approaching the zeal which inspired the crusaders who followed Peter the Hermit, our silver Democrats went forth from victory unto victory until they are now assembled, not to discuss, not to debate, but to enter up the judgment already rendered by the plain people of this country. In this contest brother has been arrayed against brother, father against son. The warmest ties of love, acquaintance, and association have been disregarded; old leaders have been cast aside when they have refused to give expression to the sentiments of those whom they would lead, and new leaders have sprung up to give direction to this cause of truth. Thus has the contest been waged, and we have assembled here under as binding and solemn instructions as were ever imposed upon representatives of the people.

We do not come as individuals. As individuals we might have been glad to compliment the gentleman from New York [Senator Hill], but we know that the people for whom we speak would never be willing to put him in a position where he could thwart the will of the Democratic party. I say it was not a question of persons; it was a question of principle, and it is not with gladness, my friends, that we find ourselves brought into conflict with those who are now arrayed on the other side.

The gentleman who preceded me [ex-Governor Russell] spoke of the State of Massachusetts; let me assure him that not one present in all this convention entertains the least hostility to the people of the State of Massachusetts, but we stand here representing people who are the equals, before the law, of the greatest citizens in the State of Massachusetts. When you (turning to the gold delegates) come before us and tell us that we are about to disturb your business interests, we reply that you have disturbed our business interests by your course.

We say to you that you have made the definition of a business man too limited in its application. The man who is employed for wages is as much a business man as his employer; the attorney in a country town is as much a business man as the corporation counsel in a great metropolis; the merchant at the cross-roads store is as much a business man as the merchant of New York; the farmer who goes forth in the morning and toils all day—who begins in the spring and toils all summer—and who by the application of brain and muscle to the natural resources of the country creates wealth, is as much a business man as the man who goes upon the board of trade and bets upon the price of grain; the miners who go down a thousand feet into the earth, or climb two thousand feet upon the cliffs, and bring forth from their hiding places the precious metals to be poured into the channels of trade are as much business men as the few financial magnates who, in a back room, corner the money of the world. We come to speak for this broader class of business men.

Ah, my friends, we say not one word against those who live upon the Atlantic coast, but the hardy pioneers who have braved all the dangers of the wilderness, who have made the desert to blossom as the rose—the pioneers away out there (pointing to the West), who rear their children near to Nature's heart, where they can mingle their voices with the voices of the birds—out there where they have erected schoolhouses for the education of their young, churches where they praise their Creator, and cemeteries where rest the ashes of their dead—these people, we say, are as deserving of the consideration of our party as any people in this country. It is for these that we speak. We do not come as aggressors. Our war is not a war of conquest; we are fighting in the defense of our homes, our families, and posterity. We have petitioned, and our petitions have been scorned; we have entreated, and our entreaties have been disregarded; we have begged, and they have mocked when our calamity came. We beg no longer; we entreat no more; we petition no more. We defy them.

The gentleman from Wisconsin has said that he fears a Robespierre. My friends, in this land of the free you need not fear that a tyrant will spring up from among the people. What we need is an Andrew Jackson to stand, as Jackson stood, against the encroachments of organized wealth.

They tell us that this platform was made to catch votes. We reply to them that changing conditions make new issues; that the principles upon which Democracy rests are as everlasting as the hills, but that they must be applied to new conditions as they arise. Conditions have arisen, and we are here to meet those conditions. They tell us that the income tax ought not to be brought in here; that it is a new idea. They criticise us for our criticism of the Supreme Court of the United States. My friends, we have not criticised; we have simply called attention to what you already know. If you want criticisms, read the dissenting opinions of the court. There you will find criticisms. They say that we passed an unconstitutional law; we deny it. The income tax law was not unconstitutional when it went before the Supreme Court for the first time; it did not become unconstitutional until one of the judges changed his mind, and we cannot be expected to know when a judge will change his mind. The income tax is just. It simply intends to put the burdens of government justly upon the backs of the people. I am in favor of an income tax. When I find a man who is not willing to bear his share of the burdens of the government which protects him, I find a man who is unworthy to enjoy the blessings of a government like ours.

They say that we are opposing national bank currency; it is true. If you will read what Thomas Benton said, you will find he said that, in searching history, he could find but one parallel to Andrew Jackson; that was Cicero, who destroyed the conspiracy of Cataline and saved Rome. Benton said that Cicero only did for Rome what Jackson did for us when he destroyed the bank conspiracy and saved America. We say in our platform that we believe that the right to coin and issue money is a function of government. We believe it. We believe that it is a part of sovereignty, and can no more with safety be delegated to private individuals than we could afford to delegate to private individuals the power to make penal statutes or levy taxes. Mr. Jefferson, who was once regarded as good Democratic authority, seems to have differed in opinion from the gentleman who has addressed us on the part of the minority. Those who are opposed to this proposition tell us that the issue of paper money is a function of the bank, and that the Government ought to go out of the banking business. I stand with Jefferson rather than with them, and tell them, as he did, that the issue of money is a function of government, and that the banks ought to go out of the governing business.

They complain about the plank which declares against life tenure in office. They have tried to strain it to mean that which it does not mean. What we oppose by that plank is the life tenure which is being built up in Washington, and which excludes from participation in official benefits the humbler members of society.

Let me call your attention to two or three important things. The gentleman from New York says that he will propose an amendment to the platform providing that the proposed change in our monetary system shall not affect contracts already made. Let me remind you that there is no intention of affecting those contracts which according to present laws are made payable in gold; but if he means to say that we cannot change our monetary system without protecting those who have loaned money before the change was made, I desire to ask him where, in law or in morals, he can find justification for not protecting the debtors when the act of 1873 was passed, if he now insists that we must protect the creditors.

He says he will also propose an amendment which will provide for the suspension of free coinage if we fail to maintain the parity within a year. We reply that when we advocate a policy which we believe will be successful, we are not compelled to raise a doubt as to our own sincerity by suggesting what we shall do if we fail. I ask him, if he would apply his logic to us, why he does not apply it to himself. He says he wants this country to try to secure an international agreement. Why does he not tell us what he is going to do if he fails to secure an international agreement? There is more reason for him to do that than there is for us to provide against the failure to maintain the parity. Our opponents have tried for twenty years to secure an international agreement, and those are waiting for it most patiently who do not want it at all.

And now, my friends, let me come to the paramount issue. If they ask us why it is that we say more on the money question than we say upon the tariff question, I reply that, if protection has slain its thousands, the gold standard has slain its tens of thousands. If they ask us why we do not employ in our platform all the things that we believe in, we reply that when we have restored the money of the Constitution all other necessary reforms will be possible; but that until this is done there is no other reform that can be accomplished.

Why is it that within three months such a change has come over the country? Three months ago, when it was confidently asserted that those who believe in the gold standard would frame our platform and nominate our candidates, even the advocates of the gold standard did not think that we could elect a president. And they had good reason for their doubt, because there is scarcely a State here today asking for the gold standard which is not in the absolute control of the Republican party. But note the change. Mr. McKinley was nominated at St. Louis upon a platform which declared for the maintenance of the gold standard until it can be changed into bimetallism by international agreement. Mr. McKinley was the most popular man among the Republicans, and three months ago everybody in the Republican party prophesied his election. How is he today? Why, the man who was once pleased to think that he looked like Napoleon—that man shudders today when he remembers that he was nominated on the anniversary of the battle of Waterloo. Not only that, but as he listens he can hear with ever increasing distinctness the sound of the waves as they beat upon the lonely shores of St. Helena.

Why this change? Ah, my friends, is not the reason for the change evident to any one who will look at the matter? No private character, however pure, no personal popularity, however great, can protect from the avenging wrath of an indignant people a man who will declare that he is in favor of fastening the gold standard upon this country, or who is willing to surrender the right of self-government and place the legislative control of our affairs in the hands of foreign potentates and powers.

We go forth confident that we shall win. Why? Because upon the paramount issue of this campaign there is not a spot of ground upon which the enemy will dare to challenge battle. If they tell us that the gold standard is a good thing, we shall point to their platform and tell them that their platform pledges the party to get rid of the gold standard and substitute bimetallism. If the gold standard is a good thing, why try to get rid of it? I call your attention to the fact that some of the very people who are in this convention today and who tell us that we ought to declare in favor of international bimetallism—thereby declaring that the gold standard is wrong and that the principle of bimetallism is better—these very people four months ago were open and avowed advocates of the gold standard, and were then telling us that we could not legislate two metals together, even with the aid of all the world. If the gold standard is a good thing, we ought to declare in favor of its retention and not in favor of abandoning it; and if the gold standard is a bad thing why should we wait until other nations are willing to help us to let go? Here is the line of battle, and we care not upon which issue they force the fight; we are prepared to meet them on either issue or on both. If they tell us that the gold standard is the standard of civilization, we reply to them that this, the most enlightened of all the nations of the earth, has never declared for a gold standard and that both the great parties this year are declaring against it. If the gold standard is the standard of civilization, why, my friends, should we not have it? If they come to meet us on that issue we can present the history of our nation. More than that, we can tell them that they will search the pages of history in vain to find a single instance where the common people of any land have ever declared themselves in favor of the gold standard. They can find where the holders of fixed investments have declared for a gold standard, but not where the masses have.

Mr. Carlisle said in 1878 that this was a struggle between "the idle holders of idle capital" and "the struggling masses, who produce the wealth and pay the taxes of the country"; and, my friends, the question we are to decide is: Upon which side will the Democratic party fight; upon the side of "the idle holders of idle capital" or upon the side of "the struggling masses"? That is the question which the party must answer first, and then it must be answered by each individual hereafter. The sympathies of the Democratic party, as shown by the platform, are on the side of the struggling masses who have ever been the foundation of the Democratic party. There are two ideas of government. There are those who believe that, if you will only legislate to make the well-to-do prosperous, their prosperity will leak through on those below. The Democratic idea, however, has been that if you legislate to make the masses prosperous, their prosperity will find its way up through every class which rests upon them.

You come to us and tell us that the great cities are in favor of the gold standard; we reply that the great cities rest upon our broad and fertile prairies. Burn down your cities and leave our farms, and your cities will spring up again as if by magic; but destroy our farms and the grass will grow in the streets of every city in the country.

My friends, we declare that this nation is able to legislate for its own people on every question, without waiting for the aid or consent of any other nation on earth; and upon that issue we expect to carry every State in the Union. I shall not slander the inhabitants of the fair State of Massachusetts nor the inhabitants of the State of New York by saying that, when they are confronted with the proposition, they will declare that this nation is not able to attend to its own business. It is the issue of 1776 over again. Our ancestors, when but three millions in number, had the courage to declare their political independence of every other nation; shall we, their descendants, when we have grown to seventy millions, declare that we are less independent than our forefathers? No, my friends, that will never be the verdict of our people. Therefore, we care not upon what lines the battle is fought. If they say bimetallism is good, but that we cannot have it until other nations help us, we reply that, instead of having a gold standard because England has, we will restore bimetallism, and then let England have bimetallism because the United States has it. If they dare to come out in the open field and defend the gold standard as a good thing, we will fight them to the uttermost. Having behind us the producing masses of this nation and the world, supported by the commercial interests, the laboring interests, and the toilers everywhere, we will answer their demand for a gold standard by saying to them: You shall not press down upon the brow of labor this crown of thorns, you shall not crucify mankind upon a cross of gold.

E. *Robert M. La Follette:*
   "The Undermining of Democracy"*

The "Progressivism" of Robert La Follette (1855-1925) may be seen as a transition between the populism of the People's Party and the diverse types of populism that Gerald Nye, William Borah, George Norris, and Huey Long brought to fruition during the 1930's.

Whatever philosophical difference existed between La Follette's populism and that of the People's Party was minor, for La Follette readily appropriated the trust-busting approach to reform, the individualist orientation, the ritual invocation of Jefferson and the slogan of "equal rights for all, special privileges for none." But Progressivism developed in a different region than Populism, and it appealed to a different demographic mix. Even in 1896, at the peak of the Populist ascendancy, its strength was mainly in the grain states of Kansas, Nebraska, and South Dakota. States like Wisconsin and Minnesota, with greater urbanization and a higher percentage of Catholics and foreigners, were not attracted to the fundamentalist style of the candidate endorsed by the People's Party; some Wisconsin German areas turned Republican for the first time since the Civil War.

But even as the death throes of Populism proceeded in the years after 1896, a maverick Republican governor in Wisconsin was getting legislation passed in his state which brought new life to the Populist dream. The "Wisconsin idea," as these measures came to be known collectively, included a system of direct primary nominations to replace the old caucus and convention system,

*Condensation prepared by Senator La Follette of a speech made in Philadelphia, February 2, 1912, and widely distributed as a pamphlet. Although this speech was made in 1912, La Follette began arguing many of the same points as early as the 1890's.

equal taxation for corporate as well as other property, regulation of railroad charges, and commissions to regulate all public services.

In 1905 La Follette was elected to the United States Senate, a post which he occupied until his death and which enabled him to bring "the Wisconsin idea" to the attention of the nation. He advocated railroad control and regulatory commissions, fought tariffs, championed the conservation movement, courageously opposed U.S. involvement in World War I, afterward opposed ratification of the League of Nations and the World Court, and wrote the resolution authorizing Senatorial investigation of Harding's oil-lease scandals.

In 1924 he ran for President on the Progressive ticket. Although by this time he had moved closer to the model of national supervision as represented by Theodore Roosevelt in his 1912 version of Progressivism, La Follette still remained fundamentally a populist reformer, relying on the laws of competition to regulate business except when state ownership became unavoidable.

La Follette's contribution to the populist tradition can be summarized under two headings. First, he kept the spirit of populism alive during the lean years, *i.e.*, after the collapse of the People's Party in 1900 and during the cynical years of the early 1920's. Second, he introduced populism to a much wider audience, an audience which had been repelled by Bryan and one which was much more representative of modern America than the old Bryan constituency—to ethnics, to labor, to intellectuals. La Follette was one of those who revitalized populism, made it popular again.

The selection is taken from *The Undermining of Democracy*.

The great issue before the American people to-day is the control of their own government. In the midst of political struggle, it is not easy to see the historical relations of the present progressive movement. But it represents a conflict as old as the history of man—the fight to maintain liberty, the rights of all the people.

A mighty power has been builded up in this country in recent years, so strong, yet so insidious and far-reaching in its influence that men are gravely inquiring whether its iron grip on government and business can ever be broken. Again and again it has proved strong enough to nominate the candidates of both political parties. It rules in the organization of legislative bodies, state and national, and of the committees which frame legislation. Its influence is felt in cabinets and in the policies of administrations, and is clearly seen in the appointment of prosecuting officers and the selection of judges upon the bench.

In business it has crippled or destroyed competition. It has stifled individual initiative. It has fixed limitations in the field of production. It makes prices and imposes its burdens upon the consuming public at will.

In transportation, after a prolonged struggle for government control, it is, with only slight check upon its great power, still master of the highways of commerce.

In finance its power is unlimited. In large affairs it gives or withholds credit, and from time to time contracts or inflates the volume of the money required for the transaction of the business of the country, regardless of everything excepting its own profits.

It has acquired vast areas of the public domain, and is rapidly monopolizing the natural resources—timber, iron, coal, oil.

And this THING has grown up in a country where, under the Constitution and the law, the citizen is sovereign!

The related events which led to this centralized control are essential to a clear understanding of the real danger—the magnitude of this danger now menacing the very existence of every independent concern remaining in the field of business enterprise.

THE FIRST PERIOD—THE INDIVIDUAL
AND THE PARTNERSHIP

For nearly a century after Jefferson declared for a government of "equal rights for all, and special privileges for none," the business of the country was conducted by individuals and partnerships. During this first period, business methods were simple, its proportions modest, and there was little call for larger capital than could be readily furnished by the individual or in the most extreme cases, a partnership of fair size.

But, as the country developed, as the population poured over the Alleghenies, occupied the Mississippi valley, pushed on to the

Rocky Mountains and down the western slope to California, dis-
covering the boundless wealth of our natural resources,—the
fields and forests, the mountains of iron and coal and precious
metals, there was a pressing call on every hand for larger capital
beyond the power of any individual or any partnership to supply.
We had outgrown the simple methods; there was a demand for a
new business device strong enough to unlock the treasure house of
the new world.

THE SECOND PERIOD—THE PRIVATE CORPORATION

The modern corporation was invented to meet that demand, and
general statutes for incorporation were soon upon the statute books
of every state. Their adoption marked the beginning of the second
period of our business life. It was the best machine ever invented
for the purpose; simple in organization, effective in operation.

Big capital behind the private corporations drove business at a
pace and upon a scale never before witnessed. Competition was at
once the spur to the highest efficiency and the check against waste
and abuse of power.
In this period of our industrial and commercial progress,
America amazed and alarmed our business rivals of the old world.
We were soon foremost among the nations of the earth in agriculture, in mines and mining, in manufactures, and in commerce as
well.
The American market became the greatest thing in all the
material world. Its control became the one thing coveted.

THE THIRD PERIOD—THE COMBINATION
OF CORPORATIONS

The evil hour was come upon us. Daring, unscrupulous men
plotted in violation of the common law, the criminal statutes and
against public right to become masters of that market and take what
toll they pleased. To do this thing it was necessary to set aside,
abrogate, nullify the natural laws of trade that had ruled in business
for centuries. Production was to be limited, competition stifled and

prices arbitrarily fixed by selfish decree. And thus we entered upon the third period of our business and commercial life—the period of a combination of the corporations under a single control in each line of business. It was not an evolution; it was a revolution.

And yet certain economists set it down in the literature of the day that the Supreme Ruler of the universe reserved in His great plan a divinely appointed place and time for a Rockefeller, a Morgan, a Carnegie, a Baer, to evolve this new law, which should enable them to appropriate the wealth of the country and Mexicanize its business and its people.

The combination became supreme in each important line, controlling the markets for the raw material and the finished product, largely dictating the price of everything we sell and the price of everything we buy—beef, sugar, woolens, cottons, coal, oil, copper, zinc, iron, steel, agricultural implements, hardware, gas, electric light, food supplies.

Monopoly acquired dominion everywhere.

It brought with it the inevitable results of monopoly, —extortionate prices, inferior products. We soon found shoddy in everything we wear, and adulteration in everything we eat.

Did these masters of business stop there? By no means! "Increase of appetite had grown by what it fed on." The flood gates of fictitious capitalization were thrown wide open. These organizations of combinations overcapitalized for a double purpose. The issue of bonds and stocks in excess of investment covered up the exaction of their immense profits, and likewise offered an unlimited field for promotion and speculation.

The establishment of this third period was the beginning of rapidly advancing prices, increasing the cost of living upon people of average earning power until the burden is greater than they can bear.

THE FOURTH PERIOD—THE COMBINATION OF COMBINATIONS

The strife for more money, more power—more power, more money—swept everything before it.

It remained only to bring together into a community of interest or ownership the great combinations which controlled, each in its own field—in short, to combine these combinations.

One needs but to study the directory of directories of the great business concerns of the country to determine the extent to which this combination of combinations has been successfully accomplished, thus carrying us over into the fourth period of our industrial and commercial life—the period of complete industrial and commercial servitude in which we now unhappily find ourselves. And this supreme control of the business of the country is the triumph of men who have at every step defied public opinion, the common law and criminal statutes.

This condition is intolerable. It is hostile to every principle of democracy. If maintained, it is the end of democracy. We may preserve the form of our representative government and lose the soul, the spirit of our free institutions.

THE CENTRALIZATION OF RAILROAD CONTROL

In the meantime, what were the powers doing in the great field of transportation? A swift backward glance reveals the fact that the same system of consolidation, centralized control and suppressed competition had been forced through in violation of law and public right.

The vital interests of organized society in commerce and the public nature of transportation impose upon government the duty to establish and maintain control over common carriers.

To discharge this obligation the government must exact from the common carrier:

(1) Reasonable rates, (2) impartial rates, (3) adequate and impartial services.

The public is interested in adequate and impartial services. The shipper is especially interested in equal and impartial rates. The consumer is especially interested in reasonable rates.

For forty years after railroads were established there was no attempt to invoke governmental control. The public depended solely upon competition between railroads for the protection of public interests.

Finally it learned the elementary lesson that the railroad is a natural monopoly; that there can be no competition excepting at common points, and that at common points the railroads were destroying all competition by pooling agreements.

Then came the demand in 1870 for governmental control—in order to secure reasonable rates. It originated in the upper Mississippi valley—in Wisconsin, Iowa, Minnesota and Illinois, for a control of rates within the state.

It spread east and west and became a national movement for controlling interstate commerce.

The supreme courts of the middle western states sustained the state legislation. The Supreme Court of the United States sustained the state courts, and the power of the state and federal governments to control and fix reasonable transportation rates, each in its own sphere, was adjudicated as a public right thirty-eight years ago.

For a generation of time since those decisions the people have struggled to secure an interstate commerce law which would establish and enforce reasonable rates. That was the relief which the consumer, the great body of the people, demanded —reasonable rates.

The shippers have no interest in reasonable rates. They do not pay the freight. The consumer pays the freight. But the shipper is at a disadvantage in supplying his trade unless he has rates relatively equal to those given to other shippers engaged in the same business.

Shippers could easily present concrete cases of injustice. They could readily organize and appear before committees and make their representatives feel their power.

Not so with the consumer, who, in the end, pays all the freight, as a part of the purchase price of everything he buys. He cannot identify the freight charge, because it is a part of the price he pays when he purchases supplies. However small the item, in the aggregate it is important to him. He cannot maintain a lobby. If his United States senators and his congressmen do not represent him, he is helpless.

What is the net result of thirty-eight years' struggle with the railroads? Congress enacted the interstate commerce law of 1887; the Elkins law of 1903; the Hepburn law of 1906; and the recent law of 1910.

Out of all this legislation the shippers have been able to secure a partial enforcement of their contention for an equalization of rates.

The consumers have lost in their long fight for reasonable rates.

After all these years it is not to-day within the power of the interstate commerce commission to take the first step to ascertain a reasonable rate. There is a vast difference between equal rates and reasonable rates.

The consumers are no nearer to securing reasonable rates than they were thirty-eight years ago.

Ninety million people are to-day paying annually to the railroads $2,500,000,000 for transportation—a sum greater than the total cost of maintaining the federal government, the state governments, the county governments, and all the municipal governments of the entire country.

The power of the railroads over Congress has been well nigh supreme. That their influence was strong enough to defeat legislation is emphatically asserted by a prominent United States senator, the writer of a letter which I quote.

"UNITED STATES SENATE.

WASHINGTON, D. C., FEB. 9, 1903.

"DEAR SIR:

Yours of the 19th ult. came duly to hand. It has happened as I feared: The interstate commerce committee will not report the measure giving power to the interstate commerce commission to fix rates. It is expecting too much from human nature that Senators whose every association is with the great railroad corporations, and whose political lives largely depend upon them, should in good faith approve a measure that would to an extent make the railroads a servant of the people, and to be subject to the decision of the commission when a question of rates is raised. The Senate committee is by a decided majority men who bear these relations to the railroads. I hope that some time in the future the committee will be so constituted that legislation of the character mentioned will issue from it, but I

am afraid you and I will be many years older when that
occurs.

Yours truly,"

THE CENTRALIZED CONTROL OF BANKING, CAPITAL, AND CREDITS

The country is only just beginning to understand how completely great banking institutions in the principal money centers
have become bound up with the control of industrial institutions,
the railroads and franchise combinations.

That there was a tendency on the part of great banking associations to merge and combine could not be overlooked. But while
financial and economic writers had directed public attention to the
fact, and had even pointed out the opportunity and temptation for
the use of this augmented power in connection with the promotion
of the speculative side of business organization, they were slow to
believe that banking institutions could be so prostituted. Certain
critical observers had, however, as long as five or six years ago,
suggested the dangerous tendencies in this direction.

Nevertheless, the most conservative authority, some five or six
years ago, suggested the dangerous tendencies then already apparent to the critical observer.

Thus early an English economist, writing in Littell's *Living
Age*, said: "The recent extreme stringency of money in New York
would probably never have arisen if the banks, instead of preparing for the autumn demands, had not locked up their funds in the
financiering of Wall Street. That the banks are, to a large extent,
under the domination of the big financiers is well known, and the
recent insurance investigations have shown how, under such
domination, private interests may be made to prevail over those of
the public."

George M. Reynolds, president of the Continental and Commercial National Bank of Chicago, at the National Business Congress, December 13, 1911, said: "I believe the money power now
lies in the hands of a dozen men. I plead guilty to being one, in the

last analysis, of those men. . . . Two or three [banks] in New York, two or three in Chicago, and two or three in St. Louis could control the question of whether or not loans should be made to correspondents throughout the country.''

This is but the barest outline of the upbuilding of this power which now controls.

Is there a way out? Let us consider.

By its decisions in the Standard Oil and Tobacco cases the Supreme Court has all at once created itself into a legislature, an interstate commerce commission and a supreme court, combined in one.

The ''rule of reason'' gives it legislative power, the power to determine according to its own opinion that some restraints of trade are lawful and other restraints unlawful. The power to carry out the dissolution and reorganization of the trusts and to work out the details is exactly the power that a legislature turns over to a commission. Punishment for contempt is the court's substitute for the criminal penalty that the legislature attaches to the violation of its statutes.

The supreme court has amended the anti-trust act in exactly the way that Congress repeatedly refused to amend it, and has usurped both legislative and executive power in doing it. Whether we wish it or not, Congress is now compelled to create an interstate trade commission to control the trusts, or else leave the control to the federal courts, acting as a commission.

Such a commission should not fix prices. Price regulation assumes that we are dealing with a necessary monopoly, as in the case of railroads and public utilities. But the commercial monopolies are based on unfair and discriminatory practices and special privileges. These can be abolished in several ways.

Amend the Sherman law by enacting specific prohibitions against well-known practices that constitute unreasonable restraints of trade. One of these is the brutal method of the Standard Oil Company of cutting prices in any place where there is a competitor in order to kill him off, while keeping up prices in other places. Another is the club wielded by the tobacco trust, which put the jobbers in a position where, unless they refrained from buying of a competitor, they could not get from the trust the brands which were indispensable to the successful conduct of their business.

These and several other obviously unreasonable restraints of trade are definitely prohibited in the bill which I have introduced in the Senate.

The bill also places the burden of proof on the trust to show that any restraint of trade which it practices is reasonable—that is, that it benefits the community.

It also provides that when the court has once entered its final decree and declared a trust illegal, any person who has suffered damages may come in under that decree and simply petition that his damages be paid without proving anything except the amount of the damages. If this had been law when the Standard Oil and Tobacco decisions were rendered, those decisions would have meant something more than mere victories on paper.

In addition to these amendments to the anti-trust law, there is need of a commission to stand between the people and the courts in order to investigate the facts and to prohibit all unreasonable restraints not specifically described in the law. This commission should have full power to ascertain the actual cost of reproduction, or physical value of the property; the reasonable value that the intangible property, such as good will, would have under conditions of fair competition, and to distinguish this from the illegal values that have been built up in violation of law. It should ascertain the values that depend on patents, monopoly of natural resources and all other forms of special privilege; the amount of property that has been paid for out of illegal profits taken from the public, distinguished from the property paid for out of legitimate profits and true investment. It should in this way ascertain the true cost of production and whether the prices charged are yielding extortionate profits or only the reasonable profits that competitors could earn. These are the facts that the people must know before they will consent to any legislation that treats illegal values as though they were legal.

With these facts ascertained and made *prima facie* evidence in court, these illegal values cannot be permanently fastened on the American people. It will take time to pull down this false structure of illegal capitalization of the trusts, but it is now the greatest menace to prosperity.

If these laws are adopted, then every business man, as well as the courts, will know definitely what is meant by the "rule of reason.'' Legitimate business will have its course laid out clear and certain before it, and every investor will know precisely what the law allows and what it prohibits.

The trust problem has become so interwoven in our legal and industrial system that no single measure or group of measures can reach all of it. It must be picked off at every point where it shows its head.

Every combination of a manufacturing business with the control of transportation, including pipe lines, should be prohibited, in order that competitors may have equal facilities for reaching markets.

The control of limited sources of raw material, like coal, iron ore or timber, by a manufacturing corporation, should be broken up and these resources should be opened to all manufacturers on equal terms.

The tariff should be brought down to the difference in labor cost of the more efficient plants and the foreign competitor, and where there is no difference the tariff should be removed. Where the protective tariff is retained its advantages must be passed along to labor, for whose benefit the manufacturer contends it is necessary.

The patent laws should be so amended that the owners of patents will be compelled to develop them fully or permit their use on equal terms by others.

More vital and menacing than any other power that supports trusts is the control of credit through the control of the people's savings and deposits. When the Emergency Currency Bill was before Congress in 1908, Senator Aldrich sneaked into the conference report certain provisions which he had withdrawn in the Senate, and withdrew provisions which he had first included. He eliminated protection against promotion schemes, excluded penalties for false reporting, dropped provisions for safeguarding reserves, inserted provisions for accepting railroad bonds as security. Now he comes with another plausible measure to remedy the admitted evils of our inelastic banking system. However innocent this plan may seem on the surface, it justifies the most careful scrutiny at every step.

When we realize that the control of credit and banking is the greatest power that the trusts possess to keep out competitors, we may well question their sincerity in offering a patriotic measure to dispossess themselves of that power. It is the people's money that is expected to give security to this plan and the people must and shall control it.

It is claimed on all sides that competition has failed. I deny it. Fair competition has not failed. It has been suppressed. When competitors are shut out from markets by discriminations, and denied either transportation, raw material or credit on equal terms, we do not have competition. We have the modern form of highway robbery. The great problem of legislation before us is first for the people to resume control of their government, and then to protect themselves against those who are throttling competition by the aid of government.

I do not say that competition does not have its evils. Labor organizations are the struggling protest against cut-throat competition. The anti-trust law was not intended or understood to apply to them. They should be exempt from its operation.

In all our plans for progressive legislation, it must not be forgotten that we are only just beginning to get control of the railroads. The present law is improvement, but the Interstate Commerce Commission requires it to be greatly strengthened. It should have a much larger appropriation, enabling it to prosecute investigations in all parts of the country. It should make physical valuations of the railroads, eliminating watered stock, monopoly values and the unwarranted inflation of railway terminals to conceal monopoly values. And the Commerce Court should be abolished as a mere subterfuge interposed to handicap the commission.

III. POPULISM AND
THE NEW DEAL

If Populism as an organized party was dead by 1908, even its spirit seemed to be crushed by 1920. A war-weary generation had had more than enough of crisis. Warren G. Harding, elected by a large majority, promised a return to "normalcy." And normalcy was to mean that American business must be undisturbed by noisy reformers. "America's business is business," said Calvin Coolidge, and he was elected in 1924 despite the scandals of the administration in which he had served as Vice President. On the surface, at least, reform had become rather quaint. William E. Leuchtenburg, in his classic study of the twenties, *The Perils of Prosperity*, quotes the economist Stuart Chase in 1926.

> Them was the days! When the muckrakers were best sellers, when trust busters were swinging their lariats over every state capitol, when "priviledge" shook in its shoes, when God was behind the initiative, the referendum and the recall—and the devil shrieked when he saw the short ballot . . . and Utopia was just around the corner. . . .
>
> Now look at the dammed thing. You could put the avowed Socialists into a roomy new house, Mr. Coolidge is compared favorably to Lincoln, the short ballot is as defunct as Mah Jong. . . .
>
> Shall we lay a wreath on the Uplift Movement in America? I suppose we might as well.*

*Stuart Chase, quoted in William E. Leuchtenburg, *The Perils of Prosperity* (Chicago: The University of Chicago, 1958), p. 137.

Yet even during these cynical years there were those who could offer more than nostalgia for the old days. The spirit of populism was being kept alive in the oddest of places, the Republican Party and the United States Senate. Besides Senator La Follette, the independent Republican who wound up his life running for President in 1924 on a populist platform, at least three other maverick Republican Senators had helped to snatch the fallen flag of the People's Party.

Its nativism, its distrust of foreign entanglements, was preserved in the Senate by William E. Borah of Idaho. Borah fought against any American involvement in the League of Nations or the World Court. This was not because he lacked enthusiasm for world peace. Quite the contrary, Borah feared that such entanglements in treaties which involved sanctions against "aggressors" would drag this country into more war. In contemporary terms, he would be almost certainly a "super-dove," for he steered through the Senate the Kellogg-Briand Pact which sought to "outlaw" war. No, the "Uplift Movement" was far from dead!

Another, more practical, populist during the lean years was George Norris. Quietly, and with inexhaustible patience, he worked all during the twenties for the passage of legislation which would provide cheap public power to the people in a depressed area of the country and, more important, would demonstrate that power, even electric power, should belong to the people. Norris was also working during these years of big business dominance for a recognition of the rights of unions. This was to bear fruit in the form of the Norris-La Guardia Act, which a reluctant President Hoover signed into law in 1932.

In 1928 there came to the Senate a young man from North Dakota. Gerald Nye's greatest moment was yet to come—his investigation of the munitions-makers—but even then he was keeping the spirit of populism alive by his attack on Eastern industrialists and bankers.

One year later the stage was set for the New Deal. The crash of the stock market destroyed more than the fragile and superficial prosperity of the twenties. It also destroyed the confidence of the American people in the spokesmen for the business community. They were told not to worry, that business knew what it was about, that prosperity would return very shortly. They were told, by the New York *Times*, that "the fundamental prescriptions for recovery [were] such homely things as savings, retrenchment, prudence and hopeful waiting for the turn." But little homilies of this kind must have sounded hollow in Cleveland, where 50 percent were jobless, or in Akron, where the figure was 60 percent, or in Toledo where 80 percent were out of work. Nor could the workers of Donora, Pennsylvania, where only 277 out of 13,900 held regular jobs, have taken very kindly to the *Times'* call for patience.

Slowly at first, but with gathering momentum, the "plain people" of America began to realize that the business community had utterly failed them. The farseeing "captains of industry" had turned out to be panic-stricken little men, unable either to anticipate or bring to an end the result of their own greed. Instead they ran for cover, deserting those who had helped them make their fortunes. In the three years after the crash, 100,000 workers were fired almost every week. This was not a time for patience but for protest, not a time for fatalism but for action. Caricatured and debunked for a decade, populism had come into its own again.

No one realized this more keenly than Franklin Delano Roosevelt. Roosevelt was the first modern President, the first to realize the enormous potential of the new technology in reaching out to the "plain people." Appealing to an audience enraged at the corporations and banks, Roosevelt excoriated "the unscrupulous money changers" who "stand indicted in the court of public opinion, rejected by the minds and hearts of men." That a number of these money changers were key figures in the Roosevelt Administration was one of the facts easily obscured by the unceasing flood of populist rhetoric.

The genius of Roosevelt lay in his ability to assume the posture of a populist without effecting any populist reforms. He did not get America out of the Depression—Hitler did. He did not destroy the trusts but worked with them, hoping to make them more statesmanlike. He did not bring power to the people but consolidated it within the Executive branch. Roosevelt was not a populist but a genial tory who combined a vague sense of *noblesse oblige* with a keen love of power. And those on the inside of the New Deal, those who knew its purposes and shared them, were not populists either, but pragmatists and social engineers. They prided themselves on their tough-mindedness; they too had learned to talk populism without taking it too seriously.

The New Deal did serve as a kind of umbrella for reform. All were welcome under it as long as they did not try to displace the man who held it. Thus Roosevelt encouraged Gerald Nye to investigate the munitions-makers, ceremoniously signed TVA into law and thanked the Republican Senator who made it possible. In train and limousine he graced the state of Idaho in the company of Senator Borah. He tried at first to associate himself with Huey Long, but Long proved to be an embarrassment, and finally an enemy, because he would not be managed. Here was one populist shrewd enough to see Roosevelt's technique, which he once described in a rural fable:

> Hoover is a hoot owl and Roosevelt is a scrootch owl. A hoot owl bangs into the nest and knocks the hen clean off and catches her while she's falling. But a scrootch owl slips into the roost and scrootches up to the hen and talks softly to her. And the hen just falls in love with him, and the next thing you know there ain't no hen.*

Long was dead, of an assassin's bullet, by 1935, but Roosevelt was still far from having ingested the kind of angry unpredictable populism that Long represented. The Depression had not died with Huey Long. It lasted another five years, until a booming war economy did what the timid Keynesianism of the New Deal had never been able to do: put America back to work and transmute protests into patriotism.

---

*Quoted in T. Harry Williams, *Huey Long: A Biography* (New York: Alfred Knopf, 1969), p. 812.

A. *William E. Borah:*
   ## "The Farmer's Enemy"*

A superficial glance at the speeches and writings of William E. Borah (1865-1940) of Idaho during his long Senate career might produce the conclusion that his foreign and domestic policy were fundamentally at odds. He was a conservative in foreign affairs, insisting upon "America first" and isolationism in the face of Nazi aggression; in domestic affairs he was a liberal, although he was not very consistent even here, since he welcomed the advent of the New Deal but grew fearful of its practices.

The superficiality of this view is evident when we examine Borah's various positions from the standpoint of the populist model outlined in the Introduction. From that perspective we can easily see the underlying unity in Borah's approach to world and domestic affairs, and see why such labels as "liberal" and "conservative" can be so misleading when applied to populism.

Borah's pride in America's revolutionary heritage was coupled with a deep and abiding suspicion of reactionary governments in the Old World. He feared that any American involvement in European affairs would ensnare this country in all Europe's petty quarrels, its atavistic wars, its greed and imperialism. For this reason he was the Senate's most uncompromising opponent of the League of Nations, seeing it as a plot to entangle our democracy in the power games of aristocratic Europe. He opposed the World Court proposal for the same reason, considering it a surrender of American sovereignty to a body that would not decide cases on their merits but on the basis of *realpolitik*.

It was not meanspiritedness or selfishness that led Borah to identify with the slogan of "America first," but quite the contrary: a conviction that America's idealism, its preference for peoples over governments, its support for the "little guy," would be compromised by membership in any organization dominated by Great Powers and staffed by their most privileged classes.

In other matters involving international relations Borah was anything but an isolationist. He supported Irish independence,

---

*From *Collier's*, XCVII (February 1, 1936).

campaigned for recognition of the Soviet Union, suggested an alternate version of a World Court, and piloted the Kellogg-Briand Pact, which sought to outlaw war, through the Senate. Considerable naiveté lay behind Borah's championship of some of these causes, particularly the last. The obvious flaw in the treaty to outlaw war was the total absence of any machinery for enforcement. But Borah's naiveté was typically populistic. So strong was his faith in a universal moral law comprehensible to a human nature which is fundamentally good, and so great was his aversion to complicated bureaucratic machinery, that he considered a declaration enough to stir the peoples of the world into forcing a renunciation of war upon their governments. His attitude toward the Soviet government followed the same lines. He was not enthusiastic about the Bolsheviks, but he believed that their revolution had at least opened the way for democracy in a country formerly ruled by the most Draconian of European authoritarians.

Borah's positions on domestic issues were also typically populistic. He was outspokenly critical of President Hoover for paralysis in the face of the worst depression in the nation's history. The scandal of the Republican Old Guard, as Borah saw it, was its refusal to provide relief lest "the dole" undermine people's incentive.

> This talk about setting a precedent or establishing the dole system is rank intellectual dishonesty. Congress is being asked to do what it has done again and again in this country and in foreign countries—appropriate money for the relief of people who are suffering from what we are pleased to call "an act of God."*

Borah then described the plight of a Tennessee mother who was trying to keep her children alive on a diet of soured meal and rancid pork.

> Yet we are told that for the government to feed this woman and her sick children would destroy her self-respect and make a bad citizen of her. Does *anyone*

*Marian C. McKenna, *Borah* (Ann Arbor: University of Michigan Press, 1961), p. 268.

> believe it? It is a cowardly imputation on the helpless. I
> resent it and I repudiate it.*

But even in this outburst we can see the note of caution. Borah
viewed the Depression as a temporary disaster, like a hurricane or
a flood. It is therefore a serious question whether he would favor
the *institution* of the right to an income, *i.e.*, a bureaucracy which
would administer a guaranteed income even during periods of
general prosperity. Borah was Hoover's most vigorous champion
during the 1928 election, and despite the Depression, his
economics never strayed very far from Hoover's "rugged individualism." This became apparent when President Roosevelt attempted to apply a program of national supervision to the problems
of the Depression. Roosevelt's National Recovery Administration
(NRA) sought to impose "codes of fair competition" upon
businessmen, exempting them from anti-trust legislation if they
complied. This combination of pragmatism in the enforcement of
the Sherman Anti-Trust Act and paternalism in industrial relations
ran counter to Borah's fundamentally *laissez-faire* orientation. He
remained convinced that the laws of competition would regulate
industries provided that these industries were cut down to size, and
he criticized what he called the "state socialism" of Roosevelt's
ill-fated experiment.

In 1936 Borah summed up his populist creed in an article
entitled "The Farmer's Enemy." This article, which constitutes
the selection, brings together a number of populist themes: hom-
age to the farmer (coupled with an opposition to "artificial" price
supports), national economic autonomy (a refusal to admit any
need for the markets of the "Old World"), an insistence that
monopoly results not from ordinary competition but from criminal
greed, and an abiding faith in trustbusting as the ultimate solution
to America's economic crisis.

Where is the American farmer to find the market upon which
alone depends his permanent prosperity? Is there a market? If so,
where is it?

Ibid.

Whatever virtues there were in the Agricultural Adjustment Act as an emergency proposition, it did not seem to me a permanent solution of the tragedy of the American farm.

Mr. Freestone, the able Master of the State Grange of the State of New York, according to the press, recently stated: "We hope that some of the experiments sincerely made in the cause of agriculture will be successful, but in the long run, on a permanent basis, government cannot save agriculture. . . . When the present emergency is over . . . when the end of experimentation comes, the organizations (farm organizations) will see new opportunities to grow in the service of agriculture."

This, I suspect, represents the view of the vast majority of the American farmers.

Notwithstanding the hog vote, the wheat vote and all other votes, the farmer does not like regimentation. He takes it because it is the only help that has been offered him in an almost indescribably distressing situation. Those who picture the farmer as anxious to let his acres lie idle and wait for his check, in my opinion, know little about his real views. He is less in love with bureaucracy than anyone in the United States. Instinctively he wants to run his farm which his own industry has carved out of perhaps a desert; he wants to enlarge and to improve. He likes to add to his acreage, his herd; and he rejoices to see things grow—"multiply and replenish the earth."

But he had seen the debenture which the Grange had urged for fifty years killed. The Tariff Act of 1929 as it passed the Senate provided for the issuance of debenture certificates to farmers exporting farm commodities equal to the amount of the duty upon such commodities.

These certificates issued to the farmer exporting his commodities were to be redeemed by the Secretary of the Treasury under proper rules and regulations. He had seen the pledge broken by which he was to be given equality of treatment under the tariff. He had seen his dollar, when measured in the commodity of his production, cut in half, and his taxes, interest and debts in the meantime increasing. So he consented to reduce acreage and to kill his pigs—something which he deplores far more than do those who criticize him for doing so.

Forced to Regimentation

Give the farmer a fair market—a market in which he can realize the cost of production with reasonable profits—and he will return the check, take back the idle acres, fight for the life of his pigs, and chase away the first representative of bureaucracy appearing at his barn gate, with a pitchfork. But until he is given a market he must take regimentation in order, as he hopes, to save his farm, his home, and afford a chance in life to his children. You cannot blame him for accepting the only program offered, however distasteful it seemed, to afford as he feels a chance, if not to pull through, at least to exist.

It is a truism, of course, to say that prosperity for agriculture depends upon an enlarged market. But it is a truism which is greatly disregarded. Refinancing of farm indebtedness is, of course, important. Reduction of taxes and cheaper freight rates are likewise important. But the fundamental and determining factor is that of increased and increasing demands for the products of the farm. Can this demand be created? Can this market be found? The demand is at hand; that we know. I feel the market can be made available. And fortunately in making this market available we will at the same time be serving the cause of humanity and strengthening our entire political structure. In other words, insofar as we serve the cause of social justice we serve the cause of agriculture by furnishing a market.

We Can't Look Abroad

It appears doubtful whether we shall realize anything like what we seem to hope for in the matter of a foreign market. Everything indicates we are not going to find any considerable demand abroad for our agricultural products. I do not mean to say that we should not by all practical and reasonable means seek to enlarge our foreign market. And to this end the debenture system will probably be of more service than anything which has been suggested. But at best the foreign market will take care of a very small percentage of the products from the farm. In normal times only about 18 per cent of farm income is represented by exports. We may not be able to maintain even that percentage.

We know that it has been the policy of all nations, particularly since the World War, to increase all agricultural output. It is estimated that some fifty million acres have been put under cultivation since the Armistice. Backward countries with fertile soil and abundance of cheap labor are supplying and building up production to such an extent that it not only reduces the demand for American products but actually threatens to invade, in fact is invading, our domestic market. It would seem that the only market for the American farmer is here in the United States, at his very door. And it seems to me that under a sound economic system that market is ample to insure, in connection with a fair system of refinancing farm indebtedness and a just tax policy, return of prosperity to American agriculture. I say a return of prosperity. The time has been so long that perhaps I should say insure prosperity to American agriculture.

I suppose we ought to gauge our farm problem by normal years rather than years of depression. It would greatly simplify the problem if it should be ascertained that in normal years the farmer was prosperous or even fairly prosperous, and that his trouble came only with the general depression. But if we ascertain that in so-called prosperous years we still had a most serious condition on the farm we will be able better to determine the seriousness of the problem, the nature of it, and possibly the solution of it.

What are the facts? The present income of the farm is about $7,300,000,000. It has been augmented since 1932 to the extent of about $1,963,000,000. I am not now subtracting anything by reason of increase in the price of the things the farmer must buy. For the purpose of this article we may credit the income with the full amount above indicated. But here is the real problem—not how much we have been able to add to an impossible minimum such as that of 1932, but what have we done or can we do to add to the income to which I now call attention? In 1928-29 the income of the farm was $11,941,000,000. The relevant question, therefore, is what was the condition of agriculture at the time it had an income in excess of the present income to the extent of $4,641,000,000?

*   *   *

A Problem We've Always Had

The income, in other words, at the present time of the American farm is about 63 per cent of the average income from 1923 to 1929. The question, therefore, is: Did this income bring prosperity to agriculture during these years? If not, can we hope to bring prosperity by curtailing production, or shall we look for enlarging and increasing markets? We know that during the years from 1923 to 1929 mortgages were increased and enlarged and foreclosed. Tax sales in agricultural regions were common. At the Republican Convention in Kansas City in 1928 the farmers marched in a body from adjoining states to make known their distressed condition.

Our farm problem did not come with the depression. It was here in a most aggravated form during the years which have been designated as years of prosperity. If the trouble on the farm had commenced with the depression we might well hope that when we get back to the "favorable" condition of 1929 the farm problem will disappear. But it will not disappear under circumstances similar to those years. In fact, I ask, when has there been prosperity on the farm during recent years except in times of war or in case of crop failures on a large scale in other countries? It is instructive to go back over the history of agriculture and learn how rarely the farmer has been prosperous in recent decades except when war or famine gave him a market. The farm question has its roots in conditions other than those superinduced by general depression.

It will not be contended that from 1923-29 the farmer was at fault. He had produced and was prepared, assuming the American people could buy, to feed the American people, pay his taxes, high as they were, pay his interest, high as it was, reduce his mortgage and, keeping step to the music of the seasons' change, reseed and replant his acres. Assuming that the American people could buy! But, badly as many needed to buy, they could not buy. A proud, strong people were by the millions without the means to supply their tables with more than the bare necessities of life, and millions more were not able to provide even the bare necessities of life. The farmer had not overproduced, measured by the needs of the people; he had not curtailed production or limited output; he had not, through agreements, fixed the price of his products. He had gone

forward and produced sufficient to make comfortable all the people of the land and in doing so had discharged his full duty to
himself, to humanity and to his country. No family need go unfed
and no child go undernourished on account of the failure of the
farmer to produce. And yet he was producing for a people, taken as
a whole, with a fabulous national income. The trouble was, this
income had been so distributed that 80,000,000 people must
confine their purchases to the bare necessities of life and
50,000,000 to be satisfied with far less. Here is where the difficulty arose.

A Libel on Civilization

It now appears that if from 1923-29 all the families in the United
States had been able to purchase sufficient to bring them up even to
the standard of bare necessities, our practical capacity production
in this country would not have been sufficient to meet the con-
sumptive demand. It would seem, wittingly or unwittingly, that
the farmer was producing on the theory that every family in the
country would have at least the bare necessities of life. Thus this
economic crisis in the life of the farm has not only revealed the
tragedy of the farm but the tragedy of the nation; to wit: must we
submit and be reconciled to the cruel and enigmatical theory that
the natural, normal workings and processes of our economic
system lead inevitably to meager existence for the millions and
incalculable plenty for the hundreds? Must we accept that as the
normal, modern civilization for which we have been striving? It
seems to me a libel upon civilization. There can be no basis in
reason or in justice in twenty per cent of the income-earning
portion of our population enjoying ninety-eight per cent of its
savings, leaving the balance, two per cent, to be divided among the
other eighty per cent of the population. Such is not an orderly,
natural result of modern civilization but a result brought about
through practices resting at last upon nothing less than extortion
and violence.

With anything like an equitable distribution of our national
income, with such a distribution as would have naturally followed
had there been no use of unfair and illegal practices, there would

have been no distress on the farm. But there was distress on the farm and there will be until a more equitable distribution takes place. There will not only be trouble ahead for agriculture but profound trouble for all, as there is at this present time. Such conditions simply cannot continue. And the more debts we incur, the more taxes we impose in an effort to counteract the effects of such inequity, the deeper grow our troubles. It is an old story that the righting of such wrongs must come through the initiative of those who suffer. It never comes from those unacquainted with the discipline of want or the wisdom acquired through self-denial.

The Source of Townsend's Strength

Things are happening under our very eyes which ought to be a warning that these conditions cannot continue. Perhaps the most extraordinary social and political movement in recent years and perhaps in our entire history is the Townsend Old-Age Pension movement. Within a few months, so rapidly have the teachings of this movement taken hold in the minds of the millions of the people that they now seem to have the balance of political power in a number of states, and are boldly bidding for national control. I am not about to discuss whether the scheme is sound or practicable but am considering it only as a barometer of the feeling of a vast number of our law-abiding people. The proposal could well be entitled Townsend's Plan for the Redistribution of Purchasing Power. It is not merely a plan to secure a pension for the aged. These elderly people are in fact to be made the agents to accomplish a much broader and more fundamental thing.

And that fundamental thing is, as they contend, the restoration of purchasing power to the masses. It is their contention that the plan, if put into operation, will bring about an equitable distribution of the national income. This, in my opinion, is the driving, impelling thought behind this movement. Regardless, therefore, of the method, which you may reject as impracticable or unworkable, the movement derives its great strength from the resentment which so many feel and which resentment the movement has summoned to its support.

There is something radically wrong. The basis upon which rests our constitutional scheme of government is that for every wrong there is a remedy. If the concentration of wealth on the one hand and the spread of distress on the other should continue to develop along the same lines for the next fifty years as it has developed during the last fifty years, just what would be the status of American institutions? We might still call this a republic but it is doubtful if we would even pay that tribute of respect to republican institutions.

No Magic in Taxing

In dealing with this problem there are some things we cannot do. We cannot confiscate and we ought not to repudiate. We cannot take the property of A and turn it over to B, C and D. And if we did so under our present system A would soon have it all back again. We cannot distribute wealth or establish equitable income through the process of taxing power. Assuming that by such methods we could break down large estates, no substantial benefit would flow to the people. The sums gathered through taxation stop at bureaus and would be consumed by unnecessary officials, resulting in mere extravagance and waste. The distribution would get very little beyond the demands of those operating the government. Taxes should be levied solely for the purpose of taking care of the necessary expense of the government.

I fully understand that, when you come to discuss the concentration of wealth and the monopolistic practices or methods by which it has been brought about and by which it is maintained, it is argued, and with an air of divine finality, that you cannot turn back the clock. For myself I am not proposing to turn back the clock. I am not proposing to take from anyone the fruits of industry, of ability, of genius. If through superior ability a better article is made, if through greater efficiency a business wins its way to the market, no one has a right to complain. On the other hand, that is in the interest of consumers provided the way is still open to compete on the basis of merit and efficiency. The people get the benefit of a better article at lower prices; and the channels of trade remain open to those who may still further produce better articles at lower prices.

Getting the Benefit

This principle has been well illustrated by the motor vehicle industry. When the depression was at its worst this industry was at its best in many ways. Its engineering and experimental departments took on new life. They did not get together and agree upon prices for the same old cars. They did not come to the Congress begging for subsidies. They devoted their efforts to solving their problems in the open field of competition. The result was the companies won out and the people got better cars at lower prices. Under a monopolistic regime, under a price-fixing agreement, under a price-fixing combine the companies might have pulled through, but the public would have been riding around in the same old singing "lizzie" at perhaps a higher price. It is in the field of competition that industry and genius win and the people get the benefit of the victory.

Justice Brandeis (before he became a member of the Supreme Court) declared that: "Experience has taught us that competition is never suppressed by the greater efficiency of one concern. It is suppressed by agreement to form a monopoly or by those excesses of competition which are designed to crush a rival. . . . No business has been so superior to its competitors in the process of manufacture or of distribution as to enable it to control the market solely by reason of its superiority. There are no natural monopolies in the industrial world."

Questions of Ethics

Is it turning back the clock to say that in the business world there shall be no squeezing out of a beginner, no discrimination against retailers who buy from a rival, no holding back of raw material, no secret agreements or arrangements against a rival, no threats against concerns who sell supplies to a rival, no agreement to impose prices upon the people regardless of the value of the goods sold? Is it turning back the clock to say that thuggery is as intolerable on the highways of commerce as it is on the highways of travel? Have we reached the point where it can be said that overreaching or illegal practices under a corporate charter are less amenable to law and the public interest than overreaching or illegal practices at the country store?

Toward Permanent Recovery

If capitalism is going to insist upon a code of conduct free from all principles of fair and honest dealing, if it is going to insist that the creed of the underworld, where cunning and deceit and ruthlessness and finally extermination are recognized as the law of life, shall be and must be the rule of capitalism, we must be prepared to meet the question of state Socialism or even Communism. I venture to prophesy that the people will not indefinitely permit private interests to fix prices either directly or indirectly. If they are to be fixed they will be fixed by public authority. If capitalism has nothing to say in the way of a more equitable distribution of the earnings of capitalism, if it is going to insist that widespread poverty in the midst of incalculable wealth, that denial of the comforts and conveniences of the modern world for the majority of the people are natural and inevitable, then capitalism must be prepared to fight for its very existence.

But is all this true? Are these things a result of natural and normal development? It does not seem to me to be so. Monopoly does not exist as a result of natural growth. It is a result of practices which between man and man no one would defend, practices definable in the law and punishable by law and enforced at little cost when compared to the cost and exertion put forth in an effort to counteract the effect of monopoly. It is much easier to define or specify those practices by which vast aggregations of economic power have been built up than it is to define or specify the practices by which the professional racketeer preys upon the public. Woodrow Wilson once declared: "I take my stand absolutely on a proposition that private monopoly is indefensible and intolerable. Any decently equipped lawyer can suggest to you statutes by which the whole business can be stopped."

We come back to the point from which we started and that is the first primary step toward permanent farm recovery—the restoration and maintenance of farm prices for farm products. To do that, a market must be found. Louis J. Taber, Master of the National Grange, speaking at Sacramento, California, November last, declared: "There can be no permanent recovery and no return to prosperity until we increase mass purchasing power, until we raise our standard of living, and until there is a better and broader distribution of the wealth we all create. Real Americans have no desire to take away the property that honestly belongs to others. But red-blooded Americans demand for every man that is willing to work the right to acquire the comforts of life."

An Exclusive Market

The market which we must have is not in Europe nor anywhere else in the old world. Those markets are ours only upon a very limited scale. It is here in the United States, in the homes of millions of common people, that our markets must be found. And they can never be found until we restore purchasing power to these people. You can never restore purchasing power while private interests through combinations and agreements fix prices. The farm purchasing problem, therefore, has its roots in the most profound problem in our whole social structure.

I conclude by saying that it would seem beyond debate that this home market belongs exclusively to the American farmer to the full extent of his ability to supply it. There can be no sound argument, it would seem, to support the contention that this market is to be divided with foreign producers so long as the American farmer is anxious and able to supply our demand.

The Most Urgent Demand

If it be said that we must let in foreign farm products in order that we may find a market for our manufactured goods, the answer seems to me to be that the finest market in the world for the American manufacturer is prosperous American agriculture. The farmer is the best of buyers when he has the means with which to buy. His fences, his barns, his granaries, his home and the clothing and schooling of his children, so long in need of what the American manufacturer has to sell, constitute the most urgent demand anywhere to be found.

Thomas B. Reed once said: "If we propose to abandon any industries, we had better not let it be the agricultural industries.

Our system of protection is not for manufacturers alone. It is for farmers also. Whoever deprives our farmers of all the American market they can occupy is false to his principles and must meet with defeat, or the system must be surrendered which proclaims that American markets are first of all for American citizens, who are engaged in developing the country we already have."

B. *George W. Norris:*
Outlawing the Yellow Dog Contract*

When George Norris (1861-1944) was growing up in rural Ohio during the 1870's, one of his neighbors ventured the opinion that a Democratic soul could not enter heaven. So he was told, at any rate, by his mother, who may have shared the opinion. For the young George Norris the rock of salvation was the Republican Party, and he would not waver from this faith even after moving to Nebraska at the time of Populist ferment. Not until his election to the U.S. House of Representatives did he begin to have any doubts about the moral firmness of the Grand Old Party. Not long after entering the House, "the light dawned upon me and I began to see for the first time that the Republican Party was subject to influences similar to those I believed controlled the Democratic Party; and soon I learned there was no difference between the parties in this respect. Both of them were machine-controlled, and the Democratic and Republican machines often worked in perfect harmony and brotherly love." After this revelation Norris became, like his colleague William Borah, a maverick Republican, ready to support anyone from any party who shared his commitment to public service. In the process he incurred the wrath of his party leaders, including two Republican Presidents, and some of the most powerful lobbies in America.

A case in point was Norris' long fight to establish the Tennessee Valley Authority. The Tennessee River, which with its tributaries

*From George W. Norris, *Fighting Liberal: The Autobiography of George W. Norris* (New York: The Macmillan Company, 1945). Ch. 29. Reprinted by permission.

flows through seven states, was subject to periodic floods that wiped out crops and destroyed homes. A few weeks after the floods the area might be plagued by equally disastrous droughts. The area drained by the Tennessee River was backward and poverty-stricken, badly in need of electrical power, soil improvement, outlets to markets. Norris conceived the idea of the government setting up a series of dams along the river to serve multiple purposes: flood control, irrigation, improved navigation, power generation, and the production of nitrates for fertilizer. The important first step was to persuade the government to retain possession of the dam and nitrate plants at Muscle Shoals, Alabama, which it had established during World War I. In the Senate during the twenties Norris managed to beat off efforts to sell the Muscle Shoals operation to commercial interests, but he was unsuccessful in getting the government to take it over. The plants remained idle because Presidents Coolidge and Hoover, fearing "socialism," vetoed the legislation that would have begun government operation of them.

But soon after President Roosevelt entered office Norris tried again, this time successfully. In 1933 a Democratic President signed the bill establishing a Tennessee Valley Authority to produce cheap power, improve navigation, and advance the "economic and social well-being of the people," then promptly gave his pen to the maverick Republican. Norris had waged his twelve-year battle, he was later to write, because he felt "the necessity of taking the unconscionable profit out of handling and development of property which belongs truly to the American people." Another cause which won Norris the lasting enmity of the magnates of the corporate world and the conservatives in his own party was the fight to outlaw the "yellow dog" contract. In the selection (which, along with all the preceding quotations, are from Norris' *Autobiography*) he provides his own poignant account of the events that culminated in the historic Norris-La Guardia Act of 1932.

For many years there had existed a most deplorable labor condition in the coal mines of the United States, particularly in Pennsylvania.

It approached semi-servitude.

Gradually that condition came to my attention. I was more conscious of it as a result of the campaign I had made in Pennsylvania against "Boss" Vare, during which I came in contact with, and had the opportunity to observe first-hand, the miners and their families. That knowledge was augmented by talks with spokesmen for organized labor.

I had relinquished the chairmanship of the Agricultural Committee, feeling its duties had become too heavy and should go to a younger man.

Senator Charles McNary of Oregon was next in line; we had worked together, and I had the highest regard for him and for his outlook on national affairs. I wanted him to have the chairmanship, and my resignation paved the way for his advancement. As ranking member next to Senator Borah on the Judiciary Committee, I became its chairman, Borah being chairman of the powerful Committee on Foreign Relations.

I was criticized by some for giving up the Agriculture chairmanship, but it was this transition which brought me squarely into some of the most important struggles—among them, that of the miners.

There had been a close organization among the coal-mine operators. They fought organized labor very bitterly, and through their close interlinking of interests, gradually had developed what became known over the country as the "yellow dog contract."

Under it, the miner practically signed away his liberties. He surrendered his right to ask for increased wages, for better working conditions, or to associate with his fellow workers in giving effectiveness to any attempt to procure changes in these working conditions. As a rule, this contract provided that he would not join a union, and that he would not associate with his fellow miners in giving effectiveness to any attempt looking toward a change in the conditions.

In the more extreme instances of the yellow dog contract, I was shocked profoundly. Through the agency of the company store I discovered that the miner and his family, accepting all of the great hazards of his occupation, its toil and its dangers, usually found himself in debt for the bare necessities of life. I found that miners or members of their families who became ill usually relied upon the company physician for medical care. The conditions in many of these mines were horrible.

The courts generally had been rather unfriendly to organizations of labor. Immense combinations of capital and monopoly had had their own way in this field of human operations. That miner who signed a yellow dog contract relinquished freedom of action. If he left one job because of dissatisfaction with conditions, his contract made it impossible for him to get another. Thus, there developed under the system a type of human bondage that enslaved the miner to a life of toil without any opportunity to make a decent effort to improve or to better his position.

The mine operators in some of these coal fields ruled the community without mercy, without compassion, without sympathy for the men who actually dug the coal out of the ground, and without respect for the rights of workmen. The condition had become intolerable. Courts had issued injunctions of the most restrictive character, and through resort to law the mine operators had invoked the aid of government to make it impossible for miners to organize and to strike.

Through the medium of the yellow dog contract, thousands of American citizens were compelled to labor under conditions too horrible to tolerate in any free country. Not only were they compelled to live under this system, but through the medium of the injunction as a process of law, government was legalizing a system that constituted a reproach to the conscience of free men.

I gave a great deal of attention to that subject long before formulating legislation to deal with it. Whenever the opportunity presented itself, I studied it to the best of my ability. I followed the developments in investigations that already had taken place, covering a period of eight years of research and legislative fight before an adequate law was enacted.

The committee had before it a bill introduced by Senator Henrik Shipstead of Minnesota.

It was well known and understood among members of the Senate that the Shipstead bill had been prepared by Andrew Furuseth. Furuseth was not a miner. He was a sailor, representing the seaman's union; but something of his ardor and his zeal in the interest of organized labor, something of his rugged, blunt honesty, something of his primitive force, had caught the attention of

Washington, and he was a well known man in the nation's capital.

He had spent his entire life in the interest of labor.

I think Andrew Furuseth in time came to command the respect of all the members of Congress who became acquainted with him. They might not agree with his passionate espousal of organized labor, but his utter sincerity and forthrightness commanded their respect. He had started life without the advantages of education—he was untutored in letters; but long experience, diligence, and unswerving loyalty to his cause had remedied the defect of early education, and at the time that I knew him there was a brilliance of mind far overshadowing his obvious defects of schooling. He understood the labor question from labor's view as completely and fully as any man I ever knew. He was perfectly conscientious. Through his years at sea in storm and in calm he knew intimately just how the seamen on the high seas were treated.

His word was good.

That rough exterior, heightened by a bluntness of speech that at times was almost offensive, melted away, once you got to know Andrew Furuseth and once you understood him. You recognized that here was a man true as burnished steel, with a throbbing sympathy for the misfortunes and struggles of his fellow men. The depth of his convictions and the strength of his philosophy were such as to inspire faith in the man and interest in the aims to which he devoted his life.

I do not know how Andrew Furuseth became interested in the coal miner; but he had very definite ideas upon coal mining, and the bill which he had prepared embraced those views. It was not a lengthy bill.

Principally it undertook to make the yellow dog contract illegal.

Beyond invalidation of the yellow dog contract, Andrew Furuseth aspired to put labor on a higher and nobler standard and give the miner a measure of equality in his fight against the organization of mine operators, who through great wealth and unlimited monopoly had been able to control the conditions in the mines and the lives of the men who worked away below the ground.

He believed his bill would accomplish its purpose.

Senator Shipstead, a man of liberal tendencies, was not very familiar with the problems of the coal miners. He was in complete sympathy with the attempts being made to improve the status of labor, and especially interested in the laboring conditions in mining but under the pressure of his work he paid very little attention to the bill after he had introduced it.

The Judiciary Committee of the Senate selected me as chairman of a subcommittee appointed to study the Shipstead bill and to hold such hearings as were deemed necessary. It authorized me to appoint two other members as my associates.

Senator William E. Borah, as a member of the Judiciary Committee, would have been entitled to be chairman of it if he had not held the chairmanship of the Foreign Affairs Committee. I endeavored to persuade him to serve with me on the subcommittee; he was sympathetic, but felt strongly he had not the time for proper investigation. Whereupon I appointed Senator Thomas J. Walsh of Montana and Senator John J. Blaine of Wisconsin, as my associates on the subcommittee.

Unanimously, we reached the conclusion that the bill introduced by Senator Shipstead, as drawn by Andrew Furuseth, did not meet the requirements fully; and especially we feared it would be held unconstitutional. We decided to prepare a new substitute bill. I was to tell Andrew Furuseth of our decision. I remember calling him to my office, and discussing with him at great length what we regarded as the defects of his proposal. He became impatient with me, and I think his anger was aroused because I did not believe his bill would meet the situation.

The subcommittee held unlimited hearings, which were very extensive.

From the very beginning, as was to be anticipated, the proposed legislation was fought bitterly by the National Association of Manufacturers. I remember that its representative, James A. Emery, a very able attorney seasoned and experienced in legislation, and a veteran of many years of struggle before various committees of Congress, appeared in opposition. He was assisted by a number of other attorneys, but he was in general command of presenting the case against any legislation relating to labor conditions in the coal mines.

No attempt was made to limit testimony. The subcommittee

permitted anybody to appear. In addition to direct evidence, every witness who took the stand was open to cross-examination if either side desired.

I believe it was one of the most comprehensive, conscientious investigations a congressional subcommittee has undertaken. I heard every syllable of testimony that was given, and my two loyal and conscientious associates heard nearly all of it. At the completion of the hearings, my associates directed me to summon to our assistance some noted attorneys, who had had long experience with labor legislation and with the trial of labor cases in the courts. The result was that I requested Felix Frankfurter of the Harvard Law School (now a justice of the United States Supreme Court), Donald Richberg of Chicago, Professor Herman Oliphant of Johns Hopkins, Edwin E. Witte, of the University of Wisconsin, and Francis B. Sayre of Harvard to aid in the preparation of the substitute bill; and they all agreed to undertake the labor. I urged them to arrange to come to Washington at the same time, so that they might not only counsel with the subcommittee but also confer and deliberate among themselves.

And then I turned over the Judiciary Committee rooms to these men.

I have always thought that the method of procedure which was adopted was significant. They locked themselves in, and for forty-eight hours gave their undivided attention and study to every court decision bearing upon the rights of organized labor. They reviewed the decisions of the United States Supreme Court with the most scrupulous care, aware that in the great conflict of interest certain to arise from legislation of this character, the constitutionality of the law would be subjected to challenge immediately.

When they had completed painstaking study of the court decisions, they consulted Senator Walsh, Senator Blaine, and myself and placed before us the results of their conclusions. The subcommittee then took the subject up again in active session and prepared a report for the full membership of the Judiciary Committee. As a result we struck from the Shipstead bill all of the provisions after the enactment clause and substituted a much more comprehensive piece of legislation. After all of the study and research and energies devoted to hearings, and the deep desire among the members of the subcommittee to remedy frightful conditions in the coal-mining industry, we were concerned chiefly with framing legislation that would pass the test of the courts. We also recognized that whatever legislation was passed would be subjected to court attack, and we felt that the failure or success of our efforts would be determined largely by perfecting a bill that could come through its legal ordeal, survive all legal assaults, and still exist as law.

I reported the redrafted bill to the Senate with the change which had been agreed upon by the subcommittee.

In the House a companion bill was introduced by Representative Fiorello La Guardia, who conducted it through the House Judiciary Committee and successfully championed its passage in the House. As the bill passed the House, it was substantially the original draft. Mr. La Guardia performed a very great service in the fight which he made for it.

In the Senate the opposition was better organized. There was a bitter contest within the Judiciary Committee, with Senator Frederick Steiwer of Oregon leading the attack. He was a very bright and able lawyer, and a fine man who had won a wide circle of friends. He wrote the opposing opinion. The Republicans were in control of the Judiciary Committee and dominated the Senate. Mr. Hoover was in the White House. So far as I know, he did not come out openly in opposition to the bill; but we never received any assistance of any kind from the Department of Justice in the Hoover administration. There was that impenetrable wall of opposition, an opposition not voiced, not out in the open, but under cover, silent and effective. The yellow dog contract legislation failed to pass the Senate of the Seventieth Congress.

Immediately upon convening of the next Congress, I reintroduced the bill in the exact form it had been reported out previously. I knew there had been a considerable shift in sentiment in the country in regard to the legislation. Many of those previously opposed had changed their attitude, and a majority of the members of the Judiciary Committee this time favored the bill. It could not have been better illustrated than by the position taken by Senator Steiwer of Oregon. Not only did he drop his opposition, but he voted for the bill in exactly the same language which he had previously opposed. Many of the Republican leaders in the Senate swung from opposition to support, either as honest and genuine converts to the purposes of the legislation, or fearful of sentiment that had developed in support of the bill.

In all of this struggle organized labor, at the time of the passage of the legislation invalidating the yellow dog contract, more completely impressed the consciousness of the American people with the inequalities which then existed in the economic structure than at any time in American history.

I always have believed and still believe that it was this remarkable upsurge of sentiment in the United States that led President Hoover to sign, instead of veto, the bill. I had no doubt then that, if he did veto it, it could be passed over his presidential veto. In the light of developments it was most fortunate that the first attempt to pass the bill had failed. I am equally certain that passage by the Seventy-first Congress, followed by a veto, would have made it fail in the next Congress.

I believe now just as firmly as I believed at the time I was sponsoring this legislation there has been written into the law of the United States a labor enactment which should appeal to the fairness and the honest judgment of any person who has given study to the subject. It embodies only matters of simple justice. The right of men to organize for the improvement of conditions under which they labor should not be open to question. The right of collective bargaining has been determined in this country. The opportunity of labor to fight for its rights should not be limited by court restrictions that in practical effect impose a condition of servitude upon men who daily go down into the bowels of the earth to extract the fuel that heats millions of homes and turns the wheels of American industry.

All that the Norris-La Guardia bill did was to give the miner emancipation from the slavery that had prevailed for years in the coal mines of America.

I believe that the anti-injunction act already has brought and will continue to bring full and honest consideration of labor questions by the American people.

I believe that in their mature judgment, with full knowledge of the facts, the new freedom for these toilers will be sustained.

Never will man's conscience permit him to restore the tyranny and injustice which long bound men to the earth in unwilling and unremitting toil.

As this is written, the American people have become concerned over labor disturbances. They are fighting a war. They are attempting to defeat armies bent upon destroying human freedom. They are endeavoring to save American civilization for posterity.

Coal miners often have been led astray, in my judgment, by ill-advised leaders; and they are now thwarting the government in its greatest war by failing to maintain production so vital to victory.

I have had few personal contacts with John L. Lewis, or with any large number of his associates, but I feel strongly that no man should strike against his country in time of war. No man, representing either management or labor, should resort to strike methods in order to enforce demands in time of deadly national peril. It seems to me that the miners have forgotten the blessings and the rights given them by the anti-injunction law, and have followed false leaders who care more for their own ambitions than they do for freedom and civilization in the world.

Nothing contained in the provisions of the Norris-La Guardia law, however, made it possible for the striking miners to take the course mapped in the recent crisis by miner leadership. Nothing in the fundamental decent principles embodied in that law—a law that attempts to safeguard and protect the liberties of the individual man—justified anyone in staying the hands of government in its glorious, noble attempts to save a civilized world from European dictatorship. Wrong committed in equalizing earlier injustices never becomes right. Right and justice are not achieved by piling wrong upon wrong.

In those quiet discussions within the circle of the Senate subcommittee I listened to the expressed aspirations of Americans to bring a larger measure of understanding and justice between the employer and the employee. Senator Walsh and Senator Blaine both were very eminent attorneys, men of judicial temperament and the very highest character. Walsh's place is secure in the hearts of his countrymen for the brave and courageous fights which he made. Senator Blaine had served as governor of Wisconsin and in that role had given great attention and energy to the type of legislation embodied in the anti-injunction law. So far as I could observe, he was as free from prejudice as any man I ever have met. The members of the committee who assisted us were outstanding lawyers; had attained prominence through their study of the subject, and commanded public confidence.

This law is labor's charter—to be guarded and protected against attack both from without and from within. It can be weakened by abuses within through the destruction of the sustaining faith of the American public. It can be destroyed only if those whom it emancipates enable those who always have opposed it to seize upon the temporary tides of American public opinion. Labor in the mines, labor everywhere, should be free from contractual relationships in its employment that strip the individual of the rights of American citizenship. The charter for labor embraced in this legislation gave labor no right that any American citizen ought not to possess in his daily life and in his day in court.

C. *Huey P. Long:*
Share Our Wealth!*

Southern populism, more than its Western counterpart, has always contained a measure of *opéra bouffe*. In both variants language is used as much to beguile as to convey meaning, but the tendency to play fast and loose with word and gesture is especially evident in the oratory of the South. "Let's vaudeville 'em," Huey Long (1893-1935) would say if he saw his audience ready for his kind of act. He became a tourist attraction in the Senate, where he represented the state of Louisiana from 1932 until his death by assassination in 1935, surpassing even Borah in filling visitors' galleries. Both were florid rhetoricians, but where Borah was grand and grave, Long was pugnacious and comic. On any day he might delight the galleries with a discourse on the merits of Louisiana potlikker, or an outrageous slander on a political oppo-

*From Huey P. Long, "An Open Letter to Members and Well-Wishers of the Share Our Wealth Society," Reprinted by permission of Senator Russell B. Long.

nent, or a self-deprecating comment about his own vulgarity, or any other choice specimen of Southern flimflammery.

It is difficult, therefore, to judge the extent to which Long took seriously his "Share-the-Wealth" plan. The plan, outlined by Long in an "Open Letter" in 1933 (which constitutes the selection) involved a scheme of capital-levy taxes which would distribute the wealth widely enough to permit every family a "homestead" (a house, car, and radio), plus an annual income of $2,000-$3,000, plus pensions for the old, free college for the young, and generous bonuses for veterans. The plan, which was far more radical than anything advocated (or retreated from) by George McGovern forty years later, was denounced as Socialistic. Long indignantly denied the charge. The Socialists, he declared, wanted government ownership of wealth, but his plan for redistributing it would retain the profit motive. By preventing concentration of wealth it would end by producing a larger number of millionaires. He would save the capitalist system and even, he ruefully admitted, save the big businessmen. "I'd cut their nails and file their teeth and let them live."

Despite his penchant for comedy Long advanced his proposals with apparent seriousness, went on speaking tours to defend them, received an enormous volume of mail in support of them, organized Share-the-Wealth clubs throughout the nation (but mainly in the South), and won somewhere between 5,000,000 and 8,000,000 registered adherents.

But, again, it is difficult to say whether Long was advancing his proposals in good faith or merely as another publicity gimmick to further his plans to run for the Presidency. Perhaps these distinctions are meaningless in the case of Huey Long. Long knew how to play the fool, but he was a political genius, having constructed a machine in Louisiana which had all but eliminated any organized opposition. His avowed purpose was to be "the champion of those little guys," the black and white poor of Louisiana, but he soon discovered that the ruthless exercise of power was required to defend the little guys against exploitation by the big guys, notably the Louisiana branch of Standard Oil. In the end, as T. H. Williams notes in his biography of Long, "he could not tell whether he wanted power as a method or for its own sake."

* * *

TO MEMBERS AND WELL-WISHERS OF THE SHARE OUR
WEALTH SOCIETY:—

For twenty years I have been in the battle to provide that, so long
as America has, or can produce, an abundance of the things which
make life comfortable and happy, that none should own so much of
the things which he does not need and cannot use, as to deprive the
balance of the people of a reasonable proportion of the necessities
and conveniences of life. The whole line of my political thought
has always been that America must face the time when the whole
country would shoulder the obligation which it owes to every child
born on earth,—that is, a fair chance to life, liberty, and happiness.

I had been in the United States Senate only a few days when I
began my effort to make the battle for a distribution of wealth
among all the people a national issue for the coming elections. . . .

It was after my disappointment over the Roosevelt policy, after
he became President, that I saw the light. I soon began to understand that, regardless of what we had been promised, our only
chance of securing the fulfillment of such pledges was to organize
the men and the women of the United States so that they were a
force capable of action, and capable of requiring such a policy
from the lawmakers and from the President, after they took office.
That was the beginning of the Share Our Wealth Society movement.

Let me say to the members and well-wishers that in this movement (the principles of which have received the endorsement of
every leader of this time, and of other times),—I am not concerned
over my personal position or political fortune; I am only interested
in the success of the cause, and on any day or at any time when, by
our going for any person or for any party, we can better, or more
surely or more quickly secure home, comfort, education and
happiness for our people, that there is no ambition of mine which
will stand in the way. But there can be no minimum of success until
every child in this land is fed, clothed and housed comfortably and
made happy with opportunity for education and a chance in life.

I delayed using this form of call to the members and well-wishers of the Share Our Wealth Society until we had progressed so far as to convince me that we could succeed either before or in the next national election of November, 1936. Until I became certain that the spirit of the people could be aroused throughout the United States, and that, without any money (because I have none, except such little as I am given), the people could be persuaded to perfect organizations throughout the counties and communities of the country, I did not want to give false hopes to any of those engaged with me in this noble work. But I have seen and checked back enough, based upon the experiences which I have had in my public career, to know that we can, with much more ease, win the present fight, either between now and the next national campaign, or else in the next national campaign;—I say with much more ease than many other battles which I have won in the past, but which did not mean near so much.

We now have enough societies and enough members, to say nothing of the well-wishers, who (if they will put their shoulder to the wheel and give us one-half of the time which they do not need for anything else), can force the principles of the Share Our Wealth Society to the forefront, to where no person participating in national affairs can ignore them further.

Now, here is what I ask the officers and members and well-wishers of all the Share Our Wealth societies to do—two things, to wit:—

1. If you have a Share Our Wealth Society in your neighborhood (or, if you have not one, organize one), meet regularly and let all members, men and women, go to work as quickly and as hard as they can, to get every person in the neighborhood to become a member, and to go out with them to get more members for the Society. If members do not want to go into the Society already organized in their community, let them organize another Society. We must have them as members in the movement, so that, by having their cooperation, on short notice we can all act as one person for the one object and purpose of providing that, in the land of plenty there shall be comfort for all. The organized 600 families who control the wealth of America have been able to keep the 125,000,000 people in bondage because they have never once known how to effectually strike for their fair demands.

2. Get a number of members of the Share Our Wealth Society to immediately go into all other neighborhoods of your county, and into the neighborhoods of the adjoining counties, so as to get the people in the other communities and in the other counties to organize more Share Our Wealth societies there; that will mean we can soon get about the work of perfecting a complete, unified organization that will not only hear promises, but will compel the fulfillment of pledges made to the people.

It is impossible for the United States to preserve itself as a republic or as a democracy, when 600 families own more of this nation's wealth—in fact, twice as much—as all the balance of the people put together. 96 per cent of our people live below the poverty line, while 4 per cent own 87 per cent of the wealth. America can have enough for all to live in comfort, and still permit millionaires to own more than they can ever use; but America cannot allow the multi-millionaires and the billionaires, a mere handful of them, to own everything unless we are willing to inflict starvation upon 125 million people.

We looked upon the year 1929 as the year when too much was produced for the people to consume. . . .

But why in the year 1929 did it appear we had too much? Because the people could not buy the things they wanted to eat, and needed to eat. That showed the need for and duty of the Government then and there, to have forced a sharing of our wealth, and a redistribution, and Roosevelt was elected on the pledge to do that very thing.

But what was done? Cotton was plowed under the ground. Hogs and cattle were burned by the millions. The same was done to wheat and corn, and farmers were paid starvation money not to raise and not to plant because of the fact that we did not want so much because of people having no money with which to buy. Less and less was produced, when already there was less produced than the people needed if they ate what the Government said they needed to sustain life. God forgive those rulers who burned hogs, threw milk in the river and plowed under cotton while little children cried for meat and milk and something to put on their naked backs!

*   *   *

And now, what of America? Will we allow the political sports, the high heelers, the wiseacres, and those who ridicule us in our misery and poverty, to keep us from organizing these societies in every hamlet so that they may bring back to life this law and custom of God and of this country? . . . Our country is calling; the laws of the Lord are calling; the graves of our forefathers would open today if their occupants could see the bloom and flower of their creation withering and dying because the greed of the financial masters of this country has starved and withheld from mankind those things produced by his own labor. To hell with the ridicule of the wise street-corner politician! Pay no attention to any newspaper or magazine that has sold its columns to perpetuate this crime against the people of America! Save this country! Save mankind! Who can be wrong in such a work, and who cares what consequences may come following the mandates of the Lord, of the Pilgrims, of Jefferson, Webster, and Lincoln? He who falls in this fight falls in the radiance of the future. Better to make this fight and lose than to be a party to a system that strangles humanity.

Here is the whole sum and substance of the Share Our Wealth movement:

1. Every family to be furnished by the government a homestead allowance, free of debt, of not less than one-third the average family wealth of the country, which means, at the lowest, that every family shall have the reasonable comforts of life up to a value of from $5,000 to $6,000: No person to have a fortune, of more than 100 to 300 times the average family fortune, which means that the limit to fortunes is between $1,500,000 and $5,000,000, with annual capital levy taxes imposed on all above $1,000,000.

2. The yearly income of every family shall be not less than one-third of the average family income, which means that, according to the estimates of the statisticians of the U.S. Government and Wall Street, no family's annual income would be less than from $2,000 to $2,500: No yearly income shall be allowed to any person larger than from 100 to 300 times the size of the average family income, which means that no person would be allowed to earn in any year more than from $600,000 to $1,800,000, all to be subject to present income tax laws.

3. To limit or regulate the hours of work to such an extent as to prevent overproduction; the most modern and efficient machinery would be encouraged so that as much would be produced as possible so as to satisfy all demands of the people, but to also allow the maximum time to the workers for recreation, convenience, education, and luxuries of life.

4. An old age pension to the persons over 60.

5. To balance agricultural production with what can be consumed according to the laws of God, which includes the preserving and storing of surplus commodities to be paid for and held by the Government for the emergencies when such are needed. Please bear in mind, however, that when the people of America have had money to buy things they needed, we have never had a surplus of any commodity. This plan of God does not call for destroying any of the things raised to eat or wear, nor does it countenance wholesale destruction of hogs, cattle or milk.

6. To pay the veterans of our wars what we owe them and to care for their disabled.

7. Education and training for all children to be equal in opportunity in all schools, colleges, universities and other institutions for training in the professions and vocations of life; to be regulated on the capacity of children to learn, and not on the ability of parents to pay the costs. Training for life's work to be as much universal and thorough for all walks in life as has been the training in the arts of killing.

8. The raising of revenue and taxes for the support of this program to come from the reduction of swollen fortunes from the top, as well as for the support of public works to give employment whenever there may be any slackening necessary in private enterprise.

I now ask those who read this circular to help us at once in this work of giving life and happiness to our people,—not a starvation dole upon which someone may live in misery from week to week. Before this miserable system of wreckage has destroyed the life germ of respect and culture in our American people, let us save what was here, merely by having none too poor and none too rich. The theory of the Share Our Wealth Society is to have enough for all, but not to have one with so much that less than enough remains for the balance of the people.

Please, therefore, let me ask you who read this document,—please help this work before it is too late for us to be of help to our people. We ask you now, (1) help to get your neighbor into the work of this Society, and (2) help get other Share Our Wealth societies started in your county and in adjoining counties and get them to go out to organize other societies.

Let everyone who feels he wishes to help in our work start right out and go ahead. One man or woman is as important as any other. Take up the fight! Do not wait for someone else to tell you what to do. There are no high lights in this effort. We have no state managers and no city managers. Everyone can take up the work and as many societies can be organized as there are people to organize them. One is the same as another. The reward and compensation is the salvation of humanity. Fear no opposition. "He who falls in this fight falls in the radiance of the future!"

Yours sincerely,

HUEY P. LONG,
United States Senator,
Washington, D.C.

D. *Gerald P. Nye:*
A Defense of Isolationism

Gerald P. Nye (1892-1971) typifies by his ambivalence the pattern of vintage populism in an important respect. When he began his career as a muckracking newspaper editor in North Dakota, he wrote of "the absolute futility of war" and commended Woodrow Wilson's efforts to maintain neutrality despite provocations from both Great Britain and Germany. But by 1917 he was urging his countrymen to be "pro-American, first, last and all the time" in supporting the war effort, and accusing Robert La

Follette of being "prejudiced, unpatriotic and dangerous" for criticizing our entry into the war. Yet seventeen years later this obscure editor, now a United States Senator, launched his famous investigation—lasting a year and half, filling thirty-nine volumes of testimony—into the influence of munition-makers in stimulating and sustaining war. One of the chief subjects for study by the Nye Committee was the case of World War I, the very war which Nye had supported so pugnaciously. At the end of the thirties Nye was a vigorous opponent of American involvement in World War II, and he later warned of the danger of American involvement in the Far East. This should not be surprising, given his indictment of the munitions-makers, but what does seem odd is his subsequent support for a large defense budget and the candidacy of Barry Goldwater.

Nye followed the same zigzag pattern in domestic policy. By 1944 the same Senator Nye who had, a decade earlier, sponsored a resolution deploring "the influence of the commercial motive" was now declaring that "the time has come to force more of business into government and less government in business."

These are tensions but not contradictions. Nye, like all populists, criticized business but did not want it abolished, and he feared that Roosevelt would replace the independent businessman with a system of "bureaucratic control operating from Washington upon everyone." (Here Nye anticipated both C. Wright Mills and George Wallace.) As for Nye's alternating isolationism and bellicosity, this is a fine specimen of populist jingoism discussed in the Introduction: avoid war, but once it becomes inevitable, then, by jingo. . . .

In the selection from Nye's "Farewell Speech,"* delivered in the Senate shortly after his defeat in the 1944 elections, we see how he characteristically combines elements both of "left" and "right" populism. This speech is, then, a fitting and significant transition from the older populisms to its contemporary manifestations. Right-wingers may find grim satisfaction in his observation that no one dares to criticize communism, and left-wingers may be struck by the accuracy of his predictions concerning "a revived

---

*From *Congressional Record*, 78th Congress, 2nd sess., 1944, vol. 70.

imperialism'' in Southeast Asia, a gigantic postwar defense budget and scandalous defense profiteering.

It should interest both "left" and "right" populists that this strangely eloquent and prophetic speech was almost totally ignored by the New York *Times*. That august organ of conservative liberalism declared, in a short editorial, that the only "good effect" of Nye's speech was that it would "prove to the complete satisfaction of the voters of North Dakota how right they were when they rejected him in the last election."

THE PREJUDICES I BROUGHT WITH ME

Mr. President, I brought with me to the Senate a prejudice against involvement in another foreign war, against the terrible economic condition which the last war had brought to our country, particularly the agricultural sections of our country, the people of which felt the penalty so much sooner than did other classes of Americans. I was prejudiced against the propaganda which had been fed to us during that war, because it had caused me and so many others to do great injustice to some men who sat in these Chambers during that war and sought to keep public thinking straight, in spite of the Government propaganda, to the end that there could be less disillusionment to suffer after the war was won and the truth came to be known. I was prejudiced against the slightest likelihood of our ever letting our country become the pawn of foreign powers in more war to save empires by throwing more sons into more wars. I was prejudiced against the countries which had found us so easy in and after the last war. My prejudice gave life to the hope that America could be on guard another time, smart, not reachable with the names and causes which would be portrayed to cover up the true and selfish causes.

I came to the Senate bearing this prejudice at a time when, led largely by the men who had fought in the last war, there was developing throughout America an overwhelming determination to be done with Europe's politics, prejudices, hates, and wars. I personally felt that determination that we must find the way to avoid repetition of that experience of 25 years ago and what followed.

CREATING THE NEUTRALITY LAWS

I sponsored the resolution, consolidated finally with another on a related subject by the senior Senator from Michigan [Mr. VANDENBERG], the approval of which authorized the conduct of what came to be known as the munitions investigation. I was honored with the chairmanship of the committee making that investigation. With the assistance of six other Senators, more unitedly cooperative than the members of any other committee with which I have had association through all these years, we plowed through nearly 4 years of intensive study, affording disclosures which could only add to American resolve to find the ways of avoiding repetition of the costly experience of World War No. 1. Our study of the causes of our involvement in that war led to legislative recommendations by our committee. I joined in introducing what came to be known as the neutrality laws. I witnessed a popular reaction to the proposals, so great that the Roosevelt administration consolidated our several proposals into one bill and introduced it as the Pittman bill. And then I saw the neutrality law adopted by overwhelming vote in both Houses of Congress, acting in the determination that America should not again become involved in Europe's wars.

Those laws of neutrality, growing out of experience leading to our involvement in the last war, came into being just at the time when it grew increasingly clear that Europe was working herself into another terrible war, were warmly received by the American people. President Roosevelt approved the law, and he took unto himself much credit for its existence. I thought much had been accomplished.

CREATE AND THEN DESTROY SAFEGUARDS

Then I saw born the concerted effort to destroy those safeguards against our involvement in war. I heard the terms "isolationism" and "isolationist" given added and new meanings. I heard the President proclaim that he was proud to be called an isolationist if that meant a person who was trying to keep our country out of other peoples' war. Then I witnessed what for long were unbelievable things. I saw a noisy drift away from the neutrality laws, those safeguards against our involvement in another foreign war. I heard the laws assailed as laws that were getting us into war. I even came to hear the administration and its leaders plead for repeal, first of this phase, then of that phase of the law, on the ground, mind you, Mr. President, that such repeal would help us keep out of the war that then was rolling onto the stage in Europe. I witnessed the President turn his back upon the law he was sworn to administer and enforce; I saw his administration decline to invoke the law against Japan. Had the law been invoked, Japan could never have so long carried on her war against China with our oil and scrap iron. Had the law been invoked against Japan, Japan could not have been the power she became; she could never have made so many thousands of American boys the targets for our own American scrap iron at Pearl Harbor and since. I shall forever wish that I might have been able to drive home the conviction which was mine when, in the Senate on August 10, 1937, I said of the scrap iron export business with Japan just this:

> It seems to me that the only return we may expect from a continuation of this exportation, aside from the munificent return in dollars to the several exporting companies, is the probability that one day we may receive this scrap back home here in the form of shrapnel in the flesh and in the bodies of our sons.

UN-AMERICAN TO BE FOR AMERICA

Piece by piece I saw the laws of neutrality whittled away, until there was no neutrality law left. Day by day I witnessed a drift or a trend to war taking the place of that long-standing and determined resolve to avoid war.

And then I witnessed our going to war and the bitter undertaking to discredit one and all of us who had labored so earnestly to avoid it. I saw and heard a word, "isolationist," pumped and stretched, repeated and paraded, until to some minds it would be made to mean everything that was bad, terrible, un-American, and indecent. The attempt to keep our country out of war had become an unforgivable sin. The position of being extremely solicitous about the fortunes of our own country suddenly became the cause for charges of un-Americanism. Because the British interest or the Russian interest in the complexities of the world were made secondary to American interest, by some of us, we were held up to scorn, and were even charged with pro-Hitler sympathies. To have been for America first came to be looked upon as treason by those who had foreign interests first at heart. All this occurred in just a few years, our own years.

To war we went, first without having to fight, but just by helping certain countries who did want to fight, and then to war to defend our country and honor when we were attacked.

When I think of those things I am living in the past, some of my colleagues will say. Very well; let us then bury it, and come right down to date. To war we went.

WE FIGHT A MILITARY WAR, OUR ALLIES A POLITICAL WAR

Then came more repetition of what we had listened to 25 years earlier—the eloquent portrayal of what a grand and beautiful job of world rebuilding and reforming would be our good fortune, once we and our allies had won this war. Democracy would be safe again, but this time for keeps. The "four freedoms," the Atlantic Charter, plenty of milk for everyone—these and more were the causes which would have us dig in and do the real job of winning the war. Our participation in the war was going to let America dictate a peace that would let Americans forevermore be joyous and proud in what their country had done for the world.

All this, Mr. President, took place during 20 years in which I have occupied a place in this great body. And now, today, just as I am about to surrender my place to a most honorable successor, I find pretty ready acknowledgment on every side line that these things we have believed to be the things we were fighting for, these things which our sons presumably were dying for, were not really what we were fighting for at all. Indeed, there is wide acknowledgment privately that we cannot hope to attain so complete a winning of the peace after we shall have won the war. We find instead, mind you, that while our country fights a bloody, heartbreaking military war some of our allies are fighting a political war, and our allies with such will to acknowledge that as true as to cause us to stand aghast for ever having thought that something lastingly good could be won as a result of this war. Clearly, while Russia fights courageously and with greater cost in lives than we know, and while Britain stubbornly resists the enemy and fights back with courage and great credit to herself, they fight for something obviously quite different from that for which we presumed we were all fighting. They have brutally kicked such causes as the "four freedoms" and the Atlantic Charter into oblivion, and are impatient at the mere thought of ever having it before them again. They give pretty emphatic notice—sometimes it seems like arrogant notice—that they are done with this tomfoolery and seem to want to know what we are going to do about it. They know, of course, that we, as an ally, will go along and finish this military job, and win the war with them and for them. They know what they want when the war is won, and who are we to say that they shall not have their way in their own realm.

TRAGEDY STALKS US

Tragedy! Tragedy no end! Today we are left by our allies and their actions with nothing but the hope that what we see with relation to Finland, Poland, Italy, Greece, India, and all the other places where human beings suffer—today we are left with nothing but the hope that what we see is only a dream, a bad dream, and that when we awaken we shall find that the chance is still here to let this war end all wars for all time. That is the tragedy of it all. We hope, but privately we dare not believe.

WIN THIS WAR, THEN PRAISE WASHINGTON

We are right, of course, in permitting no compromise of our determination to whip soundly Hitlerism and crush the arrogance of the people who call themselves the Jap civilization. We must prosecute the war to a victorious end, and we must have these allies with us if we are to do it. No other way is open to us. Our allies know it as well as we, or better. They know it so well that they have no hesitance in affording these Greek and Polish previews of what is yet to come after victory has been attained.

If there comes out of this war what seems to be in such large prospect, then perhaps once again we shall sing the praises of George Washington, and not only read his Farewell Message on each succeeding anniversary of his birth, but really pay him tribute again for that marvelous insight and foresight that caused him to plead with Americans that they and their country shun the pitfalls of foreign alliances and entanglements.

There is another approach to afford the demonstration I want so much to leave in this RECORD; namely, the demonstration of how tragic are these years of our serious striving for peace only to be moved by trends away from our high purpose, and our sincere beliefs.

IT MUST NOT HAPPEN AGAIN

My coming to the Senate was but a few years following the victorious war to end war and make the world safe for democracy. During my first years in the Senate new international agreements and arrangements followed one another in rapid succession, and all were believed to be of help in organizing the world for security and for lasting peace. Now, as I leave, all these bright hopes have turned to dust and ashes. The whole world is again plunged into war, and American boys are again being marched away as conscripts from all our American towns and homes to die on far distant battlefields for a cause that is so obscure that even the pundits and the professors cannot agree as to what it is. Nor is that the worst of it. For even as America pours out her finest blood and her treasure, the worst of it is that there is not one of us who really has full confidence that this Second World War will not be followed by a third, and that by a fourth, and that by a fifth, until our whole civilization—all that we have and hold dear—has been ground into bloody rubble.

Oh, yes, I know that we say that this must not happen. We say that this must be the last war. But we said that the last time. And we believed it the last time. The horrible thing about the situation in which we now find ourselves is that this time we do not believe it. We say it for the RECORD and for the newspapers, because we feel that we have got to say something of the sort to keep the fathers and mothers of America content to send their boys into this present conflict. But we do not believe it! When we are alone, or when we talk to one another in privacy, we know that we do not believe it. Down deep in our hearts we have no confidence whatever that this is to be the last world war, or that after another 20 years has passed—or perhaps only another 10—the nations will not be at each others' throats again and the whole world once more saturated with blood. That is the awful prospect that makes my heart heavy within me at this hour.

A NEW WORLD IN THE MAKING, ON PAPER

As I have said, the 20 years during which I have served in this body has been, both for the United States and for the whole world, a time of blighted hopes. It is painful now to recall how different the prospect was at the time I took my seat in the Senate in 1925. But then Germany had been overwhelmingly defeated, her army reduced to a smaller size than that of Czechoslovakia, her navy scuttled, her air force wiped out, her colonies and much of her richest coal and iron deposits taken from her. On the other hand, Britain had such a gigantic fleet and France such a tremendous army that between them they could do what they wished to do in order to make Europe keep the peace. In the year I became a Senator the two 9-power treaties of the Washington Conference were ratified by all the principal nations, supposedly bringing an end to all naval rivalry and threats of aggression in the Far East. The Locarno treaties were ratified in Europe, supposedly ending forever the likelihood of future trouble between Germany and any of her neighbors. In the very next year Germany was welcomed into the League of Nations and given a permanent seat on the Council. In the year after that the United States and France started the negotiations which were finally to culminate in the ratification by 62 nations of the Kellogg-Briand Pact under which they bound themselves that "the settlement or solution of all disputes or conflicts, of whatever nature or of whatever origin they may be, which may arise among them, shall never be sought except by pacific means."

SIGN WITH FINGERS CROSSED

That looked like lasting peace, did it not? Unfortunately, however, we soon found out that all the nations who signed those agreements, particularly the Kellogg-Briand Pact, had their fingers crossed when they signed. Great Britain slipped into her signature to that pact the reservation that it was not to apply to any defense of strategic places vital to the safety of the British Empire—a vitiating reservation much like the one which her representative slipped in concerning Newfoundland at the moment of signing the World Civil Aviation Pact in Chicago 3 weeks ago. And after Great Britain had done that, all the other nations, ourselves included, were under the necessity of protecting their interests and accordingly announced that "of course, they reserved the right of self-defense." They would not go to war, as they had promised in the Kellogg-Briand Pact, except in self-defense. Well, we all know what a nation intent on committing highway robbery can do with that joker about self-defense. It was not long before Mussolini was invading Ethiopia in what he claimed was self-defense. Japan had to defend herself against China. Self-defense!

BEAUTIFUL PROSPECTS AGAIN

But there was almost as much blighting of our hopes domestically as in international affairs back in those days. We had been led to believe that after the war this Nation would enter upon a new and more glorious destiny. Men and governments who are whooping it up for war always talk that way, just as they are doing today, when we are told, on the highest authority, that this war is to be followed by the golden age for America, when there will be 60,000,000 jobs paying the same kind of wages that the war has brought; when everyone will be protected against all the perils of sickness, old age, unemployment, and death; when we will fill the seven seas with our American ships crammed with American goods to flood every export market; and when our own markets and wage levels will be completely protected against being undermined by the goods produced where standards of wages and living are far below those in the United States. One would think that by this time there had been enough history to teach us that wars are not followed by great advances. Wars are followed by let-downs, and the moral let-downs that follow wars are the most tragic of all.

THE LET-DOWN WHEN WAR ENDS

As I entered the Senate, that terrible let-down which follows all wars was just beginning to register following the First World War. And thus it happened that my first important assignment as a Member of this body was to act as chairman of the committee which was investigating the Teapot Dome Continental Trading Co. and Elk Hills scandals.

There is nothing to be gained by dragging out again all the malodorous facts which were brought into the light in that investigation or the millions of dollars which were recovered for the United States; but I am bound to say that, truly as it served the cause of honest government by showing up the shameful conditions which had grown up following the other war, it has by no means ended the possibility of official corruption or of playing fast and loose with the Nation's resources. It is only 2 weeks since one of the assistant attorneys general of the United States was summarily dismissed from office, and I notice a surprising lack of interest in this body in investigating the many specific charges which he has made of the use of improper influence, in the Attorney General's office and elsewhere in connection with huge Government contracts. Incidentally, Mr. President, it is worth noticing that the most important piece of public service rendered by Mr. Littell before his dismissal in disgrace by the President was his blocking of the Elk Hills oil reserve deal which might easily have developed into another Teapot Dome, or worse.*

SCANDALS IN THE MAKING

However, the threat of vast corruption growing out of this war does not arise so much in connection with what has already happened. Some firms and some men are making a lot of money—too much money—out of this war, just as happened last time, and just as we were promised should not happen this time. But the time to be on guard against corruption on a grand scale, I

---

*During the Harding Administration the Secretary of the Interior persuaded the Navy to transfer its oil reserves in Teapot Dome, Wyoming, and Elks Hill, California, to the Interior Department. The reserves were then leased to major oil companies without competitive bidding, in exchange for bribes totaling $408,000.—*Ed.*

would remind and warn the Senate, is after the war is over. Then is when the boys who know the right people plan to "go to town." And what a chance they will have. Just think of it—more than $15,000,000,000 worth of the best designed and equipped factories in the country to be disposed of. Almost as much real estate as there is in the entire New England States. Tractors, automobiles, railway equipment, ships, food, textiles, and everything conceivable right down to safety pins, and, one suspects, perhaps, a good many million cartons of cigarettes. No one will hazard an official estimate as to the value of all this material and real estate, but the general understanding among Government officials is, as we all know, that it will represent a cost value of not a penny less than $100,000,000,000. Just think of that —$100,000,000,000 worth of Government goods to be disposed of, and in such a way as not to wreck our national economy. Talk about possible financial killings. There's the biggest meloncutting ever to take place at any time in history anywhere on God's green earth. And there is not a slicker, a something-for-nothing artist, a rascal, a corruptionist, a member of the plunderbund in this country who has not got his eye on what is coming up of this nature, and who is not getting ready right now to reap an illegitimate harvest out of this coming aftermath of the war. Teapot Dome will be kindergarten stuff alongside what the big plunderers are likely to do to that hundred billion dollars' worth of easy pickings.

THE MUNITIONS INVESTIGATION

So much for Teapot Dome. Then came the munitions investigation. With me on that committee were Senators Vandenberg, Barbour, George, Clark, Bone, and Pope, Senators whose courageous work in that investigation I shall never cease to admire. It was hard, tedious, and wearing work, carried on for nearly 4 years.

I know that it is the fashion today to minimize and deride the work done by the munitions inquiry. I know that the work of the investigation was never completed, that it always found its efforts to get at the truth hampered, sometimes by lack of funds, and that in the record of any investigation stretching over so much time and filling so many volumes of congressional reports there is bound to be a good deal of unimportant and some unproved or unprovable material. But I want to assert now, and without any hesitation or equivocation, that I am more proud of having been connected with the work of the Munitions Investigating Committee than of any other service in my 20-year career as a United States Senator. I do not account 1 day spent in the work of that committee, or 1 cent spent in its behalf, as wasted. I believe that it served a patriotic and much-needed purpose, and I confidently expect after this war is over, and men have a chance to look at the actuality of war again with some measure of objectivity and freedom of thought, that the ground work done by that committee, in spading up a field into which few had ever ventured before, will be again recognized for the important thing that it was.

DISCREDIT FACTS WHEN THEY EMBARRASS

When those who were so anxious to see this Nation enter this Second World War began to heap derision on the work of the munitions inquiry, they naturally started by trying to deceive the public as to what the inquiry had shown. They said that the inquiry had come to the conclusion that all wars are caused by merchants of death—that is to say, manufacturers of munitions and the financial interests behind them—and that if these merchants of death could be shackled there would be no more wars. They pretended that the munitions inquiry had held that if the United States would keep the Morgans and the du Ponts and Bethlehem Steel and Remington Arms and a few others from shipping munitions to other countries or financing other countries in the purchase of munitions, then there would never be any danger of the United States becoming involved in another war. President Roosevelt in one of his messages to Congress came nearer to saying that than anyone else.

Of course, the munitions investigation never said any such thing. This charge has been made only by those who maliciously wanted to falsify the record of that investigation, most of them because they did not want the United States to stay out of this war. But I find many newspapers and a good many American citizens echoing that false account of what the munitions investigation showed, and I think that something ought to be said to make clear the truth. What did the munitions inquiry actually show? Go to the 48 volumes of its hearings or to its several reports and you will get the full answer, but here are four summarized facts which I think that the inquiry established beyond any denial.

PROVED UNDERLYING CAUSES FOR WAR

First, it showed that economic interests do lie at the bottom of modern war. Mussolini may talk about have and have-not nations. Hitler may rant about Germany's need for lebensraum—living space. Churchill may declare that what Britain has she will hold. What it all comes down to is the clash of conflicting economic interests. President Wilson, in the speech he made at St. Louis during that last tour of his, said that anyone could already see—and remember, that was as far back as 1919—that the First World War had been caused by economic rivalries. The first thing the munitions investigation established was this: At the root of all war lies economic interest.

Second, our inquiry also discovered that economic interests which stand to make money out of war cannot be trusted not to work for war. I do not say, mark you, that they always do, but I do say that they cannot be trusted not to. That was what that long procession of armament salesmen who appeared before our committee proved up to the hilt. When any great company or any great bank stands to make money out of war they simply cannot be trusted not to take advantage of that opportunity. They frequently cannot be said to want war. They will be perfectly satisfied, and much happier perhaps, if the countries which buy their death-dealing manufactures only prepare for war and do not actually go to war. What they want in other words, is not war but profits. But wars always come after there has been a long period of arming, so that what the munitions companies want has little to do with the matter. It is what they do, not what they want, that counts. What they do is to go after the profits that are to be found in arms races. Therefore, I repeat, it is a fact that economic interests which stand to make money out of war cannot be trusted not to work for war.

The third fact follows, namely, that the private armament industry stands at the top of the list of those which, because they stand to make money out of the arming of nations for war, cannot be trusted to work against the coming of war. This is too clear to need any arguing.

The fourth fact brought out by our inquiry is that any portion of the banking industry which is engaged in financing the armament industry is just about as dangerous to peace as the armament industry itself. If the arms investigation begun in England had been carried through, or if the part which was carried out had not been so hedged about with restrictions from getting at the basic facts, I am sure that this would have been brought out even more clearly over there than it was here. But it is true everywhere. You cannot trust a banking industry that is making money out of financing an armament company or out of financing the purchase of armaments to work against war any more than you can trust the armament industry itself.

Still another fact developed by the munitions investigation, and of special interest now, was the extent of will in Britain, in France, and here in the United States to shut eyes to the requirements of the Versailles Treaty and help Hitler rearm Germany in violation of that treaty. There was profit for someone available through such a practice, just as there was tremendous profit in the business of selling scrap iron and oil to Japan almost up to the very hour of Japan's sneak attack at Pearl Harbor. One of my bewilderments will always be that Britain and France could have watched Germany arm, helped Germany arm, and then pretend surprise when they found how largely prepared for war Germany really was when she moved out with her heartless attack 5 years ago.

Now I say that these four facts were plainly established by the munitions investigation—the fact that economic interests underlie modern wars; the fact that economic interests that will make money out of war cannot be trusted not to work for war; the fact that the armament industry stands at the top of the list of those economic interests that cannot be trusted; and the fact that when banking is working hand in glove with armaments, banking cannot be trusted either. Those facts simply cannot be disproved. They are established beyond all doubt in the record of our inquiry. And I believe it is a good thing, a healthy thing, for the people of the United States to have them established. For that reason, I am perfectly willing to have the results and worth of the munitions investigation compared with those of any other investigation conducted by any other committee of either House of Congress during the past 20 years. . . .

NO WILL TO SAY "I TOLD YOU SO"

. . . There has been a constant temptation before me as I have been making this speech, Mr. President. Knowing that this might be the last time I will speak on this floor, there has been some temptation to make this in large measure an "I told you so" speech. But I have not done that because, great as the temptation has been, I have had no personal inclination to do so. My feeling is not at all "I told you so" as I take leave of my fellow Senators. On the contrary, I find myself deeply moved with feelings of sympathy for those of you who will remain here to wrestle with the prodigious and baffling problems of national policy which the years immediately ahead are bound to bring. This is a time, I feel, of grave peril for our country. We all feel that. Men who bear the responsibilities of United States Senators require for such an hour as this a wisdom and a purity of patriotism that all of us must despair of attaining. Therefore I have no inclination but to tell you of my earnest friendliness and good wishes for you all as you prepare to grapple with these problems.

GRAND MILITARY ALLIANCE TO RULE THE WORLD

You see the gravity of the peril in which the country stands because of the divisions within our American life produced by the growth of groups whose thinking is formed in alien molds, whose interests are primarily alien interests. And you see the gravity of the peril in which our foreign entanglements have involved us. Senators, let me ask a few candid questions about some of these things. Where do you think the end of the war is going to leave this Nation? Stripped of all partisan bravado, and of all highfalutin' oratory and of all empty talk of every kind, what do you honestly think that at the close of the war we will find ourselves in, or in for? Are we in a three-power grand military alliance to rule the world? Is that what all the talk about the Four Freedoms and the Atlantic

Charter and Dumbarton Oaks actually comes down to?* If it is—and I fear it is—then what do we do when our other two partners in this Three-Power Military Alliance fall out, as we can already see them beginning to do? What do we do then?

THE SCENERY OF DUMBARTON OAKS

Is Dumbarton Oaks going to protect us against getting caught in a jam like that? I wish I could believe it. But we know perfectly well what Dumbarton Oaks is. Dumbarton Oaks is a military alliance between the great powers to rule the world by means of regional understandings. The provisions of Dumbarton Oaks which pretend to provide means by which nations may be kept from acts of aggression are only supposed to work against the little fellows—against states like Paraguay, Rumania, and Iran. That is to say, they are not expected to work against any state that might be a real threat to world peace. John Foster Dulles is one of the men who has worked most closely with the negotiation of the Dumbarton Oaks charter, and is trying hardest to get the United States to join the new Dumbarton Oaks league; but even John Foster Dulles was forced by his honesty to say in a speech in Pittsburgh the other day that all these provisions of the Dumbarton Oaks scheme which pretend to keep the peace in the future are just so much scenery. That is all; just scenery. No; the actual truth about Dumbarton Oaks is that it is a three-power military alliance, and the actual power in the Dumbarton Oaks scheme is not even in the so-called security council, although that is where it is generally assumed to be, but in the military staff committee which is to be made up of the chiefs of staff of the permanent members of the council—the military staff committee which is to stand behind the council and tell the members of the council what they can and cannot do. That, with all the window dressing thrown out, is the actual truth about Dumbarton Oaks. . . .

*The "Four Freedoms" were defined by President Roosevelt as freedom of speech and expression, freedom of worship, freedom from want, and freedom from fear. The Atlantic Charter was a joint declaration by Roosevelt and Churchill in 1941 calling for a peaceful world after the destruction of Nazism. Dumbarton Oaks is an estate in Washington, D.C., at which the U. S., Great Britain, the U.S.S.R. and China agreed (in 1944) to create a United Nations.—*Ed.*

NO MORE IMPERIALISM IN ASIA

What is Asia going to be like after this war? Is there really going to be an end of imperialism over there? President Roosevelt has now twice declared that the Atlantic Charter must be applied to all the world at the end of this war. When Sumner Welles was Acting Secretary of State he told us, and told Asia, that the age of imperialism is ended. Do you believe that? Do you believe that the promises of self-determination for all peoples in the Atlantic Charter will actually be applied in Asia at the end of this war? It is to laugh. And Winston Churchill is laughing loudest of all. What we are actually going to get in Asia after this war is a revived imperialism, a restoration of all the European colonial empires that crumbled at the first touch, with the United States held responsible by all Asiatics for having wiped out the one nonwhite empire and having restored all the white, European empires. That is what we are going to get in Asia.

And where will the United States be when this comes to pass? Holding the bag, as usual. Our people will be staggering under a debt that may even go beyond the $300,000,000,000 mark. We shall have a standing army that will fill this capital with an officer caste with insatiable appetites for power and that will militarize the whole educational system of our Nation. We shall have the most enormous Navy that ever covered the seas, with all the enormous costs that such a Navy entails. We shall be involved in every quarrel between our partners in this new world order, for they will know how necessary it is for them to be able to count on using our power to win their quarrels, and there will be other quarrels directly between them and us. And when World War No. 3 comes along, as it certainly will as a result of this attempt to divide up Europe and the Near and Middle East between Russia and England, we will be in it from the first day. As a matter of fact, that is the real purpose of the commitments we are asked to make under the Dumbarton Oaks scheme. That is really a plan to see to it that the next time there is no such lag of 2 years and 3 months as occurred this time between the start of the Second World War and our entrance into it. . . .

* * *

THE PEOPLE TRUST PEACE JOB WITH THE SENATE

For 20 years, Mr. President, I have had the honor of representing in this body one of the States in what has been well called our valley of democracy. It is a State which lies at the very headwaters of that valley. I think I know the people of my State. They, like all of us, are susceptible to misleading for a time, but I know what is in their hearts about this war and what is to follow it. I know what they expect and what they want from the war. Very definitely they do not seek a chance for the United States to become involved in the endless intrigue about who shall control the oil fields of Persia, or about whether the British flag shall continue to wave over Hong Kong. They think the Persians and the Chinese should have the right to determine those questions. Above all else, these people want victory in this war, and then peace, peace for all the world, if we can help the world to it without surrendering our own, but surely peace for our own of America. What they seek is just a chance to mind their own business, to see their families born, reared, educated, and settled in a secure livelihood, without the prospect of being ordered off to die in some remote province over an even more remote quarrel. The responsibility is going to rest on you Senators to see that they gain, after this war, this that they seek. They cannot trust this job to those whose minds are filled with grandiose schemes for participating in a vast Great Power alliance for world rule.

I am more than ever convinced that it is the Congress of the United States, and particularly the Senate of the United States, which stands between these plain people and a future of misery and ruin, through being dragged into one world war after another.

THE HATE AND SMEAR BRIGADES

I have had my chance to serve in this body which can so largely shape the welfare of our people and contribute to the greatness, the glory, and the future of our country. I hope that in no detail have I failed my country and its people. There have been faults and frailties, to be sure. But I have made what I thought were the best possible uses of my opportunities to serve others and to serve my country. I do not think one can be rightfully expected to do more. If I had it all to do over, I do not know wherein I would want to alter the course I have pursued, even though I know what miserable attacks the course would invite from those who have been so quick to smear and to deny patriotic purpose to prompt the course. It is refreshing to contemplate having in private life a freedom from the smears which have been so plentiful in these late years of public life. I contemplate that, even though so high an authority as Walter Winchell has predicted that with my retirement from the Senate will come Government prosecution that will reveal my probable connections with the Nazis, perhaps with Hitler personally. The smear and hate brigades will find other targets, no doubt; their programs can bring profit only as they are able to find or create targets. Their targets as a rule are those who dare to think and work for the interests of their own country first. You cannot escape their wrath by being against foreign "isms" as a whole. If you would win the plaudits of the hate and smear brigades, you must be against fascism and nazi-ism. But do not go further; do not dare to speak a word that seems to condemn communism. . . .

FAITH IN SENATE AND THE FUTURE

. . . Mr. President and Senators, those of you who must remain to deal with these gigantic problems, problems which so gravely and vitally concern the future peace of our Nation and its people, deserve of all the people of America the confidence and respect which I shall always place in and with you. My faith in the good purpose and patriotic spirit of the plain people of America and in what I have come to know, during 20 years, to be the purpose and spirit of the Senate leads me to believe that somewhere you will find the answer to this terrible problem, which may be a painful and burdensome one for a long while. May our Maker bless you and our Nation always.

Part Two

The New Populism

IV. RIGHT-WING POPULISM

"Right" and "left" have always been misleading categories in the social sciences. They first came into use during the French Revolution to designate the seating positions of two prominent factions in the National Assembly. Even in European politics they proved to be clumsy tools for classification. Was Stalin "right" or "left"? What about De Gaulle?

But in America the labels are even clumsier. What are we to make of someone like Bryan, who opposed imperialism, favored wartime censorship, opposed the teaching of evolution, favored a vigorous prosecution of the trusts, opposed Wall Street, and favored Prohibition? Or for that matter Jefferson, whose states-rightism, ruralism, and individualism provide as much aid and comfort to the "right" as his defense of revolution and unbridled speech provide to the "left"? What of Gerald Nye and William Borah, who mixed antimilitarism with strident "Americanism"? Or Huey Long, who combined economic radicalism and Southern paternalism?

One way to account for all this is simply to say that no human being is perfectly consistent, and certainly not a political activist. All have certain mixtures of radical and conservative in them, and populists, being impulsive and hyperbolic souls, probably exaggerate both sides of their natures.

But such an answer assumes, once again, that we know what we are talking about when we use the terms "left" and "right." Actually the terms were hardly used in America until the 1950's, when they were first introduced by the liberals in an effort to define their own position. For they had designated themselves as "cen-

209

trists," and they needed "right" and "left" in order to highlight their own "moderation." Consequently, "right" was what the taste of liberals during the fifties decreed as "conservative," and this included an opposition to Presidential power, brain trusts, and social engineering. A "left" extremist, on the other hand, was one who ranted against Wall Street, complained about the way wealth was distributed in America and insisted that corporations were not in the process of reforming themselves. This was Communist talk, and the liberals were at pains to disassociate themselves from any position embraced by the Communists, even if it happened to be correct.

During the fifties, in short, populism was arbitrarily lopped in two. What logical incompatibility is there in denouncing both Wall Street and Harvard, decrying at once the maldistribution of wealth and the presumption of the social engineers? Are not both of these protests, the one economic and the other cultural, the two halves of populist egalitarianism? But the liberals treated them as opposites, as "left" and "right" extremism, as the carping of "ideologues" on the one hand and "neanderthals" on the other.

And, finally, each side seemed to accept the labels. "Left-wing" populists like C. Wright Mills ended up writing apologies for Castro's Cuba, and the right-wingers responded to the liberal taunts much in the manner of, "All right, call me a neanderthal and I'll *be* a neanderthal." It was in the center of this polarity, a polarity created by the misunderstood opposition between the two sides of populism, that liberalism thrived.

But liberalism disintegrated during the 1960's, and we are left today with the two poles, still raging against the vacuum at the center. Perhaps someday these two halves of the populist tradition, one economic and the other cultural, will recognize each other and be reconciled. But, more likely, liberalism, under some new name, will reconstitute itself and rush back into the center. For as long as the center holds the two halves of populism will continue to regard each other as ideological opponents.

At any rate, the categories of "economic" and "cultural" are by no means airtight. Joe McCarthy fulminated against intellectuals but also against "those born with silver spoons in their mouths." George Wallace complains about hippies but also about the "ultra-rich," the big foundations, and the system of tax loopholes. And even Kevin Phillips, the Nixon Republican, wants his party purged of "economic royalists."

A. *Joseph McCarthy:*
Communism in the State Department

> The American people have long condemned war prof-
> iteers who promptly crowd the landscape the moment
> their nation is at war. Today, Mr. President, war prof-
> iteers of a new and infinitely more debased type are
> cluttering the landscape in Washington. They are politi-
> cal war profiteers . . . They are hiding behind the word
> "unity," using it without meaning, but as a mere catch
> phrase to center the attention of the American people
> solely on the fighting front.*

The author of these words was neither Gerald Nye nor George McGovern, but Senator "Joe" (as he preferred to be called) McCarthy (1909-1957), anti-Communist crusader of the early 1950's. In this speech he was insisting on his right to investigate the State Department while the Korean War was raging. Later in this same speech he complained about those who had "wrapped themselves in the American flag," and he went on to quote Samuel Johnson's remark that "Patriotism is the last refuge of a scoun-drel."

If all of this sounds out of character for the archetypal right-winger, the *bête noire* of American liberalism, it is because McCarthy's "left" side has been insufficiently understood. McCarthy slandered many innocent people with his roundhouse punches, but his chief targets were neither humble, nor defense-less, nor, always, perfectly innocent: Harvard University, the State Department, the Army, and, finally, his own Senate. Indeed, it was McCarthy's choice of such powerful enemies that proved his

---

*U. S. Congress, Senate, *Congressional Record*, 81st Congress, 2nd Session, 1950, Vol. 96, p. 9715.

ultimate undoing. When he began browbeating a brigadier general, reminding him that "You are an employee of the people," the machinery was set in motion which culminated in censure by the Senate. He was censured not for all the harm he had done to individuals by accusing them of being Communists, but because his conduct impaired the dignity of the Senate.

Whether cynically or not, McCarthy drew heavily upon the folklore of populism in his campaign to root out "Communism" in high places. Whether his following was as massive or as dedicated as it seemed at the time, the fact is beyond dispute that he won the support of many normally Democratic voters, particularly among lower-class Catholics, who had been staunch New Dealers. Republican conservatives had been ranting against "Bolsheviks" for decades, with little appreciable effect upon the lower classes except to confirm their suspicions of big business rhetoric. But the young Senator from Wisconsin—a Catholic, a war veteran, a hard drinker, and a tough talker—managed to fit anti-Communism into the populist "underdog" tradition, to turn the key and open the door to millions who had been unreceptive to traditional Republican red-baiting. In the process he may have perverted populism, but he also revivified it, purging it of its rural and Protestant bias.

McCarthy's trick was to turn Marxism on its head, associating it not with the masses but with the sons and daughters of the privileged. The inversion contained a kernel of truth. During the 1930's Communism did fascinate a small but influential number of adherents in academia, young people who saw the only hope for America in a radical departure from the *status quo*. Many of these idealists did come from the upper-middle classes, and some of them did indeed end up in the Communist Party, which at that time was utterly servile to the interests of the Soviet Union.

The most sensational case of this sort, a case which set the stage for Joe McCarthy, was that of Alger Hiss.

In 1949 Whittaker Chambers, a senior editor of *Time* magazine and a repentant ex-Communist, alleged that he used to collect Party dues from a number of Communists who were on their way up in the federal bureaucracy, and that he had personal knowledge of espionage activities they had conducted for the Soviet government. Among the individuals named was Alger Hiss, a former high-ranking career official in the State Department, a member of the U.S. delegation at Yalta, and, since 1946, president of the Carnegie Endowment for International Peace. Hiss seemed the very embodiment of the Establishment—his Ivy League education, his career as diplomat and brain truster, his Eastern manners—yet Chambers' charges stood up in court: Hiss was convicted of perjury for denying that he had ever been a member of the Communist Party.

In the 1950 speech excerpted here,* McCarthy refers to Hiss as one "who is important not as an individual any more, but rather because he is representative of a group in the State Department." To McCarthy Hiss represented not only Communism and treason but a whole way of life which he professed to hate. He associated Communism with fancy manners, Anglophilism, Harvard, pretensions to high culture, all the qualities that vintage populism had associated with the Eastern Establishment. Dean Acheson, Truman's Secretary of State, occupied such a high position on McCarthy's hate list not only because he had once defended Hiss but also because he was so like him in background and life-style. He was "the great Red Dean of fashion," part of the "lace handkerchief crowd," "the elegant and alien Acheson—Russian as to heart, British as to manner."

Ladies and gentlemen, tonight as we celebrate the one hundred and forty-first birthday of one of the greatest men in American history, I would like to be able to talk about what a glorious day today is in the history of the world. As we celebrate the birth of this man who with his whole heart and soul hated war, I would like to be able to speak of peace in our time, of war being outlawed, and of worldwide disarmament. These would be truly appropriate things to be able to mention as we celebrate the birthday of Abraham Lincoln.

Five years after a world war has been won, men's hearts should anticipate a long peace, and men's minds should be free from the heavy weight that comes with war. But this is not such a period

*Speech in Wheeling, W. Va. (quoted by Senator McCarthy in Senate Speech), U. S. Congress, Senate, *Congressional Record*, 81st Congress, 2nd Session, 1950, vol. 96.

—for this is not a period of peace. This is a time of the "cold war." This is a time when all the world is split into two vast, increasingly hostile armed camps—a time of a great armaments race.

Today we can almost physically hear the mutterings and rumblings of an invigorated god of war. You can see it, feel it, and hear it all the way from the hills of Indochina, from the shores of Formosa, right over into the very heart of Europe itself.

The one encouraging thing is that the "mad moment" has not yet arrived for the firing of the gun or the exploding of the bomb which will set civilization about the final task of destroying itself. There is still a hope for peace if we finally decide that no longer can we safely blind our eyes and close our ears to those facts which are shaping up more and more clearly. And that is that we are now engaged in a show-down fight—not the usual war between nations for land areas or other material gains, but a war between two diametrically opposed ideologies.

The great difference between our western Christian world and the atheistic Communist world is not political, ladies and gentlemen, it is moral. There are other differences, of course, but those could be reconciled. For instance, the Marxian idea of confiscating the land and factories and running the entire economy as a single enterprise is momentous. Likewise, Lenin's invention of the one-party police state as a way to make Marx's idea work is hardly less momentous.

Stalin's resolute putting across of these two ideas, of course, did much to divide the world. With only those differences, however, the East and the West could most certainly still live in peace.

The real, basic difference, however, lies in the religion of immoralism—invented by Marx, preached feverishly by Lenin, and carried to unimaginable extremes by Stalin. This religion of immoralism, if the Red half of the world wins—and well it may —this religion of immoralism will more deeply wound and damage mankind than any conceivable economic or political system.

Karl Marx dismissed God as a hoax, and Lenin and Stalin have added in clear-cut, unmistakable language their resolve that no nation, no people who believe in a God, can exist side by side with their Communistic state.

Karl Marx, for example, expelled people from his Communist

Party for mentioning such things as justice, humanity, or morality. He called this soulful ravings and sloppy sentimentality.

While Lincoln was a relatively young man in his late thirties, Karl Marx boasted that the Communist specter was haunting Europe. Since that time, hundreds of millions of people and vast areas of the world have fallen under Communist domination. Today, less than 100 years after Lincoln's death, Stalin brags that this Communist specter is not only haunting the world, but is about to completely subjugate it.

Today we are engaged in final, all-out battle between communistic atheism and Christianity. The modern champions of communism have selected this as the time. And, ladies and gentlemen, the chips are down—they are truly down.

Lest there be any doubt that the time has been chosen, let us go directly to the leader of communism today—Joseph Stalin. Here is what he said—not back in 1928, not before the war, not during the war—but 2 years after the last war was ended: "To think that the Communist revolution can be carried out peacefully, within the framework of a Christian democracy, means one has either gone out of one's mind and lost all normal understanding, or has grossly and openly repudiated the Communist revolution."

And this is what was said by Lenin in 1919, which was also quoted with approval by Stalin in 1947:

"We are living," said Lenin, "not merely in a state, but in a system of states, and the existence of the Soviet Republic side by side with Christian states for a long time is unthinkable. One or the other must triumph in the end. And before that end supervenes, a series of frightful collisions between the Soviet Republic and the Bourgeois states will be inevitable."

Ladies and gentlemen, can there be anyone here tonight who is so blind as to say that the war is not on? Can there be anyone who fails to realize that the Communist world has said, "The time is now"—that this is the time for the show-down between the democratic Christian world and the Communist atheistic world?

Unless we face this fact, we shall pay the price that must be paid by those who wait too long.

Six years ago, at the time of the first conference to map out the peace—Dumbarton Oaks—there was within the Soviet orbit

180,000,000 people. Lined up on the antitotalitarian side there were in the world at that time roughly 1,625,000,000 people. Today, only 6 years later, there are 800,000,000 people under the absolute domination of Soviet Russia—an increase over 400 per cent. On our side, the figure has shrunk to around 500,000,000. In other words, in less than 6 years the odds have changed from 9 to 1 in our favor to 8 to 5 against us. This indicates the swiftness of the tempo of Communist victories and American defeats in the cold war. As one of our outstanding historical figures once said, "When a great democracy is destroyed, it will not be because of enemies from without, but rather because of enemies from within."

The truth of this statement is becoming terrifyingly clear as we see this country each day losing on every front.

At war's end we were physically the strongest nation on earth and, at least potentially, the most powerful intellectually and morally. Ours could have been the honor of being a beacon in the desert of destruction, a shining living proof that civilization was not yet ready to destroy itself. Unfortunately, we have failed miserably and tragically to arise to the opportunity.

The reason why we find ourselves in a position of impotency is not because our only powerful potential enemy has sent men to invade our shores, but rather because of the traitorous actions of those who have been treated so well by this Nation. It has not been the less fortunate or members of minority groups who have been selling this Nation out, but rather those who have had all the benefits that the wealthiest nation on earth has had to offer—the finest homes, the finest college education, and the finest jobs in Government we can give.

This is glaringly true in the State Department. There the bright young men who are born with silver spoons in their mouths are the ones who have been worst.

Now I know it is very easy for anyone to condemn a particular bureau or department in general terms. Therefore, I would like to cite one rather unusual case—the case of a man who has done much to shape our foreign policy.

When Chiang Kai-shek was fighting our war, the State Department had in China a young man named John S. Service. His task, obviously, was not to work for the communization of China.

Strangely, however, he sent official reports back to the State Department urging that we torpedo our ally Chiang Kai-shek and stating, in effect, that communism was the best hope of China.

Later, this man—John Service—was picked up by the Federal Bureau of Investigation for turning over to the Communists secret State Department information. Strangely, however, he was never prosecuted. However, Joseph Grew, the Under Secretary of State, who insisted on his prosecution, was forced to resign. Two days after Grew's successor, Dean Acheson, took over as Under Secretary of State, this man—John Service—who had been picked up by the FBI and who had previously urged that communism was the best hope of China, was not only reinstated in the State Department but promoted. And finally, under Acheson, placed in charge of all placements and promotions.

Today, ladies and gentlemen, this man Service is on his way to represent the State Department and Acheson in Calcutta—by far and away the most important listening post in the Far East.

Now, let's see what happens when individuals with Communist connections are forced out of the State Department. Gustave Duran, who was labeled as (I quote) "a notorious international Communist," was made assistant to the Assistant Secretary of State in charge of Latin American affairs. He was taken into the State Department from his job as a lieutenant colonel in the Communist International Brigade. Finally, after intense congressional pressure and criticism, he resigned in 1946 from the State Department—and, ladies and gentlemen, where do you think he is now? He took over a high-salaried job as Chief of Cultural Activities Section in the office of the Assistant Secretary General of the United Nations.

Then there was a Mrs. Mary Jane Kenny, from the Board of Economic Warfare in the State Department, who was named in an FBI report and in a House committee report as a courier for the Communist Party while working for the Government. And where do you think Mrs. Kenny is—she is now an editor in the United Nations Document Bureau.

Another interesting case was that of Julian H. Wadleigh, economist in the Trade Agreements Section of the State Department for 11 years and [sic] was sent to Turkey and Italy and other countries as United States representative. After the statute of limitations had run so he could not be prosecuted for treason, he openly and brazenly not only admitted but proclaimed that he had been a member of the Communist Party . . . that while working for the State Department he stole a vast number of secret documents . . . and furnished these documents to the Russian spy ring of which he was a part.

You will recall last spring there was held in New York what was known as the World Peace Conference—a conference which was labeled by the State Department and Mr. Truman as the sounding board for Communist propaganda and a front for Russia. Dr. Harlow Shapley was the chairman of that conference. Interestingly enough, according to the new release put out by the Department in July, the Secretary of State appointed Shapley on a commission which acts as liaison between UNESCO and the State Department.

This, ladies and gentlemen, gives you somewhat of a picture of the type of individuals who have been helping to shape our foreign policy. In my opinion the State Department, which is one of the most important government departments, is thoroughly infested with Communists.

I have in my hand 57 cases of individuals who would appear to be either card carrying members or certainly loyal to the Communist Party, but who nevertheless are still helping to shape our foreign policy.

One thing to remember in discussing the Communists in our Government is that we are not dealing with spies who get 30 pieces of silver to steal the blueprints of a new weapon. We are dealing with a far more sinister type of activity because it permits the enemy to guide and shape our policy. . . .

This brings us down to the case of one Alger Hiss who is important not as an individual any more, but rather because he is so representative of a group in the State Department. It is unnecessary to go over the sordid events showing how he sold out the Nation which had given him so much. Those are rather fresh in all of our minds.

However, it should be remembered that the facts in regard to his connection with this international Communist spy ring were made known to the then Under Secretary of State Berle 3 days after Hitler and Stalin signed the Russo-German alliance pact. At that time one Whittaker Chambers—who was also part of the spy ring—apparently decided that with Russia on Hitler's side, he could no longer betray our Nation to Russia. He gave Under Secretary of State Berle—and this is all a matter of record —practically all, if not more, of the facts upon which Hiss' conviction was based.

Under Secretary Berle promptly contacted Dean Acheson and received word in return that Acheson (and I quote) "could vouch for Hiss absolutely"—at which time the matter was dropped. And this, you understand, was at a time when Russia was an ally of Germany. This condition existed while Russia and Germany were invading and dismembering Poland, and while the Communist groups here were screaming "warmonger" at the United States for their support of the allied nations.

Again in 1943, the FBI had occasion to investigate the facts surrounding Hiss' contacts with the Russian spy ring. But even after that FBI report was submitted, nothing was done.

Then late in 1948—on August 5—when the Un-American Activities Committee called Alger Hiss to give an accounting, President Truman at once issued a Presidential directive ordering all Government agencies to refuse to turn over any information whatsoever in regard to the Communist activities of any Government employee to a congressional committee.

Incidentally, even after Hiss was convicted—it is interesting to note that the President still labeled the exposé of Hiss as a "red herring."

If time permitted, it might be well to go into detail about the fact that Hiss was Roosevelt's chief adviser at Yalta when Roosevelt was admittedly in ill health and tired physically and mentally . . . and when, according to the Secretary of State, Hiss and Gromyko drafted the report on the conference.

According to the then Secretary of State Stettinius, here are some of the things that Hiss helped to decide at Yalta. (1) The establishment of a European High Commission; (2) the treatment of Germany—this you will recall was the conference at which it was decided that we would occupy Berlin with Russia occupying an area completely circling the city, which, as you know, resulted in the Berlin airlift which cost 31 American lives; (3) the Polish question; (4) the relationship between UNRRA and the Soviet; (5) the rights of Americans on control commissions of Rumania,

Bulgaria, and Hungary; (6) Iran; (7) China—here's where we gave away Manchuria; (8) Turkish Straits question; (9) international trusteeships; (10) Korea.

Of the results of this conference, Arthur Bliss Lane of the State Department had this to say: "As I glanced over the document, I could not believe my eyes. To me, almost every line spoke of a surrender to Stalin."

As you hear this story of high treason, I know that you are saying to yourself, "Well, why doesn't the Congress do something about it?" Actually, ladies and gentlemen, one of the important reasons for the graft, the corruption, the dishonesty, the disloyalty, the treason in high Government positions—one of the most important reasons why this continues is a lack of moral uprising on the part of the 140,000,000 American people. In the light of history, however, this is not hard to explain.

It is the result of an emotional hang-over and a temporary moral lapse which follows every war. It is the apathy to evil which people who have been subjected to the tremendous evils of war feel. As the people of the world see mass murder, the destruction of defenseless and innocent people, and all of the crime and lack of morals which go with war, they become numb and apathetic. It has always been thus after war.

However, the morals of our people have not been destroyed. They still exist. This cloak of numbness and apathy has only needed a spark to rekindle them. Happily, this spark has finally been supplied.

As you know, very recently the Secretary of State proclaimed his loyalty to a man guilty of what has always been considered as the most abominable of all crimes—of being a traitor to the people who gave him a position of great trust. The Secretary of State in attempting to justify his continued devotion to the man who sold out the Christian world to the atheistic world, referred to Christ's Sermon on the Mount as a justification and reason therefor, and the reaction of the American people to this would have made the heart of Abraham Lincoln happy.

When this pompous diplomat in striped pants, with a phony British accent, proclaimed to the American people that Christ on the Mount endorsed communism, high treason, and betrayal of a sacred trust, the blasphemy was so great that it awakened the dormant indignation of the American people.

He has lighted the spark which is resulting in a moral uprising and will end only when the whole sorry mess of twisted, warped thinkers are swept from the national scene so that we may have a new birth of national honesty and decency in Government.

B. *George C. Wallace:*
In Praise of "The Average Man"

"He was the leading liberal in the legislature, no doubt about that. He was regarded as a dangerous left-winger. A lot of people even looked on him as downright pink." The speaker (quoted by Marshall Frady in his biography of George Wallace) is a former staff member of Gordon Persons, Alabama governor during the early fifties. At that time George Wallace (1919-   ) was beginning his second term as state legislator and had already achieved a reputation as a leading sponsor of social welfare legislation—veterans' benefits, tuberculosis hospitals, antipoverty legislation, and aid to education. "The Number-One Do-Gooder in the legislature," one newsman called him, and another columnist warned that "house members would do well to look more closely at these do-good bills that are siphoning off tax funds." The Chamber of Commerce summed it up by giving him a "C," one of their lowest ratings, and adding the comment: "Radical."

Wallace was no radical, but he did fit squarely into the tradition of Southern populism. His mentor and sponsor was "Big Jim" Folsom, an epic figure in Alabama politics during the forties. In winning the governorship, Folsom had wrenched power away from the "big mules," as he called the industrial and land barons, and introduced a free-wheeling populist administration which actively courted the returning war veterans, the dirt farmers, and the workers of Alabama.

The young George Wallace regarded Folsom with the greatest of awe, even imitating some of his speech patterns. More important, he followed the same pattern of populist politics which Folsom had brought to the governorship. "He really believed in all that stuff that Folsom wanted to do for the common folks," said one former state senator. "With Folsom, he felt his kind of people were getting a hook into things finally."

But one of Folsom's policies turned out to be a liability to Wallace. Folsom's populism had led him toward a modification of white supremacy, at one point urging black and white to stand together against the rich. In Wallace's first bid for the governorship in 1958 he may have been experimenting, however cautiously, with this policy. He denounced the Ku Klux Klan and promptly won the endorsement of the state NAACP.

After his defeat by John Patterson, however, a somewhat different Wallace emerged. "John Patterson out nigguhed me," he told a group of politicians. "And boys, I'm not goin' to be out-nigguhed again." This was the Wallace who won the governorship in 1962 on the promise to stand in the schoolhouse door—and he did. Then, as Robert Kennedy conferred with him in a vain effort to prevent this showdown, Wallace gave evidence of a still larger ambition. "I believe all over this nation we get thousands of letters from Michigan and former Southerners in California, in Michigan—automobile workers. . . ."

Nine years later many of those Michigan automobile workers contributed to Wallace's first majority in a Northern state. He had first come North in 1964 to enter the Wisconsin primary, where he captured almost 30 percent of the vote; in Maryland the same year he won 45 percent of the vote. In 1968 he continued to worry the major party contenders, almost costing Nixon the election. But 1972 became the memorable breakthrough as Wallace successfully exploited the busing issue to win a victory in one of the most liberal states in the Union.

In the meantime the image had changed again—and yet again. "Nigguh," or any direct reference to race, was out. The rhetorical staple was now "law and order." Then, somewhere between 1968 and 1972, Wallace began to absorb this conservative theme into his earlier framework of populism. He was now addressing both blacks and whites (acquiring some black supporters in the process), and listing among his pet villains "those ultra-rich who escape taxation."

The first part of the selection consists of his Declaration of Candidacy, in the Florida Democratic Primary, January 13, 1972; the second part of the selection is from his address to the Democratic National Convention on July 12, 1972, Miami, Florida. Both are taken from mimeographed press releases.

At this writing Wallace is still attempting to recover from the effects of five bullets pumped into his body during the Maryland primary campaign in May of 1972. He is described as mellowed and subdued, noncommittal about future plans except to say, "I'm still very much interested in the future of politics in this country and I'm going to stay involved." Although paralyzed from the waist down and suffering intense pain, he says, "My mind's still here and my heart is still strong. I intend to make the best of things."

The people of Florida, many who come from all over the United States and thus represent a cross section of American public opinion, have a unique opportunity. They can start the grass roots movement to take back the National Democratic Party unto themselves. Too long this party has been controlled by the so-called intellectual snobs who feel that big government should control the lives of American citizens from the cradle to the grave. The people want to be left alone from the unnecessary control of big government. As a candidate for the Democratic Party nomination, I ask for the support of Floridians whether white or black, rich or poor, whether they belong to management, labor or business, or whether they are in active pursuits or retired, whether they are native-born citizens or citizens by choice. Yes, our offering is a new beginning of hope for the American people.

The essential stands I take among others will be: peace through strength; superior offensive and defensive capabilities of our military forces second to none; then we will always be in a position to negotiate with our enemies.

A continuation of a viable space program which is tied directly to national defense.

A fair tax system that levies taxes on the multi-billion and multi-million dollar foundations which are now virtually tax exempt, whose purposes are other than strictly charitable. The levying of taxes upon the estimated 150 billion dollars' worth of church commercial property now in competition with businesses and industries in our free enterprise system.

A reduction in taxes for the individual and businesses and industry to be replaced with revenues from those now evading taxes through special laws passed in their special interest. This will put people back to work because the demand for consumer goods by individuals will stimulate production activity. This should be of the highest priority. Get people back to work.

Protection of the social security trust fund from other uses so that pensions can be raised and social security taxes reduced on individuals and those whose incomes are low.

The discontinuance of foreign aid programs except where determined to be in our national interest, and no foreign aid to Communist countries or those countries who aid the Communists.

Continued withdrawal from Vietnam and never again commit American troops to fight a no win war. No recognition of Castro Cuba.

Curtailment of Federal spending to bring about a balanced budget.

A farm program that will not have the farmer at the bottom of the economic ladder as he is now.

Reasonable restrictions, but not prohibiting the investment of American capital to build plants in foreign countries when the loss of jobs to American workers in those plants not built are relocated abroad was not offset by gains to the overall economy of the Nation and to the Nation's work force.

The restoration of our maritime fleet to the position of No. 1 in the world.

A return to law and order. Action by the Federal Government in its proper role in cooperation with the States and political subdivisions to make it safe to walk on the streets of the cities of our nation and for the curtailment of other criminal activities and 100 percent support for the law enforcement personnel and firemen of the Nation.

The appointment of Judges to the Supreme Court who will not

decree their own political, social and economic philosophy into court-made law.

A reasonable welfare program for those who are disabled and blind and handicapped and for the elderly, but a curtailment of welfare programs that are designed to pay able-bodied individuals not to work.

The return to local control of public education on a nondiscriminatory basis. A return to freedom of choice and the neighborhood school concept. A complete halt to involuntary busing to achieve any sort of balance, and the reopening of schools now closed under Federal Court orders, HEW departmental regulations and/or by action of the Justice Department where such openings are desired by the citizens and officials of the States and/or local school districts.

Those in this campaign who have served in the Congress of the United States have had their opportunity to keep our military strength superior but have either failed in their efforts or have supported a weakened military posture.

They have made no significant effort to tax those ultra-rich who escape taxation and give relief to lower income groups proportionately.

They have failed to keep social security taxes reasonable and to give meaningful social security benefits to those entitled, especially to our senior citizens.

They have voted to give away our money by the billions to those who not only did not appreciate it, but who in many cases worked against the interests of the United States. They voted to give aid to our Communist enemies and those who were aiding the Communists.

We are the leaders of the free world, but we cannot act as the world's policemen. We should require our allies in the NATO Alliances and other parts of the world to shoulder a larger burden of the manpower requirements and cost involved in these alliances. We do not have sufficient manpower to shoulder over and above our share of the burden, and the cost over the years has aided in bringing on our balance of payment problem which threatens our economic well being and the economic stability of the free world.

Mr. Chairman, delegates to the Democratic National Convention, and ladies and gentlemen. I appreciate the opportunity to address this convention tonight, on the party platform, and on the amendments that are included in the minority report that will be offered to this convention. So, I do appreciate this unique opportunity. As I left the hotel tonight, my young eleven-year-old daughter asked me, "Daddy, you are going to speak to a political rally?" I told her, "No, I'm not going to speak to a political rally tonight—I've spoken to one political rally too many already this year." But, anyway, I am grateful for the opportunity to come before this convention.

I do know that I have some experience that I have acquired during the primary campaigns all the way from the great State of Florida, to the State of Michigan, and all the way to California. I can recall that in the State of Florida, this great cosmopolitan state in which this convention is being held, that I received a plurality of the vote, having carried every single county in this state. As a result of that campaign, most of the columnists and editors in the country wrote that "George Wallace has touched the issues that today frustrate the American people, and as a result of his campaign, and as a result of his being in Florida, we now find that other politicians and others seeking public office are beginning to say identically the same things." It was not George Wallace. It was the thousands of people that listened to me in this state, that caused others to see that people in our country had grown cynical of government—that they were frustrated—and that they were tired of big government and they knew that big government could not solve all of the problems that confront the American people. Some problems must be solved by the individuals themselves or those back in the respective states from which they come. So, I am here to give you the benefit of that which I have learned, and which I believe that the average citizen today feels and is so concerned about in these United States.

You know the average citizen in our country—and that's who I spoke about all the way from Florida to Michigan—knows that those in the National Democratic Party and the National Republican Party and in the government in the past, had payed [sic] attention to the noise-makers, and to the exotic, and they had ignored that average citizen who works each day for a living, and pays the taxes and holds the country together. They only payed [*sic*] attention to him on tax paying day and on election day. But the average citizen in this country today—the average woman is the queen of American politics and the average man is the king of American politics. What are they most interested in and why are we offering minority reports to the platform? Because we believe that this is in the interest of the Democratic Party and that it will aid it in the campaign this coming November.

The platform calls for tax reform. In 1968 I spoke about tax reform all over these United States. I was the only candidate that did, that said that the income tax was regressive and that the average citizen payed [*sic*] through the nose, while the tax free foundations went Scott-free, with their multi-billions and multi-millions of dollars. So, I am for tax reform, and I raise the issue of tax reform. But the minority plank that we will present to this platform, calls not only for reform, but calls for tax relief, because I believe there is almost a tax revolt among the average citizens. The average middle class and low income citizen in this country can hardly make ends meet as a result, not only of inflation, but the high taxation at the level of the federal government. So, our plank will call for relief from taxes for the average citizen in our country.

And I might say to this convention, that maybe you haven't thought about it, but I know when I go to Washington, that all the Governors themselves sometimes wonder what all the hundreds of thousands of bureaucrats do. The administrative cost of government can be cut in this country—and ought to be cut. When we go to Washington and when we visit with one another—the Governors—we whisper in one another's ears and ask, "What do all of them do?"—the hundreds of thousands of bureaucrats that draw twenty-five and forty thousand dollars a year of the average working man's money looking after matters that ought to be looked after, and could be looked after, by those elected back in the local states and local political subdivisions. So, we are offering a plank on the matter of administrative cost of government.

We are offering a plank on the matter of foreign aid. Since 1946 the American people have given two-hundred and twelve billion dollars of our money, including interest, to every country from A to Z, throughout the world. I can think of one country that received

nearly ten billion dollars in the last ten years of American taxpayers money, that spit in our face, called us an aggressor nation,
an imperialist nation, votes against us in the United Nations, and
aids our enemies in Viet Nam. The average citizen is sick and
tired, and fed up to his ears in his hard earned tax money going to
countries that spit in our face in the United Nations and actively aid
our enemies in Viet Nam.

We shall offer a plank on the matter of welfare. We have heard
so much talk about welfare in this country, and I am sure that
everybody in the democratic party, and everybody in government,
and everybody in this country wants to help the elderly and the
blind and the maimed—and they ought to—but the welfare programs today in our country are out of hand, and the platform that
has been offered to the American people by the democratic party
calls for more welfare. A screening of the welfare program in this
country, which has been tried in some of the largest cities in our
country, show that fifteen to twenty-five percent of those who are
on the rolls are ineligible. So our plank will call for less welfare
spending instead of more, because the average working citizen in
this country is tired of some of his money going to those who have
made it a profession to draw welfare and wouldn't work if they
could find a job in this country.

We shall offer a plank on the matter of law and order. Regardless of what anyone might say, today the thugs have taken over the
streets of every large city in the United States. No average citizen,
at night, can leave his home for fear of something happening to
him. He cannot ride the subway system, the rapid transit
system—his wife cannot go to the supermarket. I hope that this
convention will adopt a platform that will impress the average
citizen—that the next president of the United States will go on
record as being for the enforcement of the law, and the taking of
the thugs in this country off the streets and turning those streets
back over to the average man and woman, who are entitled to be
able to walk in safety in whatever city they happen to live in, large
or small, in the United States.

We shall offer a minority plank on the matter of national defense. I do not believe that any party can win the presidency and
the election in November that offers a party platform that will cut
our defense forces, offensive and defensive, to that below that of

any other power. And so, I hope that this national convention will adopt the minority report, that says that we shall never be relegated to a second rate power.

I wind up my brief remarks, ladies and gentlemen, because there are those that will speak briefly to each one of the minority report planks, that we hope that you will include in the National Democratic Party platform, that I honestly believe will aid it in the coming campaign in November.

I believe in quality education. I want to see the American dream realized by everyone in this country regardless of their race or color—and that has always been my desire—it is my desire at the present time. But the people, the average citizen in this country —and I can say that maybe the State of Michigan is one example that we can think about today—no one is against quality education in this country. But the Gallup Poll, the Harris Poll, and every other poll, shows that seventy-five to eighty-five percent of the American people are against the senseless asinine busing of little school children to achieve racial balance throughout the United States. And I would like to advise the delegates to this great convention assembled here on Miami Beach, that I ran in the State of Florida where that issue was an acute, sensitive issue. As you recall, the people of this state voted overwhelmingly against it. I recently carried fifty-one percent of the vote in the great industrial and agricultural State of Michigan. So, I can tell you, that any party that doesn't confront this issue, and confront it in the right manner, is going to be in jeopardy as far as success is concerned this coming November.

So, I hope that this convention will adopt those items of the minority that we have offered, because we offer them in the interest of the Democratic Party. I am here because I want to help the Democratic Party. I want it again to become the party of the average citizen in this country as it used to be, and not the party of the intellectual pseudo-snobbery that has controlled it for so many years.

Thank you very much ladies and gentlemen.

C. *Kevin Phillips:*
The Future of American Politics*

Writing books on voting behavior is an activity which used to be limited mainly to liberal intellectuals. Kevin Phillips (1940-) is a conservative intellectual, and it appears that he has beaten the liberals at their own game. In the mid-sixties, seemingly the darkest period for conservative Republicans, he conceived the idea for a book which would predict, on the basis of Presidential voting trends, the emergence of a Republican majority by the end of the decade. A first draft was completed by October of 1967, but Phillips delayed publication until after the 1968 election, the results of which "happily . . . meshed with the trends I had projected." The selection is taken from his 1969 book, *The Emerging Republican Majority*.

Phillips' intellectual credentials are impressive. His undergraduate work was at Colgate University, which he attended as a National Merit Scholar and a Phi Beta Kappa member. He graduated *magna cum laude*, with highest honors in political science, then went on for graduate work at the University of Edinburgh. Later he received an LLB from Harvard Law School, where he won the Bureau of National Affairs Prize in 1964.

In spite of this brilliant background in the citadels of academic liberalism, Phillips' political career immediately veered in the opposite direction. After graduating from Harvard Law School he served as administrative assistant to Paul Fino, the archconservative Congressman from the Bronx. Four years later he was special assistant to John Mitchell, President Nixon's campaign manager and Attorney General.

Whether these experiences induced or merely reinforced Phillips' attitudes, he appears today as an uncompromising and unapologetic opponent of all the social innovations of the sixties: wars on poverty, busing, maximum feasible participation, low-income housing, quota systems, counterculture, permissiveness, everything associated with Great Society liberalism. And, more to

*From Kevin Phillips, *The Emerging Republican Majority*, Ch. 6. Copyright © 1969 by Arlington House, New Rochelle, New York. All rights reserved. Reprinted by permission.

the point, Phillips believes that the great masses of Americans share his viewpoint. His thesis is that the party cleavage of the New Deal has now become inverted: whereas in the 1930's the Republicans were the party of a minority "Establishment"—voters in silk-stocking districts, rich suburbs, Boston's Beacon Hill, Eastern universities—today the Democrats have acquired this mantle, while the broad masses of nonaffluent whites have drifted into the waiting arms of the Republicans. The reason for this turnabout, Phillips believes, is that the leadership of the Democratic Party has been taken over by patronizing do-gooders, affluent liberals no less hostile to the working class than were their conservative counterparts a generation ago, only more disposed to hide their hostility behind a façade of social radicalism. Accordingly the working class, farmers and small businessmen—those "plain people" eulogized in the old Populist platform—have found a new home in a reconstructed Republican Party. "Sure, Hubert will carry Riverside Drive in November," Phillips told columnist Garry Wills in 1968. "La-de-dah. What will he do in Oklahoma?" As for the future, "When Hubie loses, [Eugene] McCarthy and Lowenstein backers are going to take the party so far to the Left they'll just become irrelevant. They'll do to it what our economic royalists did to us in 1936." He predicted a close election in 1968. "But you watch us in seventy-two. . . . I'd hate to be the opponent in that race."

The long-range meaning of the political upheaval of 1968 rests on the Republican opportunity to fashion a majority among the 57 per cent of the American electorate which voted to eject the Democratic Party from national power. To begin with, more than half of this protesting 57 per cent were firm Republicans from areas—Southern California to Long Island's Suffolk County—or sociocultural backgrounds with a growing GOP bias. Some voted for George Wallace, but most backed Richard Nixon, providing the bulk of his Election Day support. Only a small minority of 1968 Nixon backers—perhaps several million liberal Republicans and independents from Maine and Oregon to Fifth Avenue—cast what may be their last Republican presidential ballots because of the partisan re-alignment taking place. The third major anti-

Democratic voting stream of 1968—and the most decisive—was that of the fifteen million or so conservative Democrats who shunned Hubert Humphrey to divide about evenly between Richard Nixon and George Wallace. Such elements stretched from the "Okie" Great Central Valley of California to the mountain towns of Idaho, Florida's space centers, rural South Carolina, Bavarian Minnesota, the Irish sidewalks of New York and the Levittowns of Megalopolis. . . .

Although most of George Wallace's votes came from Democrats rather than Republicans, they were conservatives—Southerners, Borderers, German and Irish Catholics—who had been trending Republican prior to 1968. . . . The Wallace vote followed the cultural geography of obsolescent conservative (often Southern) Democratic tradition. There was no reliable Wallace backing among blue-collar workers and poor whites as a class; industrial centers in the Yankee sphere of influence from Duluth to Scranton, Fall River and Biddeford shunned the Alabama ex-governor with a mere 2 per cent to 3 per cent of the vote. Areas of eroding Democratic tradition were the great breeding grounds of Wallace voters.

In the South, Wallace drew principally on conservative Democrats quitting the party they had long succored and controlled. Generally speaking, Wallace's Southern strength was greatest in the Democratic Party's historic (pre-1964) lowland strongholds, while the Alabaman's worst Southern percentages came in the Republican highlands. White voters throughout most sections of the Deep South went two-to-one for Wallace. In the more Republican Outer South, only one white voter out of three supported the third-party candidate. In the South as a whole, 85 to 90 per cent of the white electorate cast Nixon or Wallace votes against the realigning national Democratic Party in 1968, an unprecedented magnitude of disaffection which indicates the availability of the Wallace vote to the future GOP.

Four of the five Wallace states had gone Republican in 1964, and although the Alabaman greatly enlarged the scope of Southern revolt by attracting most of the (poor white or Outer South Black Belt) Southerners who had hitherto resisted Republican or States Rights candidacies, much of his tide had already been flowing for

Goldwater. Nor does the Nixon Administration have to bid much ideologically for this electorate. Despite his success in enlarging the scope of white Southern revolt, George Wallace failed to reach far enough or strongly enough beyond the Deep South to give his American Independent Party the national base required for a viable future. Republican Nixon won most of the Outer South, establishing the GOP as the ascending party of the local white majority. Having achieved statewide success only in the Deep South, and facing competition from a Southern Republicanism mindful of its opportunity, the Wallace movement cannot maintain an adequate political base and is bound to serve, like past American third parties, as a way station for groups abandoning one party for another. Some Wallace voters were longtime Republicans, but the great majority were conservative Democrats who have been moving—and should continue to do so—towards the GOP.

The linkage of Wallace voting to the obsolescent Democratic loyalties of certain areas and groups can also be proved far beyond the old Confederacy. . . . The pattern of Wallace support in the Ohio Valley, instead of standing out in backlash-prone industrial areas, followed rural contours of traditional Democratic strength, moving farthest north along the Scioto River, central Ohio's roadway of Virginia and Kentucky migration. And in New York and Pennsylvania, . . . certain levels of Wallace support probed farthest north along the Susquehanna, Delaware and Hudson valleys, outliers of traditionally Democratic non-Yankee rural strength. Out West, Wallace percentages were greatest in the Oklahoma- and Texas-settled towns of California's Central Valley, the populist mining and logging counties of the Rocky Mountains, the traditionally Democratic Mormon reaches of Idaho, and in Alaska's long-Democratic sluice and sawmill districts.

In addition to Western or Southern Democrats of conservative or populist bent, Wallace also scored well among Catholics, but only in certain areas. From Maine to Michigan, across most of the belt of Yankee-settled territory where local cleavage, though changing, still pits Protestant Republicans against urban Catholic Democrats, the Catholic trend away from the Democrats was slight. However, in the greater New York area, as well as Gary and Cleveland, where minority group (Negro and/or Jewish) power has taken control of local Democratic machinery, Catholic backing of Wallace was considerable. Here . . . Catholics are leaving the Democratic Party.

The common denominator of Wallace support, Catholic or Protestant, is alienation from the Democratic Party and a strong trend—shown in other years and other contests—towards the GOP. Although most of Wallace's votes came from Democrats, he principally won those in motion between a Democratic past and a Republican future. In the last few weeks of the campaign, labor union activity, economic issues and the escalating two-party context of October, 1968, drew many Wallace-leaning Northern blue-collar workers back into the Democratic fold. Only those fully alienated by the national Democratic Party stuck with Wallace in the voting booth. Offered a three-party context, these sociopolitical streams preferred populist Wallace; a two-party context would have drawn them into the GOP. Three quarters or more of the Wallace electorate represented lost Nixon votes.

A few states—Mississippi or Alabama—may indulge in future third-party or states rights efforts. The Wallace party itself, however, has dubious prospects, being not a broad-based national grouping but a transient 1968 aggregation of conservative Democrats otherwise trending into the Republican Party. Generally speaking, the South is more realistic than its critics believe, and nothing more than an effective and responsibly conservative Nixon Administration is necessary to bring most of the Southern Wallace electorate into the fold against a Northeastern liberal Democratic presidential nominee. Abandonment of civil rights enforcement would be self-defeating. Maintenance of Negro voting rights in Dixie, far from being contrary to GOP interests, is essential if southern conservatives are to be pressured into switching to the Republican Party—for Negroes are beginning to seize control of the national Democratic Party in some Black Belt areas.

Successful moderate conservatism is also likely to attract to the Republican side some of the Northern blue-collar workers who flirted with George Wallace but ultimately backed Hubert Humphrey. Fears that a Republican administration would undermine Social Security, Medicare, collective bargaining and aid to education played a major part in keeping socially conservative blue-collar workers and senior citizens loyal to the 1968 Democratic candidate. Assuming that a Nixon administration can dispel these apprehensions, it ought to be able to repeat—with much more permanence—Eisenhower's great blue-collar success of 1956. Sociologically, the Republican Party is becoming much more lower-middle class and much less establishmentarian than it was during the Nineteen-Fifties, and pursuit of an increasing portion of the Northern blue-collar electorate—an expansion of its 1968 Catholic triumph in greater New York City—would be a logical extension of this trend.

Although the appeal of a successful Nixon Administration and the lack of a Wallace candidacy would greatly swell the 1972 Republican vote in the South, West, Border and the Catholic North, the 1972 GOP may well simultaneously lose a lesser number of 1968 supporters among groups reacting against the party's emerging Southern, Western and New York Irish majority . . . Yankees, Megalopolitan silk-stocking voters and Scandinavians from Maine across the Great Lakes to the Pacific all showed a distinct Democratic trend in the years between 1960 and 1968. Such disaffection will doubtlessly continue, but its principal impact has already been felt. Richard Nixon won only 38 per cent of the total 1968 presidential vote on Manhattan's rich East Side; he took only 44 per cent of the ballots in Scarsdale, the city's richest suburb; New England's Yankee counties and towns produced Nixon majorities down 10 per cent to 15 per cent from 1960 levels; fashionable San Francisco shifted toward the Democrats; and Scandinavian Minnesota and Washington state backed Humphrey, as did the Scandinavian northwest of Wisconsin.

. . . All of these locales shifted *towards* the Democrats during the 1960-68 period. Because the local re-alignment pivoted on liberal Republicans rather than conservative Democrats, these areas evidenced little or no support for George Wallace. . . . Beyond the bounds of states that went Democratic in 1968, the Yankee, silk-stocking establishmentarian and Scandinavian trends predominate only in Vermont, New Hampshire and Oregon. Although Northern California, Wisconsin, Ohio's old Western Reserve, central Iowa and parts of the Dakotas are likewise influenced, other conservative trends—those of Southern California suburbanites, German Catholics of the upper Farm Belt and the quasi-Southern Democrats of the Ohio Valley—should keep those states Republican. Yankee, Northeastern silk-stocking and Scandinavian disaffection with the GOP is concentrated in states which the party has already lost, and it menaces only a few states which the GOP won in 1968.

The upcoming cycle of American politics is likely to match a dominant Republican Party based in the Heartland, South and California against a minority Democratic Party based in the Northeast and the Pacific Northwest (and encompassing Southern as well as Northern Negroes). With such support behind it, the GOP can easily afford to lose the states of Massachusetts, New York and Michigan—and is likely to do so except in landslide years. Together with the District of Columbia, the top ten Humphrey states—Hawaii, Washington, Minnesota, Michigan, West Virginia, New York, Connecticut, Rhode Island, Massachusetts and Maine—should prove to be the core of national Democratic strength. . . . The new battlegrounds of quadrennial presidential politics are likely to be California, Ohio and Pennsylvania.

Unluckily for the Democrats, their major impetus is centered in stagnant Northern industrial states—and within those states, in old decaying cities, in a Yankee countryside that has fewer people than in 1900, and in the most expensive suburbs. Beyond this, in the South and West, the Democrats dominate only two expanding voting blocs—Latins and Negroes. From space-center Florida across the booming Texas plains to the Los Angeles-San Diego suburban corridor, the nation's fastest-growing areas are strongly Republican and conservative. Even in the Northeast, the few rapidly growing suburbs are conservative-trending areas. . . . Because of this demographic pattern, the South and West are gaining electoral votes and national political power at the expense of the Northeast. . . . The conservative Sun Belt cities are undergoing a population boom—and getting more conservative—while the old liberal cities of the Northeast decline. . . . The Northeast is steadily losing relative political importance to the Sun Belt.

One of the greatest political myths of the decade—a product of liberal self-interest—is that the Republican Party cannot attain national dominance without mobilizing liberal support in the big cities, appealing to "liberal" youth, empathizing with "liberal" urbanization, gaining substantial Negro support and courting the affluent young professional classes of "suburbia." The actual

CHART 142

The Decline in the Big City Presidential Vote, 1960-68

City*	Total Major Party Vote for President (In Thousands)		
	1960	1964	1968
New York City	3,081	2,811	2,591
Chicago	1,674	1,607	1,433
Los Angeles	1,053	1,079	1,012
Philadelphia	914	910	826
Detroit	743	681	598
Baltimore	317	317	290
Cleveland	338	302	263
St. Louis	304	268	221
Milwaukee	309	298	256
San Francisco	341	324	272
Boston	292	255	225

demographic and political facts convey a very different message.
. . . The big city political era is over in the United States. Chart
142 lists the considerable 1960-68 slippage in the presidential vote
cast by the leading big cities. With Negroes moving into the cities,
whites have moved out. Moreover, white urban populations are
getting increasingly conservative. Richard Nixon and George
Wallace together won 40 per cent of the vote in liberal New York
City. Perhaps more to the point, leading big city states like New
York, Michigan and Massachusetts are no longer necessary for
national Republican victory.

Youth is important, but voters under 25 cast only 7.4 per cent of
the nation's ballots in 1968. And while many Northeastern young
people are more liberal and Democratic than their parents
—especially the affluent and anarchic progeny of the
Establishment—the reverse seems to be true in Southern, Border,
Rocky Mountain, Catholic, lower middle class and working-class
areas. In these locales, the young electorate's trend against local
political tradition helps the GOP, as does resentment of the blyth
[*sic*] nihilism of the children of the affluent society.

While urbanization *is* changing the face of America, and the

*The eleven largest cities of 1960 (excluding Sun Belt Houston); several will no longer
be on the list when the 1970 Census is completed.

GOP must take political note of this fact, it presents the opposite of a problem. A generation ago, the coming of age of the working-class central cities condemned the Republican Party to minority status, but the new "urbanization"—suburbanization is often a better description—is a middle-class impetus shaping the same ignominy for the Democrats. All across the nation, the fastest-growing urban areas are steadily increasing their *Republican* pluralities, while the old central cities—seat of the New Deal era—are casting steadily fewer votes for Democratic liberalism. No major American city is losing population so rapidly as arch-Democratic and establishmentarian Boston, while the fastest-growing urban area in the nation is Southern California's staunchly conservative Orange County, and the fastest growing cities are conservative strongholds like Phoenix, Dallas, Houston, Anaheim, San Diego and Fort Lauderdale.

Substantial Negro support is not necessary to national Republican victory in light of the 1968 election returns. Obviously, the GOP can build a winning coalition without Negro votes. Indeed, Negro-Democratic mutual identification was a major source of Democratic loss—and Republican or American Independent Party profit—in many sections of the nation.

. . . The liberal and Democratic 1960-68 shifts of a few (now atypical) silk-stocking counties were dwarfed by the conservative trends of the vast new tracts of middle-class suburbia. Actually, the Democratic upswing in a number of rich suburban areas around New York, Boston and Philadelphia is nothing more than an extension of the liberal establishmentarian behavior of Manhattan's East Side, Boston's Beacon Hill and Philadelphia's Rittenhouse Square. Typical suburban behavior is something else again.

Centered in the Sun Belt, the nation's heaviest suburban growth is solidly middle-class and conservative. Contemporary suburban expansion in the Northeast pales next to the spread of the Florida, Texas, Arizona and Southern California suburbs. Rapid, although less spectacular, suburban growth is occurring in the areas around Camden (New Jersey), Washington, D.C., Richmond, Atlanta, Memphis, St. Louis, Chicago, Oklahoma City, Tulsa and Denver. These suburbs are also conservative, often highly so. And even the few fast-growing Northeastern suburban counties—Suffolk, New

York; Burlington, New Jersey; Prince Georges, Maryland—are conservative-trending, middle-class sections. . . . The principal exception is Maryland's rich but fast-expanding Montgomery County, liberal seat of the upper echelons of Washington's federal bureaucracy.

From a national perspective, the silk-stocking liberal suburbs of Boston, New York, Philadelphia, San Francisco and (to a lesser extent) Chicago and Washington cast only a minute fraction of the ballots wielded by the preponderance of unfashionable lower-middle- and middle-income suburbs. And because more and more new suburbanites come from lower-middle-income backgrounds, this gap should widen.

The National Commission on Urban Problems, chaired by former Illinois Senator Paul Douglas, has drawn attention to the increasingly powerful shift of blue-collar and lower-middle-class population to suburbia, but surprisingly few establishment liberals understand or admit these demographic facts of life. Instead, they typically portray the large conservative majority of Americans as a mere obsolescent and shrinking periphery of society, meanwhile painting their own peer group as the expanding segment of the nation committed to cosmopolitan thinking, technological sophistication and cultural change.

This myopia has considerable precedent. Since the days of Alexander Hamilton and the Federalists, the United States—and the Northeast in particular—has periodically supported a privileged elite, blind to the needs and interests of the large national majority. The corporate welfarists, planners and academicians of the Liberal Establishment are the newest of these elites, and their interests—for one thing, a high and not necessarily too productive rate of government social, educational, scientific and research spending—are as vested as those of Coolidge-Hoover era financiers and industrialists. The great political upheaval of the Nineteen-Sixties is not that of Senator Eugene McCarthy's relatively small group of upper-middle-class and intellectual supporters, but a populist revolt of the American masses who have been elevated by prosperity to middle-class status and conservatism. *Their* revolt is against the caste, policies and taxation of the mandarins of Establishment liberalism.

Granted that the new populist coalition includes very few

CHART 143

Central City-Surburban Apartheid: The Demographic Projections of the President's National Commission on Urban Problems, July, 1968

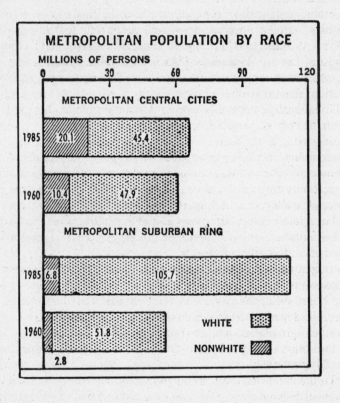

Note—As the chart indicates, the Commission expects the nation's growth over the next twenty years to ignore the cities and focus on suburbia. Indeed, only the urban growth of the South and West will prevent a sharp decline in the nation's central city population based on the steady shrinkage of northeastern central cities.

Negroes—they have become almost entirely Democratic and exert very little influence on the GOP—black solidarity within the Democratic Party is rapidly enlarging Negro influence and job opportunities in many old Northern central cities. In New York, few Negroes have deserted the Democratic Party even to support

Republican liberals Rockefeller, Javits, and Lindsay. . . . These intensely Democratic Negro loyalties are not rooted in fear of the GOP or its promise of a return to law and order, but in a realization that the Democratic Party can serve as a vehicle for Negro advancement—just as other groups have used politics to climb the social and economic ladder of urban America.

Ethnic polarization is a longstanding hallmark of American politics, not an unprecedented and menacing development of 1968. As illustrated throughout this book, ethnic and cultural division has so often shaped American politics that, given the immense midcentury impact of Negro enfranchisement and integration, reaction to this change almost inevitably had to result in political realignment. Moreover, American history has another example of a persecuted minority—the Nineteenth-Century Irish—who, in the face of considerable discrimination and old-stock animosity, likewise poured their ethnic numbers into the Democratic Party alone, winning power, jobs and socioeconomic opportunity through local political skill rather than the benevolence of usually-Republican national administrations.

For a half-century after the Civil War, the regular Democratic fidelity of the unpopular Irish city machines helped keep much of the nation Republican, and it seems possible that rising Negro participation in (national) Democratic politics from Manhattan to Mississippi may play a similar role in the post-1968 cycle. Growing Negro influence in—and conservative Southern, Western and Catholic departure from—the Democratic Party also suggests that Northeastern liberals ought to be able to dominate the party, which in turn must accelerate the sectional and ideological re-alignment already underway.

To the extent that the ethnic and racial overtones of American political behavior and alignment are appreciated, they are often confused or mis-stated. For example, far from being opposed by all non-whites, Richard Nixon was strongly supported by one non-white group—the Chinese. San Francisco's Chinese electorate was more Republican in 1968 than the city's white population. Nor is today's Republican Party Protestant rather than Catholic. In New York City, the party is becoming the vehicle of the Italians and Irish, and in the Upper Farm Belt—Wisconsin, Minnesota and North Dakota—German Catholics are moving to the fore. From the first days of the Republic, American politics have been a maze of ethnic, cultural and sectional oppositions and loyalties, and this has not deterred progress or growth. The new popular conservative majority has many ethnic strains, and portraits showing it as a white Anglo-Saxon Protestant monolith are highly misleading.

The emerging Republican majority spoke clearly in 1968 for a shift away from the sociological jurisprudence, moral permissiveness, experimental residential, welfare and educational programing and massive federal spending by which the Liberal (mostly Democratic) Establishment sought to propagate liberal institutions and ideology—and all the while reap growing economic benefits. The dominion of this impetus is inherent in the list of Republican-trending groups and potentially Republican Wallace electorates of 1968: Southerners, Borderers, Germans, Scotch-Irish, Pennsylvania Dutch, Irish, Italians, Eastern Europeans and other urban Catholics, middle-class suburbanites, Sun Belt residents, Rocky Mountain and Pacific Interior populists. Democrats among these groups were principally alienated from their party by its social programs and increasing identification with the Northeastern Establishment and ghetto alike. Except among isolationist Germans, resentment of the Vietnamese war, far from helping to forge the GOP majority, actually produced *Democratic* gains among the groups most affected: silk-stocking Megalopolitans, the San Francisco-Berkeley-Madison-Ann Arbor electorate, Scandinavian progressives and Jews. As for the Republican trend groups, nothing characterizes their outlook so much as a desire to dispel the Liberal Establishment's philosophy of taxation and redistribution (partly to itself) and reverse the encroachment of government in the social life of the nation.

Shorn of power, stripped of vested interests in misleading and unsuccessful programs, the Liberal Establishment may narrow its gap between words and deeds which helped to drive racial and youthful minorities into open revolt. So changed, Democratic liberalism will once again become a vital and creative force in national politics, usually too innovative to win a presidential race, but injecting a needed leavening of humanism into the middle-class *realpolitik* of the new Republican coalition.

Because the Republicans are little dependent on the Liberal

Establishment or urban Negroes—the two groups most intimately, though dissimilarly, concerned with present urban and welfare policies—they have the political freedom to disregard the multitude of vested interests which have throttled national urban policy. The GOP is particularly lucky not to be weighted down with commitment to the political blocs, power brokers and poverty concessionaires of the decaying central cities of the North, now that national growth is shifting to suburbia, the South and the West. The American future lies in a revitalized countryside, a demographically ascendant Sun Belt and suburbia, and new towns—perhaps mountainside linear cities astride monorails 200 miles from Phoenix, Memphis or Atlanta. National policy will have to direct itself towards this future and its constituencies; and perhaps an administration so oriented can also deal realistically with the central cities where Great Society political largesse has so demonstrably failed.

When new eras and alignments have evolved in American politics, the ascending party has ridden the economic and demographic wave of the future: with Jefferson, a nation pushing inland from the Federalist seaboard and Tidewater; with Jackson, the trans-Appalachian New West; with Lincoln, the free-soil West and industrial North; with McKinley, a full-blown industrial North feeding from a full dinner pail; and with Roosevelt, the emergence of the big cities and the coming of age of the immigrant masses. Now it is Richard Nixon's turn to build a new era on the immense middle-class impetus of Sun Belt and suburbia. Thus, it is appropriate that much of the emerging Republican majority lies in the top growth states (California, Arizona, Texas and Florida) or new suburbia, while Democratic trends correlate with stability and decay (New England, New York City, Michigan, West Virginia and San Francisco-Berkeley).

. . . The GOP core areas are the Mountain, Farm and Outer South states. The Deep South will become a GOP core area once it abandons third-party schemes. The Democratic stronghold is obvious: New York and New England. Most of the upcoming cycle's serious presidential campaign strategy will relate to three battleground areas: (1) the Pacific; (2) the Ohio-Mississippi Valley (Ohio, Indiana, Illinois, Kentucky and Missouri); and (3) the non-Yankee Northeast (New Jersey, Pennsylvania, Delaware and

Maryland). Overall trends favor the Republicans in each of these battlegrounds.

It is doubtful whether either party could turn back the clock, but neither has attempted to do so. The 1968 election returns were barely final before Richard Nixon announced that he was transferring his voting residence from New York to Florida, and picked a cabinet notably short on representatives of the Northeastern Establishment. And the Democrats waited only a little longer to replace Louisiana's Russell Long with Massachusetts' Edward Kennedy as their Senate Whip. A new era has begun.

V. LEFT-WING POPULISM

The movement somewhat inaccurately labeled "the New Left" was born in the early 1960's. It was born, at least partly, out of disgust at the liberalism inherited from the 1950's.

Arthur Schlesinger helped to set the mood of 1950's liberalism in a book entitled *The Vital Center*, published in 1949. The true reformer, Schlesinger contended, must not be a "wailer," criticizing our political system from the sidelines while "rejecting practical responsibility." He must instead learn "the facts of life through the exercise of power." The liberal strategy for reform was not to fight the establishment but to join it. The moral polarities of radical movements were to be replaced by an objective and clinical approach to reform. The liberal always liked to think of himself as tough-minded; he did not see heroes and villains but a set of problems in America which needed solutions. What America needed, Schlesinger and his colleagues believed, were not banner-waving movements outside of government but intellectual elites within it, elites prepared to approach social problems in a calm and scientific atmosphere. They welcomed a strong Presidency as a means of effecting reforms through administrative means, free from politics and passion. By the end of the decade they believed that the stage was set for this problem-solving approach to reform: Daniel Bell and Seymour Martin Lipset, both prominent liberals, published essays on "The End of Ideology."

But to many, particularly the young civil rights workers who had risked their lives down South in the early sixties, these liberal promises seemed hollow. They had experienced a particularly vicious side of America, an America beyond the reach of reason or calm mediation. They had met not "problems" but villains—the very creatures which Schlesinger had consigned to "political soap opera." And they endured the most horrifying persecution with little or no assistance from the Kennedy Administration. The last point needs emphasis. Here was the archetypal liberal President, who had promised "vigor" in solving the nation's ills, delaying and temporizing in the enforcement of the most basic rights: to vote, to petition and demonstrate peacefully, to go to school with people of other races. Life is "complicated," Schlesinger had said. But there was nothing at all complicated here; the Constitution and the Supreme Court had put these questions beyond the reach of dispute. To the young activists of the early sixties it was liberalism, not life, which was excessively complicated.

As the decade wore on, liberalism took on a more sinister aspect in the minds of the young idealists. When President Johnson, aided and abetted by his liberal advisers, escalated the war in Vietnam and invaded the Dominican Republic, they began to suspect not merely that liberalism was not solving the problems but that it *was* the problem. The young people had by now rediscovered C. Wright Mills, who had excoriated the Pentagon planners all during the 1950's. What was Cold War "tough-mindedness" to the liberals was "crackpot realism" to Mills. What was "practical responsibility" to Schlesinger was "cooptation" to Mills. What was a benevolent federal government to the liberals was an "interlocking directorate" of generals, bureaucrats, and corporate chieftains to Mills. All of this seemed frighteningly relevant to the New Left in the mid-sixties.

Aside from the substantive issues of racism and imperialism, and perhaps more important than either, was what Mills had called "the conservative mood" in America. Schlesinger's "realism" seemed too much like cynicism to the young idealists of the sixties. The liberal's "end of ideology" had itself become an ideology —an apology for the *status quo*, a convenient cop-out for young men on the make, concentrating on grades, social life, draft deferments, and the academic rat race.

One cannot read many New Left tracts without seeing that the real thrust was not political or economic, but moral. It would banish war, poverty, and racism on the way to the larger end of dispelling the spiritual emptiness of America. This is what distinguished it both from liberalism and from the Old (Marxist) Left, neither of which would have anything to do with such "sentimental" questions. And it was this emphasis on renewal and regeneration that raised again what the liberals of the fifties had scorned and debunked and, they thought, interred forever: the old-old left, the populist tradition of revivalist politics.

The differences between vintage populism and the New Left are obvious. The constituencies are almost exactly antithetical, since the New Left attracted university students from affluent families—those whom vintage populism identified with wealth and privilege. (Sometimes members of the New Left reinforced these suspicions by sneering at "the middle classes," who comprise a large part of the "plain people" in America.) But in one important respect—in what Richard Hofstadter called its "traffic in moral absolutes, its exalted moral tone"—there can be no doubt that the populist tradition was revived and reinvigorated by the young moralists of the 1960's.

And with much the same results. Like the populists of old, the New Leftists were long on moral uplift but short on doctrinal discipline. They were from the outset incorrigible individualists, each following his own personal, "authentic" interpretation of the grandiose goals it had set for itself—"participatory democracy," "a humanist reformation," and so on. There was to be no need for ideological consensus. They would change the world, Carl Oglesby declared, "not in the name of this or that blueprint or 'ism,' but in the name of simple human decency and democracy and the vision that wise and brave men saw in the time of our own Revolution."

The result of this doctrinal vacuity should have been predictable. By the end of the 1960's the Students for a Democratic Society, the central organization of the New Left, had broken into a spectrum of factions ranging from metaphysicians to bomb-throwers, each with its own version of what the wise and brave men saw during the American Revolution.

At the beginning of the 1970's some ambitious attempts were made to pick up some of the pieces of the New Left and graft them more securely to the old populist tradition. Jack Newfield, who had earlier eulogized "the prophetic minority," co-authored a tract which combined excellent muckraking with a somewhat more dubious attempt to put together a new majority composed of everyone from Gloria Steinem to the Irish cop from Bay Ridge. On the dustjacket of the book Nicholas Johnson, commissioner of the Federal Communications Commission, is quoted as saying that "Any Presidential candidate who would read, believe and run on this book would win. . . ." Whether or not George McGovern read the book, his campaign did attempt to forge such a coalition in the 1972 Presidential race. At its conclusion it was clear that McGovern had won only the Gloria Steinem part of the coalition. The Irish cop, perversely enough, insisted on *his* version of populism.

A. *C. Wright Mills:* "The Power Elite"*

Sociology, especially American sociology, would seem to be an unlikely environment for producing populists. From its introduction at the end of the nineteenth century, American sociology has been conservative and fatalistic, contemplating with awe a social system which seemed bound to iron laws of nature. By the 1940's sociology in America had become, if anything, more timid and scholastic. Mountains of data were assembled to "prove" trivialities. "Value judgments" were discouraged, as were any attempts to posit alternatives to the *status quo*. A patina of pretentious jargon had been acquired, tending to isolate the profession from the general public.

C. Wright Mills (1916-1962) was a unique sociologist in his time, then, because he brought to the profession a quality conspicuously lacking among his colleagues: the capacity for indignation. By the end of his life he had, quite openly, taken to pamphleteering, but even in his earlier and more scholarly writings he never concealed his outrage at what he saw as the domination of

America by an irresponsible triumvirate of administrators, generals, and the very rich.

Mills' perspective, which seemed shocking to many of his colleagues during the forties and fifties, is not an unfamiliar one to the student of American populism. What Mills did, in fact, was to forge a link between sociology and the great tradition of populist muckraking from Henry Demarest Lloyd to Gerald Nye. Mills may not have been fully conscious of this relationship, since he considered populism only in the historical form it had assumed during the 1890's.

But the similarities between Mills and his populist predecessors are much too plain to be ignored. Like them, and unlike the New Deal liberals, he detested government bureaucrats, and big government in general, as heartily as he detested big business. Like the populists he had no hesitation in describing the various elites in America as linked together in a gigantic conspiracy against the public—a contention regarded as either naive or paranoidal by his liberal critics. Like any good populist he had the grandest of scorn for the proposition, dear to liberal economists like A. A. Berle, that big business was gradually reforming itself. Like the populists, and unlike his *wertfrei* colleagues, he was a moralist, deploring the "higher immorality" of government and corporate corruption. Consequently he was not merely a social scientist but a reformer, committed not merely to describing the world but to changing it. "Mills," says Irving Horowitz in his introduction to Mills' collected essays, "had a populist suspicion for any measure of a man that failed to begin and conclude with what he could do in the world and make of the world."

In reaching back, whether consciously or not, to an old tradition of American populism he was to find the ingredients for a new activism during the sixties: an insistence on the social relevance of knowledge, a suspicion of "official" reform, and, despite his fears of an emerging "mass society," an ultimate trust in the wisdom and common sense of the general public.

Reprinted as the selection is Chapter One of Mills' *The Power Elite*.

The powers of ordinary men are circumscribed by the everyday worlds in which they live, yet even in these rounds of job, family, and neighborhood they often seem driven by forces they can neither understand nor govern. "Great changes" are beyond their control, but affect their conduct and outlook none the less. The very framework of modern society confines them to projects not their own, but from every side, such changes now press upon the men and women of the mass society, who accordingly feel that they are without purpose in an epoch in which they are without power.

But not all men are in this sense ordinary. As the means of information and of power are centralized, some men come to occupy positions in American society from which they can look down upon, so to speak, and by their decisions mightily affect, the everyday worlds of ordinary men and women. They are not made by their jobs; they set up and break down jobs for thousands of others; they are not confined by simple family responsibilities; they can escape. They may live in many hotels and houses, but they are bound by no one community. They need not merely "meet the demands of the day and hour"; in some part, they create these demands, and cause others to meet them. Whether or not they profess their power, their technical and political experience of it far transcends that of the underlying population. What Jacob Burkhardt said of "great men," most Americans might well say of their elite: "They are all that we are not."[1]

The power elite is composed of men whose positions enable them to transcend the ordinary environments of ordinary men and women; they are in positions to make decisions having major consequences. Whether they do or do not make such decisions is less important than the fact that they do occupy such pi tal positions: their failure to act, their failure to make decision is itself an act that is often of greater consequence than the decisions they do make. For they are in command of the major hierarchies and organizations of modern society. They rule the big corporations. They run the machinery of the state and claim its prerogatives. They direct the military establishment. They occupy the strategic command posts of the social structure, in which are now centered the effective means of the power and the wealth and the celebrity which they enjoy.

The power elite are not solitary rulers. Advisers and consultants, spokesmen and opinion-makers are often the captains of their higher thought and decision. Immediately below the elite are the professional politicians of the middle levels of power, in the Congress and in the pressure groups, as well as among the new and old upper classes of town and city and region. Mingling with them, in curious ways which we shall explore, are those professional celebrities who live by being continually displayed but are never, so long as they remain celebrities, displayed enough. If such celebrities are not at the head of any dominating hierarchy, they do often have the power to distract the attention of the public or afford sensations to the masses, or, more directly, to gain the ear of those who do occupy positions of direct power. More or less unattached, as critics of morality and technicians of power, as spokesmen of God and creators of mass sensibility, such celebrities and consultants are part of the immediate scene in which the drama of the elite is enacted. But that drama itself is centered in the command posts of the major institutional hierarchies.

1

The truth about the nature and the power of the elite is not some secret which men of affairs know but will not tell. Such men hold quite various theories about their own roles in the sequence of event and decision. Often they are uncertain about their roles, and even more often they allow their fears and their hopes to affect their assessment of their own power. No matter how great their actual power, they tend to be less acutely aware of it than of the resistances of others to its use. Moreover most American men of affairs have learned well the rhetoric of public relations, in some cases even to the point of using it when they are alone, and thus coming to believe it. The personal awareness of the actors is only one of the several sources one must examine in order to understand the higher circles. Yet many who believe that there is no elite, or at any rate none of any consequence, rest their argument upon what men of affairs believe about themselves, or at least assert in public.

There is, however, another view: those who feel, even if vaguely, that a compact and powerful elite of great importance does now prevail in America often base that feeling upon the

historical trend of our time. They have felt, for example, the
domination of the military event, and from this they infer that
generals and admirals, as well as other men of decision influenced
by them, must be enormously powerful. They hear that the Congress has again abdicated to a handful of men decisions clearly
related to the issue of war or peace. They know that the bomb was
dropped over Japan in the name of the United States of America,
although they were at no time consulted about the matter. They
feel that they live in a time of big decisions; they know that they are
not making any. Accordingly, as they consider the present as
history, they infer that at its center, making decisions or failing to
make them, there must be an elite of power.

On the one hand, those who share this feeling about big historical events assume that there is an elite and that its power is great.
On the other hand, those who listen carefully to the reports of men
apparently involved in the great decisions often do not believe that
there is an elite whose powers are of decisive consequence.

Both views must be taken into account, but neither is adequate.
The way to understand the power of the American elite lies neither
solely in recognizing the historic scale of events nor in accepting
the personal awareness reported by men of apparent decision.
Behind such men and behind the events of history, linking the two,
are the major institutions of modern society. These hierarchies of
state and corporation and army constitute the means of power; as
such they are now of a consequence not before equaled in human
history—and at their summits, there are now those command posts
of modern society which offer us the sociological key to an
understanding of the role of the higher circles in America. Within
American society, major national power now resides in the
economic, the political, and the military domains. Other institutions seem off to the side of modern history, and, on occasion, duly
subordinated to these. No family is as directly powerful in national
affairs as any major corporation; no church is as directly powerful
in the external biographies of young men in America today as the
military establishment; no college is as powerful in the shaping of
momentous events as the National Security Council. Religious,
educational, and family institutions are not autonomous centers of
national power; on the contrary, these decentralized areas are

increasingly shaped by the big three, in which developments of decisive and immediate consequence now occur.

Families and churches and schools adapt to modern life; governments and armies and corporations shape it; and, as they do so, they turn these lesser institutions into means for their ends. Religious institutions provide chaplains to the armed forces where they are used as a means of increasing the effectiveness of its morale to kill. Schools select and train men for their jobs in corporations and their specialized tasks in the armed forces. The extended family has, of course, long been broken up by the industrial revolution, and now the son and the father are removed from the family, by compulsion if need be, whenever the army of the state sends out the call. And the symbols of all these lesser institutions are used to legitimate the power and the decisions of the big three.

The life-fate of the modern individual depends not only upon the family into which he was born or which he enters by marriage, but increasingly upon the corporation in which he spends the most alert hours of his best years; not only upon the school where he is educated as a child and adolescent, but also upon the state which touches him throughout his life; not only upon the church in which on occasion he hears the word of God, but also upon the army in which he is disciplined.

If the centralized state could not rely upon the inculcation of nationalist loyalties in public and private schools, its leaders would promptly seek to modify the decentralized educational system. If the bankruptcy rate among the top five hundred corporations were as high as the general divorce rate among the thirty-seven million married couples, there would be economic catastrophe on an international scale. If members of armies gave to them no more of their lives than do believers to the churches to which they belong, there would be a military crisis.

Within each of the big three, the typical institutional unit has become enlarged, has become administrative, and, in the power of its decisions, has become centralized. Behind these developments there is a fabulous technology, for as institutions, they have incorporated this technology and guide it, even as it shapes and paces their developments.

The economy—once a great scatter of small productive units in autonomous balance—has become dominated by two or three hundred giant corporations, administratively and politically interrelated, which together hold the keys to economic decisions.

The political order, once a decentralized set of several dozen states with a weak spinal cord, has become a centralized, executive establishment which has taken up into itself many powers previously scattered, and now enters into each and every cranny of the social structure.

The military order, once a slim establishment in a context of distrust fed by state militia, has become the largest and most expensive feature of government, and, although well versed in smiling public relations, now has all the grim and clumsy efficiency of a sprawling bureaucratic domain.

In each of these institutional areas, the means of power at the disposal of decision makers have increased enormously; their central executive powers have been enhanced; within each of them modern administrative routines have been elaborated and tightened up.

As each of these domains becomes enlarged and centralized, the consequences of its activities become greater, and its traffic with the others increases. The decisions of a handful of corporations bear upon military and political as well as upon economic developments around the world. The decisions of the military establishment rest upon and grievously affect political life as well as the very level of economic activity. The decisions made within the political domain determine economic activities and military programs. There is no longer, on the one hand, an economy, and, on the other hand, a political order containing a military establishment unimportant to politics and to money-making. There is a political economy linked, in a thousand ways, with military institutions and decisions. On each side of the world-split running through central Europe and around the Asiatic rimlands, there is an ever-increasing interlocking of economic, military, and political structures.[2] If there is government intervention in the corporate economy, so is there corporate intervention in the governmental process. In the structural sense, this triangle of power is the source of the interlocking directorate that is most important for the historical structure of the present.

The fact of the interlocking is clearly revealed at each of the points of crisis of modern capitalist society—slump, war, and boom. In each, men of decision are led to an awareness of the interdependence of the major institutional orders. In the nineteenth century, when the scale of all institutions was smaller, their liberal integration was achieved in the automatic economy, by an autonomous play of market forces, and in the automatic political domain, by the bargain and the vote. It was then assumed that out of the imbalance and friction that followed the limited decisions then possible a new equilibrium would in due course emerge. That can no longer be assumed, and it is not assumed by the men at the top of each of the three dominant hierarchies.

For given the scope of their consequences, decisions—and indecisions—in any one of these ramify into the others, and hence top decisions tend either to become co-ordinated or to lead to a commanding indecision. It has not always been like this. When numerous small entrepreneurs made up the economy, for example, many of them could fail and the consequences still remain local; political and military authorities did not intervene. But now, given political expectations and military commitments, can they afford to allow key units of the private corporate economy to break down in slump? Increasingly, they do intervene in economic affairs, and as they do so, the controlling decisions in each order are inspected by agents of the other two, and economic, military, and political structures are interlocked.

At the pinnacle of each of the three enlarged and centralized domains, there have arisen those higher circles which make up the economic, the political, and the military elites. At the top of the economy, among the corporate rich, there are the chief executives; at the top of the political order, the members of the political directorate; at the top of the military establishment, the elite of soldier-statesmen clustered in and around the Joint Chiefs of Staff and the upper echelon. As each of these domains has coincided with the others, as decisions tend to become total in their consequence, the leading men in each of the three domains of power —the warlords, the corporation chieftains, the political directorate —tend to come together, to form the power elite of America.

* * *

2

The higher circles in and around these command posts are often thought of in terms of what their members possess: they have a greater share than other people of the things and experiences that are most highly valued. From this point of view, the elite are simply those who have the most of what there is to have, which is generally held to include money, power, and prestige—as well as all the ways of life to which these lead.[3] But the elite are not simply those who have the most, for they could not "have the most" were it not for their positions in the great institutions. For such institutions are the necessary bases of power, of wealth, and of prestige, and at the same time, the chief means of exercising power, of acquiring and retaining wealth, and of cashing in the higher claims for prestige.

By the powerful we mean, of course, those who are able to realize their will, even if others resist it. No one, accordingly, can be truly powerful unless he has access to the command of major institutions, for it is over these institutional means of power that the truly powerful are, in the first instance, powerful. Higher politicians and key officials of government command such institutional power; so do admirals and generals, and so do the major owners and executives of the larger corporations. Not all power, it is true, is anchored in and exercised by means of such institutions, but only within and through them can power be more or less continuous and important.

Wealth also is acquired and held in and through institutions. The pyramid of wealth cannot be understood merely in terms of the very rich; for the great inheriting families, as we shall see, are now supplemented by the corporate institutions of modern society: every one of the very rich families has been and is closely connected—always legally and frequently managerially as well—with one of the multi-million dollar corporations.

The modern corporation is the prime source of wealth, but, in latter-day capitalism, the political apparatus also opens and closes many avenues to wealth. The amount as well as the source of income, the power over consumer's goods as well as over productive capital, are determined by position within the political economy. If our interest in the very rich goes beyond their lavish or their miserly consumption, we must examine their relations to modern forms of corporate property as well as to the state; for such relations now determine the chances of men to secure big property and to receive high income.

Great prestige increasingly follows the major institutional units of the social structure. It is obvious that prestige depends, often quite decisively, upon access to the publicity machines that are now a central and normal feature of all the big institutions of modern America. Moreover, one feature of these hierarchies of corporation, state, and military establishment is that their top positions are increasingly interchangeable. One result of this is the accumulative nature of prestige. Claims for prestige, for example, may be initially based on military roles, then expressed in and augmented by an educational institution run by corporate executives, and cashed in, finally, in the political order where, for General Eisenhower and those he represents, power and prestige finally meet at the very peak. Like wealth and power, prestige tends to be cumulative: the more of it you have the more you can get. These values also tend to be translatable into one another: the wealthy find it easier than the poor to gain power; those with status find it easier than those without it to control opportunities for wealth.

If we took the one hundred most powerful men in America, the one hundred wealthiest, and the one hundred most celebrated away from the institutional positions they now occupy, away from their resources of men and women and money, away from the media of mass communication that are now focused upon them—then they would be powerless and poor and uncelebrated. For power is not of a man. Wealth does not center in the person of the wealthy. Celebrity is not inherent in any personality. To be celebrated, to be wealthy, to have power requires access to major institutions, for the institutional positions men occupy determine in large part their chances to have and to hold these valued experiences.

3

The people of the higher circles may also be conceived as members of a top social stratum, as a set of groups whose members know one another, see one another socially and at business, and so, in making decisions, take one another into account. The elite, according to this conception, feel themselves to be, and are felt by others to be, the inner circle of "the upper social classes."[4] They form a more or less compact social and psychological entity; they have become self-conscious members of a social class. People are either accepted into this class or they are not, and there is a qualitative split, rather than merely a numerical scale, separating them from those who are not elite. They are more or less aware of themselves as a social class and they behave toward one another differently from the way they do toward members of other classes. They accept one another, understand one another, marry one another, tend to work and to think if not together at least alike.

Now, we do not want by our definition to prejudge whether the elite of the command posts are conscious members of such a socially recognized class, or whether considerable proportions of the elite derive from such a clear and distinct class. These are matters to be investigated. Yet in order to be able to recognize what we intend to investigate, we must note something that all biographies and memoirs of the wealthy and the powerful and the eminent make clear: no matter what else they may be, the people of these higher circles are involved in a set of overlapping "crowds" and intricately connected "cliques." There is a kind of mutual attraction among those who "sit on the same terrace"—although this often becomes clear to them, as well as to others, only at the point at which they feel the need to draw the line; only when, in their common defense, they come to understand what they have in common, and so close their ranks against outsiders.

The idea of such ruling stratum implies that most of its members have similar social origins, that throughout their lives they maintain a network of informal connections, and that to some degree there is an interchangeability of position between the various hierarchies of money and power and celebrity. We must, of course, note at once that if such an elite stratum does exist, its social visibility and its form, for very solid historical reasons, are quite different from those of the noble cousinhoods that once ruled various European nations.

That American society has never passed through a feudal epoch is of decisive importance to the nature of the American elite, as well as to American society as a historic whole. For it means that no nobility or aristocracy, established before the capitalist era, has stood in tense opposition to the higher bourgeoisie. It means that this bourgeoisie has monopolized not only wealth but prestige and power as well. It means that no set of noble families has commanded the top positions and monopolized the values that are generally held in high esteem; and certainly that no set has done so explicitly by inherited right. It means that no high church dignitaries or court nobilities, no entrenched landlords with honorific accouterments, no monopolists of high army posts have opposed the enriched bourgeoisie and in the name of birth and prerogative successfully resisted its self-making.

But this does *not* mean that there are no upper strata in the United States. That they emerged from a "middle class" that had no recognized aristocratic superiors does not mean they remained middle class when enormous increases in wealth made their own superiority possible. Their origins and their newness may have made the upper strata less visible in America than elsewhere. But in America today there are in fact tiers and ranges of wealth and power of which people in the middle and lower ranks know very little and may not even dream. There are families who, in their well-being, are quite insulated from the economic jolts and lurches felt by the merely prosperous and those farther down the scale. There are also men of power who in quite small groups make decisions of enormous consequence for the underlying population.

The American elite entered modern history as a virtually unopposed bourgeoisie. No national bourgeoisie, before or since, has had such opportunities and advantages. Having no military neighbors, they easily occupied an isolated continent stocked with natural resources and immensely inviting to a willing labor force. A framework of power and an ideology for its justification were already at hand. Against mercantilist restriction, they inherited the principle of *laissez-faire*; against Southern planters, they imposed the principle of industrialism. The Revolutionary War put an end to colonial pretensions to nobility, as loyalists fled the country and many estates were broken up. The Jacksonian upheaval with its status revolution put an end to pretensions to monopoly of descent by the old New England families. The Civil War broke the power, and so in due course the prestige, of the ante-bellum South's claimants for the higher esteem. The tempo of the whole capitalist development made it impossible for an inherited nobility to develop and endure in America.

No fixed ruling class anchored in agrarian life and coming to flower in military glory, could contain in America the historic thrust of commerce and industry, or subordinate to itself the capitalist elite—as capitalists were subordinated, for example, in Germany and Japan. Nor could such a ruling class anywhere in the world contain that of the United States when industrialized violence came to decide history. Witness the fate of Germany and Japan in the two world wars of the twentieth century; and indeed the fate of Britain herself and her model ruling class, as New York became the inevitable economic, and Washington the inevitable political capital of the western capitalist world.

4

The elite who occupy the command posts may be seen as the possessors of power and wealth and celebrity; they may be seen as members of the upper stratum of a capitalistic society. They may also be defined in terms of psychological and moral criteria, as certain kinds of selected individuals. So defined, the elite, quite simply, are people of superior character and energy.

The humanist, for example, may conceive of the "elite" not as a social level or category, but as a scatter of those individuals who attempt to transcend themselves, and accordingly, are more noble, more efficient, made out of better stuff. It does not matter whether they are poor or rich, whether they hold high position or low, whether they are acclaimed or despised; they are elite because of the kind of individuals they are. The rest of the population is mass, which, according to this conception, sluggishly relaxes into uncomfortable mediocrity.[5]

This is the sort of socially unlocated conception which some American writers with conservative yearnings have recently sought to develop. But most moral and psychological conceptions of the elite are much less sophisticated, concerning themselves not with individuals but with the stratum as a whole. Such ideas, in fact, always arise in a society in which some people possess more than do others of what there is to possess. People with advantages are loath to believe that they just happen to be people with advantages. They come readily to define themselves as inherently worthy of what they possess; they come to believe themselves "naturally" elite; and, in fact, to imagine their possessions and their privileges as natural extensions of their own elite selves. In this sense, the idea of the elite as composed of men and women having a finer moral character is an ideology of the elite as a privileged ruling stratum, and this is true whether the ideology is elite-made or made up for it by others.

In eras of equalitarian rhetoric, the more intelligent or the more articulate among the lower and middle classes, as well as guilty members of the upper, may come to entertain ideas of a counter-elite. In western society, as a matter of fact, there is a long tradition and varied images of the poor, the exploited, and the oppressed as the truly virtuous, the wise, and the blessed. Stemming from Christian tradition, this moral idea of a counter-elite, composed of essentially higher types condemned to a lowly station, may be and has been used by the underlying population to justify harsh criticism of ruling elites and to celebrate utopian images of a new elite to come.

The moral conception of the elite, however, is not always merely an ideology of the overprivileged or a counter-ideology of the underprivileged. It is often a fact: having controlled experiences and select privileges, many individuals of the upper stratum do come in due course to approximate the types of character they claim to embody. Even when we give up—as we must—the idea that the elite man or woman is born with an elite character, we need not dismiss the idea that their experiences and trainings develop in them characters of a specific type.

Nowadays we must qualify the idea of elite as composed of higher types of individuals, for the men who are selected for and shaped by the top positions have many spokesmen and advisers and ghosts and make-up men who modify their self-conceptions and create their public images, as well as shape many of their decisions. There is, of course, considerable variation among the elite in this respect, but as a general rule in America today, it would be naive to interpret any major elite group merely in terms of its ostensible personnel. The American elite often seems less a collection of persons than of corporate entities, which are in great part created and spoken for as standard types of "personality." Even the most apparently free-lance celebrity is usually a sort of synthetic production turned out each week by a disciplined staff which systematically ponders the effect of the easy ad-libbed gags the celebrity "spontaneously" echoes.

Yet, in so far as the elite flourishes as a social class or as a set of men at the command posts, it will select and form certain types of personality, and reject others. The kind of moral and psychological beings men become is in large part determined by the values they experience and the institutional roles they are allowed and expected to play. From the biographer's point of view, a man of the upper classes is formed by his relations with others like himself in a series of small intimate groupings through which he passes and to which throughout his lifetime he may return. So conceived, the elite is a set of higher circles whose members are selected, trained and certified and permitted intimate access to those who command the impersonal institutional hierarchies of modern society. If there is any one key to the *psychological* idea of the elite, it is that they combine in their persons an awareness of impersonal decision-making with intimate sensibilities shared with one another. To understand the elite as a social class we must examine a whole series of smaller face-to-face milieux, the most obvious of which, historically, has been the upper-class family, but the most important of which today are the proper secondary school and the metropolitan club.[6]

5

These several notions of the elite, when appropriately understood, are intricately bound up with one another, and we shall use them all in this examination of American success. We shall study each of several higher circles as offering candidates for the elite, and we shall do so in terms of the major institutions making up the total society of America; within and between each of these institutions, we shall trace the interrelations of wealth and power and prestige. But our main concern is with the power of those who now occupy the command posts, and with the role which they are enacting in the history of our epoch.

Such an elite may be conceived as omnipotent, and its powers thought of as a great hidden design. Thus, in vulgar Marxism, events and trends are explained by reference to "the will of the bourgeoisie"; in Nazism, by reference to "the conspiracy of the Jews"; by the petty right in America today, by reference to "the hidden force" of Communist spies. According to such notions of the omnipotent elite as historical cause, the elite is never an entirely visible agency. It is, in fact, a secular substitute for the will of God, being realized in a sort of providential design, except that usually non-elite men are thought capable of opposing it and eventually overcoming it.*

The opposite view—of the elite as impotent—is now quite popular among liberal-minded observers. Far from being omnipotent, the elites are thought to be so scattered as to lack any coherence as a historical force. Their invisibility is not the invisibility of secrecy but the invisibility of the multitude. Those who occupy the formal places of authority are so check-mated—by other elites exerting pressure, or by the public as an electorate, or by constitutional codes—that, although there may be upper classes, there is no ruling class; although there may be men of power, there is no power elite; although there may be a system of stratification, it has no effective top. In the extreme, this view of the elite, as weakened by compromise and disunited to the point of nullity, is a substitute for impersonal collective fate; for, in this view, the decisions of the visible men of the higher circles do not count in history.**

---

*Those who charge that Communist agents have been or are in the government, as well as those frightened by them, never raise the question: "Well, suppose there are Communists in high places, how much power do they have?" They simply assume that men in high places, or in this case even those in positions from which they might influence such men, do decide important events. Those who think Communist agents lost China to the Soviet bloc, or influenced loyal Americans to lose it, simply assume that there is a set of men who decide such matters, actively or by neglect or by stupidity. Many others, who do not believe that Communist agents were so influential, still assume that loyal American decision-makers lost it all by themselves.

**The idea of the impotent elite, as we shall have occasion to see, in ELEVEN: The Theory of Balance, is mightily supported by the notion of an automatic economy in which the problem of power is solved for the economic elite by denying its existence. No one has enough power to make a real difference; events are the results of an anonymous balance. For

Internationally, the image of the omnipotent elite tends to prevail. All good events and pleasing happenings are quickly imputed by the opinion-makers to the leaders of their own nation; all bad events and unpleasant experiences are imputed to the enemy abroad. In both cases, the omnipotence of evil rulers or of virtuous leaders is assumed. Within the nation, the use of such rhetoric is rather more complicated: when men speak of the power of their own party or circle, they and their leaders are, of course, impotent; only "the people" are omnipotent. But, when they speak of the power of their opponent's party or circle, they impute to them omnipotence; "the people" are now powerlessly taken in.

More generally, American men of power tend, by convention, to deny that they are powerful. No American runs for office in order to rule or even govern, but only to serve; he does not become a bureaucrat or even an official, but a public servant. And nowadays, as I have already pointed out, such postures have become standard features of the public-relations programs of all men of power. So firm a part of the style of power-wielding have they become that conservative writers readily misinterpret them as indicating a trend toward an "amorphous power situation."

But the "power situation" of America today is less amorphous than is the perspective of those who see it as a romantic confusion. It is less a flat momentary "situation" than a graded, durable structure. And if those who occupy its top grades are not omnipotent, neither are they impotent. It is the form and the height of the gradation of power that we must examine if we would understand the degree of power held and exercised by the elite.

If the power to decide such national issues as are decided were shared in an absolutely equal way, there would be no power elite; in fact, there would be no *gradation* of power, but only a radical homogeneity. At the opposite extreme as well, if the power to decide issues were absolutely monopolized by one small group, there would be no gradation of power; there would simply be this small group in command, and below it, the undifferentiated, dominated masses. American society today represents neither the

---

the political elite too, the model of balance solves the problem of power. Parallel to the market-economy, there is the leaderless democracy in which no one is responsible for anything and everyone is responsible for everything; the will of men acts only through the impersonal workings of the electoral process.

one nor the other of these extremes, but a conception of them is none the less useful: it makes us realize more clearly the question of the structure of power in the United States and the position of the power elite within it.

Within each of the most powerful institutional orders of modern society there is a gradation of power. The owner of a roadside fruit stand does not have as much power in any area of social or economic or political decision as the head of a multi-million-dollar fruit corporation; no lieutenant on the line is as powerful as the Chief of Staff in the Pentagon; no deputy sheriff carries as much authority as the President of the United States. Accordingly, the problem of defining the power elite concerns the level at which we wish to draw the line. By lowering the line, we could define the elite out of existence; by raising it, we could make the elite a very small circle indeed. In a preliminary and minimum way, we draw the line crudely, in charcoal as it were: By the power elite, we refer to those political, economic, and military circles which as an intricate set of overlapping cliques share decisions having at least national consequences. In so far as national events are decided, the power elite are those who decide them.

To say that there are obvious gradations of power and of opportunities to decide within modern society is not to say that the powerful are united, that they fully know what they do, or that they are consciously joined in conspiracy. Such issues are best faced if we concern ourselves, in the first instance, more with the structural position of the high and mighty, and with the consequences of their decisions, than with the extent of their awareness or the purity of their motives. To understand the power elite, we must attend to three major keys:

I. One, which we shall emphasize throughout our discussion of each of the higher circles, is the psychology of the several elites in their respective milieux. In so far as the power elite is composed of men of similar origin and education, in so far as their careers and their styles of life are similar, there are psychological and social bases for their unity, resting upon the fact that they are of similar social type and leading to the fact of their easy intermingling. This kind of unity reaches its frothier apex in the sharing of that prestige that is to be had in the world of the celebrity; it achieves a more solid culmination in the fact of the interchangeability of positions within and between the three dominant institutional orders.

II. Behind such psychological and social unity as we may find, are the structure and the mechanics of those institutional hierarchies over which the political directorate, the corporate rich, and the high military now preside. The greater the scale of these bureaucratic domains, the greater the scope of their respective elite's power. How each of the major hierarchies is shaped and what relations it has with the other hierarchies determine in large part the relations of their rulers. If these hierarchies are scattered and disjointed, then their respective elites tend to be scattered and disjointed; if they have many interconnections and points of coinciding interest, then their elites tend to form a coherent kind of grouping.

The unity of the elite is not a simple reflection of the unity of institutions, but men and institutions are always related, and our conception of the power elite invites us to determine that relation. Today in America there are several important structural coincidences of interest between these institutional domains, including the development of a permanent war establishment by a privately incorporated economy inside a political vacuum.

III. The unity of the power elite, however, does not rest solely on psychological similarity and social intermingling, nor entirely on the structural coincidences of commanding positions and interests. At times it is the unity of a more explicit co-ordination. To say that these three higher circles are increasingly co-ordinated, that this is *one* basis of their unity, and that at times—as during the wars—such co-ordination is quite decisive, is not to say that the co-ordination is total or continuous, or even that it is very surefooted. Much less is it to say that willful co-ordination is the sole or the major basis of their unity, or that the power elite has emerged as the realization of a plan. But it is to say that as the institutional mechanics of our time have opened up avenues to men pursuing their several interests, many of them have come to see that these several interests could be realized more easily if they worked together, in informal as well as in more formal ways, and accordingly they have done so.

6

It is not my thesis that for all epochs of human history and in all nations, a creative minority, a ruling class, an omnipotent elite, shape all historical events. Such statements, upon careful examination, usually turn out to be mere tautologies,[7] and even when they are not, they are so entirely general as to be useless in the attempt to understand the history of the present. The minimum definition of the power elite as those who decide whatever is decided of major consequence, does not imply that the members of this elite are always and necessarily the history-makers; neither does it imply that they never are. We must not confuse the conception of the elite, which we wish to define, with one theory about their role: that they are the history-makers of our time. To define the elite, for example, as "those who rule America" is less to define a conception than to state one hypothesis about the role and power of that elite. No matter how we might define the elite, the extent of its members' power is subject to historical variation. If, in a dogmatic way, we try to include that variation in our generic definition, we foolishly limit the use of a needed conception. If we insist that the elite be defined as a strictly coordinated class that continually and absolutely rules, we are closing off from our view much to which the term more modestly defined might open to our observation. In short, our definition of the power elite cannot properly contain dogma concerning the degree and kind of power that ruling groups everywhere have. Much less should it permit us to smuggle into our discussion a theory of history.

During most of human history, historical change has not been visible to the people who were involved in it, or even to those enacting it. Ancient Egypt and Mesopotamia, for example, endured for some four hundred generations with but slight changes in their basic structure. That is six and a half times as long as the entire Christian era, which has only prevailed some sixty generations; it is about eighty times as long as the five generations of the United States' existence. But now the tempo of change is so rapid, and the means of observation so accessible, that the interplay of event and decision seems often to be quite historically visible, if we will only look carefully and from an adequate vantage point.

When knowledgeable journalists tell us that "events, not men, shape the big decisions," they are echoing the theory of history as Fortune, Chance, Fate, or the work of The Unseen Hand. For "events" is merely a modern word for these older ideas, all of which separate men from history-making, because all of them lead us to believe that history goes on behind men's backs. History is drift with no mastery; within it there is action but no deed; history is mere happening and the event intended by no one.[8]

The course of events in our time depends more on a series of human decisions than on any inevitable fate. The sociological meaning of "fate" is simply this: that, when the decisions are innumerable and each one is of small consequence, all of them add up in a way no man intended—to history as fate. But not all epochs are equally fateful. As the circle of those who decide is narrowed as the means of decision are centralized and the consequences of decisions become enormous, then the course of great events often rests upon the decisions of determinable circles. This does not necessarily mean that the same circle of men follow through from one event to another in such a way that all of history is merely their plot. The power of the elite does not necessarily mean that history is not also shaped by a series of small decisions, none of which are thought out. It does not mean that a hundred small arrangements and compromises and adaptations may not be built into the going policy and the living event. The idea of the power elite implies nothing about the process of decision-making as such: it is an attempt to delimit the social areas within which that process, whatever its character, goes on. It is a conception of who is involved in the process.

The degree of foresight and control of those who are involved in decisions that count may also vary. The idea of the power elite does not mean that the estimations and calculated risks upon which decisions are made are not often wrong and that the consequences are sometimes, indeed often, not those intended. Often those who make decisions are trapped by their own inadequacies and blinded by their own errors.

Yet in our time the pivotal moment does arise, and at that moment, small circles do decide or fail to decide. In either case, they are an elite of power. The dropping of the A-bombs over Japan was such a moment; the decision on Korea was such a moment; the confusion about Quemoy and Matsu, as well as before Dienbienphu were such moments; the sequence of maneuvers which involved the United States in World War II was such a "moment." Is it not true that much of the history of our times is composed of such moments? And is not that what is meant when it is said that we live in a time of big decisions, of decisively centralized power?

Most of us do not try to make sense of our age by believing in a Greek-like, eternal recurrence, nor by a Christian belief in a salvation to come, nor by any steady march of human progress. Even though we do not reflect upon such matters, the chances are we believe with Burckhardt that we live in a mere succession of events; that sheer continuity is the only principle of history. History is merely one thing after another; history is meaningless in that it is not the realization of any determinate plot. It is true, of course, that our sense of continuity, our feeling for the history of our time, is affected by crisis. But we seldom look beyond the immediate crisis or the crisis felt to be just ahead. We believe neither in fate nor providence; and we assume, without talking about it, that "we"—as a nation—can decisively shape the future but that "we" as individuals somehow cannot do so.

Any meaning history has, "we" shall have to give to it by our actions. Yet the fact is that although we are all of us within history we do not all possess equal powers to make history. To pretend that we do is sociological nonsense and political irresponsibility. It is nonsense because any group or any individual is limited, first of all, by the technical and institutional means of power at its command; we do not all have equal access to the means of power that now exist, nor equal influence over their use. To pretend that "we" are all history-makers is politically irresponsible because it obfuscates any attempt to locate responsibility for the consequential decisions of men who do have access to the means of power.

From even the most superficial examination of the history of the western society we learn that the power of decision-makers is first of all limited by the level of technique, by the *means* of power and violence and organization that prevail in a given society. In this connection we also learn that there is a fairly straight line running upward through the history of the West; that the means of oppression and exploitation, of violence and destruction, as well as the means of production and reconstruction, have been progressively enlarged and increasingly centralized.

As the institutional means of power and the means of communications that tie them together have become steadily more efficient, those now in command of them have come into command of instruments of rule quite unsurpassed in the history of mankind. And we are not yet at the climax of their development. We can no longer lean upon or take soft comfort from the historical ups and downs of ruling groups of previous epochs. In that sense, Hegel is correct: we learn from history that we cannot learn from it.

For every epoch and for every social structure, we must work out an answer to the question of the power of the elite. The ends of men are often merely hopes, but means are facts within some men's control. That is why all means of power tend to become ends to an elite that is in command of them. And that is why we may define the power elite in terms of the means of power—as those who occupy the command posts. The major questions about the American elite today—its composition, its unity, its power—must now be faced with due attention to the awesome means of power available to them. Caesar could do less with Rome than Napoleon with France; Napoleon less with France than Lenin with Russia; and Lenin less with Russia than Hitler with Germany. But what was Caesar's power at its peak compared with the power of the changing inner circle of Soviet Russia or of America's temporary administrations? The men of either circle can cause great cities to be wiped out in a single night, and in a few weeks turn continents into thermonuclear wastelands. That the facilities of power are enormously enlarged and decisively centralized means that the decisions of small groups are now more consequential.

But to know that the top posts of modern social structures now permit more commanding decisions is not to know that the elite who occupy these posts are the history-makers. We might grant that the enlarged and integrated economic, military, and political structures are shaped to permit command decisions, yet still feel that, as it were, "they run themselves," that those who are on top, in short, are determined in their decisions by "necessity," which presumably means by the instituted roles that they play and the situation of these institutions in the total structure of society.

Do the elite determine the roles that they enact? Or do the roles that institutions make available to them determine the power of the elite? The general answer—and no general answer is sufficient—is that in different kinds of structures and epochs elites are quite differently related to the roles that they play: nothing in the nature of the elite or in the nature of history dictates an answer. It is also true that if most men and women take whatever roles are permitted to them and enact them as they are expected to by virtue of their position, this is precisely what the elite need *not* do, and often do not do. They may call into question the structure, their position within it, or the way in which they are to enact that position.

Nobody called for or permitted Napoleon to chase *Parlement* home on the 18 *Brumaire*, and later to transform his consulate into an emperorship.[9] Nobody called for or permitted Adolf Hitler to proclaim himself "Leader and Chancellor" the day President Hindenburg died, to abolish and usurp roles by merging the presidency and the chancellorship. Nobody called for or permitted Franklin D. Roosevelt to make the series of decisions that led to the entrance of the United States into World War II. It was no "historical necessity," but a man named Truman who, with a few other men, decided to drop a bomb on Hiroshima. It was no historical necessity, but an argument within a small circle of men that defeated Admiral Radford's proposal to bomb troops before Dienbienphu. Far from being dependent upon the structure of institutions, modern elites may smash one structure and set up another in which they then enact quite different roles. In fact, such destruction and creation of institutional structures, with all their means of power, when events seem to turn out well, is just what is involved in "great leadership," or, when they seem to turn out badly, great tyranny.

Some elite men *are*, of course, typically role-determined, but others are at times role-determining. They determine not only the role they play but today the roles of millions of other men. The creation of pivotal roles and their pivotal enactment occurs most readily when social structures are undergoing epochal transitions. It is clear that the international development of the United States to one of the two "great powers"—along with the new means of

annihilation and administrative and psychic domination—have
made of the United States in the middle years of the twentieth
century precisely such an epochal pivot.

There is nothing about history that tells us that a power elite
cannot make it. To be sure, the will of such men is always limited,
but never before have the limits been so broad, for never before
have the means of power been so enormous. It is this that makes
our situation so precarious, and makes even more important an
understanding of the powers and the limitations of the American
elite. The problem of the nature and the power of this elite is now
the only realistic and serious way to raise again the problem of
responsible government.

7

Those who have abandoned criticism for the new American
celebration take readily to the view that the elite is impotent. If
they were politically serious, they ought, on the basis of their
view, to say to those presumably in charge of American
policy:[10]

"One day soon, you may believe that you have an opportunity
to drop a bomb or a chance to exacerbate further your relations
with allies or with the Russians who might also drop it. But don't
be so foolish as to believe that you really have a choice. You have
neither choice nor chance. The whole Complex Situation of which
you are merely one balancing part is the result of Economic and
Social Forces, and so will be the fateful outcome. So stand by
quietly, like Tolstoy's general, and let events proceed. Even if you
did act, the consequences would not be what you intended, even if
you had an intention.

"But—if events come out well, talk as though you had decided.
For then men have had moral choices and the power to make them
and are, of course, responsible.

"If events come out badly, say that *you* didn't have the real
choice, and are, of course, not accountable: *they*, the others, had
the choice and they are responsible. You can get away with this
even though you have at your command half the world's forces and
God knows how many bombs and bombers. For you are, in fact, an

impotent item in the historical fate of your times; and moral responsibility is an illusion, although it is of great use if handled in a really alert public relations manner.''

The one implication that can be drawn from all such fatalisms is that if fortune or providence rules, then no elite of power can be justly considered a source of historical decisions, and the idea —much less the demand—of responsible leadership is an idle and an irresponsible notion. For clearly, an impotent elite, the plaything of history, cannot be held accountable. If the elite of our time do not have power, they cannot be held responsible; as men in a difficult position, they should engage our sympathies. The people of the United States are ruled by sovereign fortune; they, and with them their elite, are fatally overwhelmed by consequences they cannot control. If that is so, we ought all to do what many have in fact already done: withdraw entirely from political reflection and action into a materially comfortable and entirely private life.

If, on the other hand, we believe that war and peace and slump and prosperity are, precisely now, no longer matters of "fortune" or "fate," but that, precisely now more than ever, they are controllable, then we must ask—controllable by whom? The answer must be: By whom else but those who now command the enormously enlarged and decisively centralized means of decision and power? We may then ask: Why don't they, then? And for the answer to that, we must understand the context and the character of the American elite today.

There is nothing in the idea of the elite as impotent which should deter us from asking just such questions, which are now the most important questions political men can ask. The American elite is neither omnipotent nor impotent. These are abstract absolutes used publicly by spokesmen, as excuses or as boasts, but in terms of which we may seek to clarify the political issues before us, which just now are above all the issues of responsible power.

There is nothing in "the nature of history" *in our epoch* that rules out the pivotal function of small groups of decision-makers. On the contrary, the structure of the present is such as to make this not only a reasonable, but a rather compelling, view.

There is nothing in "the psychology of man," or in the social manner in which men are shaped and selected for and by the command posts of modern society, that makes unreasonable the view that they do confront choices and that the choices they make—or their failure to confront them—are history-making in their consequences.

Accordingly, political men now have every reason to hold the American power elite accountable for a decisive range of the historical events that make up the history of the present.

It is as fashionable, just now, to suppose that there is no power elite, as it was fashionable in the 'thirties to suppose a set of ruling-class villains to be the source of all social injustice and public malaise. I should be as far from supposing that some simple and unilateral ruling class could be firmly located as the prime mover of American society, as I should be from supposing that all historical change in America today is merely impersonal drift.

The view that all is blind drift is largely a fatalist projection of one's own feeling of impotence and perhaps, if one has ever been active politically in a principled way, a salve of one's guilt.

The view that all of history is due to the conspiracy of an easily located set of villains, or of heroes, is also a hurried projection from the difficult effort to understand how shifts in the structure of society open opportunities to various elites and how various elites take advantage or fail to take advantage of them. To accept either view—of all history as conspiracy or of all history as drift—is to relax the effort to understand the facts of power and the ways of the powerful.

8

In my attempt to discern the shape of the power elite of our time, and thus to give a responsible meaning to the anonymous "They," which the underlying population opposes to the anonymous "We," I shall begin by briefly examining the higher elements which most people know best: the new and the old upper classes of local society and the metropolitan 400. I shall then outline the world of the celebrity, attempting to show that the prestige system of American society has now for the first time become truly national in scope; and that the more trivial and glamorous aspects of this national system of status tend at once to distract attention from its more authoritarian features and to justify the power that it often conceals.

In examining the very rich and the chief executives, I shall indicate how neither "America's Sixty Families" nor "The Managerial Revolution" provides an adequate idea of the transformation of the upper classes as they are organized today in the privileged stratum of the corporate rich.

After describing the American statesman as a historical type, I shall attempt to show that what observers in the Progressive Era called "the invisible government" has now become quite visible; and that what is usually taken to be the central content of politics, the pressures and the campaigns and the congressional maneuvering, has, in considerable part, now been relegated to the middle levels of power.

In discussing the military ascendancy, I shall try to make clear how it has come about that admirals and generals have assumed positions of decisive political and economic relevance, and how, in doing so, they have found many points of coinciding interests with the corporate rich and the political directorate of the visible government.

After these and other trends are made as plain as I can make them, I shall return to the master problems of the power elite, as well as take up the complementary notion of the mass society.

What I am asserting is that in this particular epoch a conjunction of historical circumstances has led to the rise of an elite of power; that the men of the circles composing this elite, severally and collectively, now make such key decisions as are made; and that, given the enlargement and the centralization of the means of power now available, the decisions that they make and fail to make carry more consequences for more people than has ever been the case in the world history of mankind.

I am also asserting that there has developed on the middle levels of power, a semi-organized stalemate, and that on the bottom level there has come into being a mass-like society which has little resemblance to the image of a society in which voluntary associations and classic publics hold the keys to power. The top of the American system of power is much more unified and much more powerful, the bottom is much more fragmented, and in truth, impotent, than is generally supposed by those who are distracted by the middling units of power which neither express such will as exists at the bottom nor determine the decisions at the top.

Notes

1. Jacob Burckhardt, *Force and Freedom* (New York: Pantheon Books, 1943), pp. 303 ff.

2. Cf. Hans Gerth and C. Wright Mills, *Character and Social Structure* (New York: Harcourt, Brace, 1953), pp. 457 ff.

3. The statistical idea of choosing some value and calling those who have the most of it an elite derives, in modern times, from the Italian economist, Pareto, who puts the central point in this way: "Let us assume that in every branch of human activity each individual is given an index which stands as a sign of his capacity, very much the way grades are given in the various subjects in examinations in school. The highest type of lawyer, for instance, will be given 10. The man who does not get a client will be given 1—reserving zero for the man who is an out-and-out idiot. To the man who has made his millions—honestly or dishonestly as the case may be—we will give 10. To the man who has earned his thousands we will give 6; to such as just manage to keep out of the poor-house, 1, keeping zero for those who get in . . . So let us make a class of people who have the highest indices in their branch of activity, and to that class give the name of *elite*." Vilfredo Pareto, *The Mind and Society* (New York: Harcourt, Brace, 1935), par. 2027 and 2031. Those who follow this approach end up not with one elite, but with a number corresponding to the number of values they select. Like many rather abstract ways of reasoning, this one is useful because it forces us to think in a clear-cut way. For a skillful use of this approach, see the work of Harold D. Lasswell, in particular, *Politics: Who Gets What, When, How* (New York: McGraw-Hill, 1936); and for a more systematic use, H. D. Lasswell and Abraham Kaplan, *Power and Society* (New Haven: Yale University Press, 1950).

4. The conception of the elite as members of a top social stratum, is, of course, in line with the prevailing common-sense view of stratification. Technically, it is closer to "status group" than to "class," and has been very well stated by Joseph A. Schumpeter, "Social Classes in an Ethically Homogeneous Environment," *Imperialism and Social Classes* (New York: Augustus M. Kelley, Inc., 1951), pp. 133 ff., especially pp. 137-47. Cf. also his *Capitalism, Socialism and Democracy*, 3rd ed. (New York: Harper, 1950), Part II. For the distinction between class and status groups, see *From Max Weber: Essays in Sociology* (trans. and ed. by Gerth and Mills; New York: Oxford University Press, 1946). For an analysis of Pareto's conception of the elite compared with Marx's conception of classes, as well as data on France, see Raymond Aron, "Social Structure and Ruling Class," *British Journal of Sociology*, vol. I, nos. 1 and 2 (1950).

5. The most popular essay in recent years which defines the elite and the mass in terms of a morally evaluated character-type is probably José Ortega y Gasset's *The Revolt of the Masses*, 1932 (New York: New American Library, Mentor Edition, 1950), esp. pp. 91 ff.

6. "The American elite" is a confused and confusing set of images, and yet when we hear or when we use such words as Upper Class, Big Shot, Top Brass, The Millionaire Club, The High and The Mighty, we feel at least vaguely that we know what they mean, and often do. What we do not often do, however, is connect each of these images with the others; we make little effort to form a coherent picture in our minds of the elite as a whole. Even when, very occasionally, we do try to do this, we usually come to believe that it is

indeed no "whole"; that, like our images of it, there is no one elite, but many, and that they are not really connected with one another. What we must realize is that until we *do* try to see it as a whole, perhaps our impression that it may not be is a result merely of our lack of analytic rigor and sociological imagination.

The first conception defines the elite in terms of the sociology of institutional position and the social structure these institutions form; the second, in terms of the statistics of selected values; the third, in terms of membership in a clique-like set of people; and the fourth, in terms of the morality of certain personality types. Or, put into inelegant shorthand: what they head up, what they have, what they belong to, who they really are.

In this chapter, as in this book as a whole, I have taken as generic the first view—of the elite defined in terms of institutional position—and have located the other views within it. This straight-forward conception of the elite has one practical and two theoretical advantages. The practical advantage is that it seems the easiest and the most concrete "way into" the whole problem—if only because a good deal of information is more or less readily available for sociological reflection about such circles and institutions.

But the theoretical advantages are much more important. The institutional or structural definition, first of all, does not force us to prejudge by definition what we ought properly to leave open for investigation. The elite conceived morally, for example, as people having a certain type of character is not an ultimate definition, for apart from being rather morally arbitrary, it leads us immediately to ask *why* these people have this or that sort of character. Accordingly, we should leave open the type of characters which the members of the elite in fact turn out to have, rather than by definition select them in terms of one type or another. In a similar way, we do not want, by mere definition, to prejudge whether or not the elite are conscious members of a social class. The second theoretical advantage of defining the elite in terms of major institutions, which I hope this book as a whole makes clear, is the fact that it allows us to fit the other three conceptions of the elite into place in a systematic way: (1) The institutional positions men occupy throughout their lifetime determine their chances to get and to hold selected values. (2) The kind of psychological beings they become is in large part determined by the values they thus experience and the institutional roles they play. (3) Finally, whether or not they come to feel that they belong to a select social class, and whether or not they act according to what they hold to be its interests—these are also matters in large part determined by their institutional position, and in turn, the select values they possess and the characters they acquire.

7. As in the case, quite notably, of Gaetano Mosca, *The Ruling Class* (New York: McGraw-Hill, 1939). For a sharp analysis of Mosca, see Fritz Morstein Marx, "The Bureaucratic State," *Review of Politics*, vol. 1, 1939, pp. 457 ff. Cf. also Mills, "On Intellectual Craftsmanship," April 1952, mimeographed, Columbia College, February 1955.

8. Cf. Karl Löwith, *Meaning in History* (Chicago: University of Chicago Press, 1949), pp. 125 ff. for concise and penetrating statements of several leading philosophies of history.

9. Some of these items are taken from Gerth and Mills, *Character and Social Structure*, pp. 405 ff. On role-determined and role-determining men, see also Sidney Hook's discussion, *The Hero in History* (New York: John Day, 1943).

10. I have taken the idea of the following kind of formulation from Joseph Wood Krutch's presentation of the morality of choice. See *The Measure of Man* (Indianapolis: Bobbs-Merrill, 1954), p. 52.

B. *Carl Oglesby:*
"Trapped in a System"*

Students for a Democratic Society (SDS) was the major forum for the evolution of New Left opinion during the 1960's. It was founded in 1962 as a somewhat heretical offshoot of the League for Industrial Democracy, a socialist organization. Its first convention, in Port Huron, Michigan, produced a sixty-page manifesto which came to be known as the "Port Huron Statement." It was a tedious document, written in the leaden prose of Tom Hayden, but it touched upon the themes which seemed critical to a new generation of activist reformers: the need for new departures in politics, the inadequacy of liberalism, the insensitivity of the Establishment, the cynicism of the campus as then constituted, its enormous potential for reform if properly reconstituted. In five years more than 100,000 copies of the "Port Huron Statement" were distributed, and excerpts from it have become the *sine qua non* of any New Left anthology.

But a much better sample of New Left sentiment is provided in the following address in 1965 by Carl Oglesby (1935-   ), then president of SDS. It is a riper statement of SDS views, since it takes into account the escalating Vietnam War, along with other American interventions, and brings into sharper focus its indictment of corporate liberalism. It deserves to be called a classic because it represents "The Movement" just as it peaked, and it captures—as the "Port Huron Statement" does not—all of its sauciness and verve.

Like the Populists of old, Oglesby excoriates "our American corporate system," invokes the names of Jefferson and Paine, avoids class analysis, rejects ideology or any attempt at ideologizing, and finishes up with a rousing appeal to "shape the future in the name of plain human hope." Lenin might sneer, but William Jennings Bryan. . . .

*From Carl Oglesby, "Trapped in a System," Speech at the October 27, 1965 anti war march in Washington, in Massimo Teodori, ed., *The New Left: A Documentary History* (Indianapolis: The Bobbs-Merrill Company, 1969). Reprinted by permission of Bobbs-Merrill Company.

Seven months ago at the April March on Washington, Paul Potter, then President of Students for a Democratic Society, stood in approximately this spot and said that we must name the system that creates and sustains the war in Vietnam—name it, describe it, analyze it, understand it, and change it.

Today I will try to name it—to suggest an analysis which, to be quite frank, may disturb some of you—and to suggest what changing it may require of us.

We are here again to protest again a growing war. Since it is a very bad war, we acquire the habit of thinking that it must be caused by very bad men. But we only conceal reality, I think, by denouncing on such grounds the menacing coalition of industrial and military power, or the brutality of the blitzkrieg we are waging against Vietnam, or the ominous signs around us that heresy may soon no longer be permitted. We must simply observe, and quite plainly say that this coalition, this blitzkrieg, and this demand for acquiescence are creatures, all of them, of a Government that since 1932 has considered itself to be fundamentally *liberal*.

The original commitment in Vietnam was made by President Truman, a mainstream liberal. It was seconded by President Eisenhower, a moderate liberal. It was intensified by the late President Kennedy, a flaming liberal. Think of the men who now engineer that war—those who study the maps, give the commands, push the buttons, and tally the dead: Bundy, McNamara, Rusk, Lodge, Goldberg, the President himself.

They are not moral monsters.

They are all honorable men.

They are all liberals.

But so, I'm sure, are many of us who are here today in protest. To understand the war, then, it seems necessary to take a closer look at this American liberalism. Maybe we are in for some surprises. Maybe we have here two quite different liberalisms: one authentically humanist; the other not so human at all.

Not long ago, I considered myself a liberal. And if someone had asked me what I meant by that, I'd perhaps have quoted Thomas Jefferson or Thomas Paine, who first made plain our nation's unprovisional commitment to human rights. But what do you think would happen if these two heroes could sit down now for a chat with President Johnson and McGeorge Bundy?

They would surely talk of the Vietnam war. Our dead revolutionaries would soon wonder why their country was fighting
against what appeared to be a revolution. The living liberals would
hotly deny that it is one: there are troops coming in from outside,
the rebels get arms from other countries, most of the people are not
on their side, and they practice terror against their own. Therefore,
not a revolution.

What would our dead revolutionaries answer? They might say:
"What fools and bandits, sir, you make then of us. Outside help?
Do you remember Lafayette? Or the 3,000 British freighters the
French navy sunk for our side? Or the arms and men we got from
France and Spain? And what's this about terror? Did you never
hear what we did to our own loyalists? Or about the thousands of
rich American Tories who fled for their lives to Canada? And as for
popular support, do you not know that we had less than one-third
of our people with us? That, in fact, the colony of New York
recruited more troops for the British than for the revolution?
Should we give it all back?"

Revolutions do not take place in velvet boxes. They never have.
It is only the poets who make them lovely. What the National
Liberation Front is fighting in Vietnam is a complex and vicious
war. This war is also a revolution, as honest a revolution as you can
find anywhere in history. And this is a fact which all our intricate
official denials will never change.

But it doesn't make any difference to our leaders anyway. Their
aim in Vietnam is really much simpler than this implies. It is to
safeguard what they take to be American interests around the
world against revolution or revolutionary change, which they
always call Communism—as if that were that. In the case of
Vietnam, this interest is, first, the principle that revolution shall
not be tolerated anywhere, and second, that South Vietnam shall
never sell its rice to China—or even to North Vietnam.

There is simply no such thing now, for us, as a just revolution—never mind that for two-thirds of the world's people the
20th Century might as well be the Stone Age; never mind the
melting poverty and hopelessness that are the basic facts of life for
most modern men; and never mind that for these millions there is
now an increasingly perceptible relationship between their sorrow
and our contentment.

Can we understand why the Negroes of Watts rebelled? Then why do we need a devil theory to explain the rebellion of the South Vietnamese? Can we understand the oppression in Mississippi, or the anguish that our Northern ghettos make epidemic? Then why can't we see that our proper human struggle is not with Communism or revolutionaries, but with the social desperation that drives good men to violence, both here and abroad?

To be sure, we have been most generous with our aid, and in Western Europe, a mature industrial society, that aid worked. But there are always political and financial strings. And we have never shown ourselves capable of allowing others to make those traumatic institutional changes that are often the prerequisites of progress in colonial societies. For all our official feeling for the millions who are enslaved to what we so self-righteously call the yoke of Communist tyranny, we make no real effort at all to crack through the much more vicious right-wing tyrannies that our businessmen traffic with and our nation profits from every day. And for all our cries about the international Red conspiracy to take over the world, we take only pride in the fact of our 6,000 military bases on foreign soil.

We gave Rhodesia a grave look just now—but we keep on buying her chromium, which is cheap because black slave labor mines it.

We deplore the racism of Verwoerd's fascist South Africa—but our banks make big loans to that country and our private technology makes it a nuclear power.

We are saddened and puzzled by random back-page stories of revolt in this or that Latin American state—but are convinced by a few pretty photos in the Sunday supplement that things are getting better, that the world is coming our way, that change from disorder can be orderly, that our benevolence will pacify the distressed, that our might will intimidate the angry.

Optimists, may I suggest that these are quite unlikely fantasies. They are fantasies because we have lost that mysterious social desire for human equity that from time to time has given us genuine moral drive. We have become a nation of young, bright-eyed, hard-hearted, slim-waisted, bullet-headed make-out artists. A nation—may I say it?—of beardless liberals.

You say I am being hard? Only think.

This country, with its thirty-some years of liberalism, can send 200,000 young men to Vietnam to kill and die in the most dubious of wars, but it cannot get 100 voter registrars to go into Mississippi.

What do you make of it?

The financial burden of the war obliges us to cut millions from an already pathetic War on Poverty budget. But in almost the same breath, Congress appropriates $140 million for the Lockheed and Boeing companies to compete with each other on the supersonic transport project—that Disneyland creation that will cost us all about $2 billion before it's done.

What do you make of it?

Many of us have been earnestly resisting for some years now the idea of putting atomic weapons into West German hands, an action that would perpetuate the division of Europe and thus the Cold War. Now just this week we find out that, with the meagerest of security systems, West Germany has had nuclear weapons in her hands for the past six years.

What do you make of it?

Some will make of it that I overdraw the matter. Many will ask: What about the other side? To be sure, there is the bitter ugliness of Czechoslovakia, Poland, those infamous Russian tanks in the streets of Budapest. But my anger only rises to hear some say that sorrow cancels sorrow, or that *this* one's shame deposits in *that one's* account the right to shamefulness.

And others will make of it that I sound mighty anti-American. To these, I say: Don't blame *me* for *that*! Blame those who mouthed my liberal values and broke my American heart.

Just who might they be, by the way? Let's take a brief factual inventory of the latter-day Cold War.

In 1953 our Central Intelligence Agency managed to overthrow Mossadegh in Iran, the complaint being his neutralism in the Cold War and his plans to nationalize the country's oil resources to improve his people's lives. Most evil aims, most evil man. In his place we put in General Zahedi, a World War II Nazi collaborator. New arrangements on Iran's oil gave 25-year leases on 40% of it to three U.S. firms, one of which was Gulf Oil. The CIA's leader for this coup was Kermit Roosevelt. In 1960 Kermit Roosevelt became a vice president of Gulf Oil.

In 1954, the democratically elected Arbenz of Guatemala wanted to nationalize a portion of United Fruit Company's plantations in his country, land he needed badly for a modest program of agrarian reform. His government was overthrown in a CIA-supported right-wing coup. The following year, Gen. Walter Bedell Smith, director of the CIA when the Guatemala venture was being planned, joined the board of directors of the United Fruit Company.

Comes 1960 and Castro cries we are about to invade Cuba. The Administration sneers, "poppycock," and we Americans believe it. Comes 1961 and the invasion. Comes with it the awful realization that the United States Government had lied.

Comes 1962 and the missile crisis, and our Administration stands prepared to fight global atomic war on the curious principle that another state does not have the right to its own foreign policy.

Comes 1963 and British Guiana, where Cheddi Jagan wants independence from England and a labor law modelled on the Wagner Act. And Jay Lovestone, the AFL-CIO foreign policy chief, acting, as always, quite independently of labor's rank and file, arranges with our Government to finance an eleven-week dock strike that brings Jagan down, ensuring that the state will remain *British* Guiana, and that any workingman who wants a wage better than 50¢ a day is a dupe of Communism.

Comes 1964. Two weeks after Under Secretary Thomas Mann announces that we have abandoned the *Alianza's* principle of no aid to tyrants, Brazil's Goulart is overthrown by the vicious right-winger, Ademar Barros, supported by a show of American gunboats at Rio de Janeiro. Within 24 hours, the new head of state, Mazzilli, receives a congratulatory wire from our President.

Comes 1965. The Dominican Republic. Rebellion in the streets. We scurry to the spot with 20,000 neutral Marines and our neutral peacemakers—like Ellsworth Bunker, Jr., Ambassador to the Organization of American States. Most of us know that our neutral Marines fought openly on the side of the junta, a fact that the Administration still denies. But how many also know that what was at stake was our new Caribbean Sugar Bowl? That this same neutral peacemaking Bunker is a board member and stock owner of the National Sugar Refining Company, a firm his father founded in the good old days, and one which has a major interest in maintaining the status quo in the Dominican Republic? Or that the President's close personal friend and advisor, our new Supreme Court Justice Abe Fortas, has sat for the past 19 years on the board of the Sucrest Company, which imports black-strap molasses from the Dominican Republic? Or that the rhetorician of corporate liberalism and the late President Kennedy's close friend Adolf Berle, was chairman of the same board? Or that our roving ambassador Averell Harriman's brother Roland is on the board of National Sugar? Or that our former ambassador to the Dominican Republic, Joseph Farland is a board member of the South Puerto Rico Sugar Co., which owns 275,000 acres of rich land in the Dominican Republic and is the largest employer on the island—at about one dollar a day?

Neutralists! God save the hungry people of the world from such neutralists!

We do not say these men are evil. We say rather, that good men can be divided from their compassion by the institutional system that inherits us all. Generation in and out, we are put to use. People become instruments. Generals do not hear the screams of the bombed; sugar executives do not see the misery of the cane cutters—for to do so is to be that much *less* the general, that much *less* the executive.

The foregoing facts of recent history describe one main aspect of the estate of Western liberalism. Where is our American humanism here? What went wrong?

Let's stare our situation coldly in the face. All of us are born to the colossus of history, our American corporate system—in many ways, an awesome organism. There is one fact that describes it: With about 5% of the world's people, we consume about half the world's goods. We take a richness that is in good part not our own, and we put it in our pockets, our garages, our split-levels, our bellies, and our futures.

On the *face* of it, it is a crime that so few should have so much at the expense of so many. Where is the moral imagination so abused as to call this just? Perhaps many of us feel a bit uneasy in our sleep. We are not, after all, a cruel people. And perhaps we don't really need this super-dominance that deforms others. But what can we do? The investments are made. The financial ties are established. The plants abroad are built. Our system *exists*. One is swept up into it. How intolerable—to be born moral, but addicted to a stolen and maybe surplus luxury. Our goodness threatens to become counterfeit before our eyes—unless we change. But change threatens us with uncertainty—at least.

Our problem, then, is to justify this system and give its theft another name—to make kind and moral what is neither, to perform some alchemy with language that will make this injustice seem to be a most magnanimous gift.

A hard problem. But the Western democracies, in the heyday of their colonial expansionism, produced a hero worthy of the task.

Its name was free enterprise, and its partner was an *illiberal liberalism* that said to the poor and the dispossessed: What we acquire of your resources we repay in civilization. The white man's burden. But this was too poetic. So a much more hard-headed theory was produced. This theory said that colonial status is in fact a *boon* to the colonized. We give them technology and bring them into modern times.

But this deceived no one but ourselves. We were delighted with this new theory. The poor saw in it merely an admission that their claims were irrefutable. They stood up to us, without gratitude. We were shocked—but also confused, for the poor seemed again to be right. How long is it going to be the case, we wondered, that the poor will be right and the rich will be wrong?

Liberalism faced a crisis. In the face of the collapse of the European empires, how could it continue to hold together our twin need for richness and righteousness? How can we continue to sack the ports of Asia and still dream of Jesus?

The challenge was met with a most ingenious solution: the ideology of anti-Communism. This was the bind: we cannot call revolution bad, because we started that way ourselves, and because it is all too easy to see why the dispossessed should rebel. So we will call revolution *Communism*. And we will reserve for ourselves the right to say what Communism means. We take note of revolution's enormities, wrenching them where necessary from their historical context and often exaggerating them, and say: Behold, Communism is a bloodbath. We take note of those reactionaries who stole the revolution, and say: Behold, Communism is a betrayal of the people. We take note of the revolution's need to consolidate itself, and say: Behold, Communism is a tyranny.

It has been all these things, and it will be these things again, and we will never be at a loss for those tales of atrocity that comfort us so in our self-righteousness. Nuns will be raped and bureaucrats will be disembowelled. Indeed, revolution is a fury. For it is a letting loose of outrages pent up sometimes over centuries. But the more brutal and longer-lasting the suppression of this energy, all the more ferocious will be its explosive release.

Far from helping Americans deal with this truth, the anti-Communist ideology merely tries to disguise it so that things may stay the way they are. Thus, it depicts our presence in other lands not as a coercion, but a protection. It allows us even to say that the napalm in Vietnam is only another aspect of our humanitarian love—like those exorcisms in the Middle Ages that so often killed the patient. So we say to the Vietnamese peasant, the Cuban intellectual, the Peruvian worker: "You are better dead than Red. If it hurts or if you don't understand why—sorry about that."

This is the action of *corporate liberalism*. It performs for the corporate state a function quite like what the Church once performed for the feudal state. It seeks to justify its burdens and protect it from change. As the Church exaggerated this office in the Inquisition, so with liberalism in the McCarthy time—which, if it was a reactionary phenomenon, was still made possible by our anti-Communist corporate liberalism.

Let me then speak directly to humanist liberals. If my facts are wrong, I will soon be corrected. But if they are right, then you may face a crisis of conscience. Corporatism or humanism: which? For it has come to that. Will you let your dreams be used? Will you be a grudging apologist for the corporate state? Or will you help try to change it—not in the name of this or that blueprint or "ism," but in the name of simple human decency and democracy and the vision that wise and brave men saw in the time of our own Revolution?

And if your commitment to human value is unconditional, then disabuse yourselves of the notion that statements will bring change, if only the right statements can be written, or that interviews with the mighty will bring change if only the mighty can be reached, or that marches will bring change if only we can make them massive enough, or that policy proposals will bring change if only we can make them responsible enough.

We are dealing now with a colossus that does not want to be changed. It will not change itself. It will not cooperate with those who want to change it. Those allies of ours in the Government —are they really our allies? If they *are*, then they don't need advice, they need *constituencies*; they don't need study groups, they need a *movement*. And if they are *not*, then all the more reason for building that movement with a most relentless conviction.

There are people in this country today who are trying to build that movement, who aim at nothing less than a humanist reformation. And the humanist liberals must understand that it is this movement with which their own best hopes are most in tune. We radicals know the same history that you liberals know, and we can understand your occasional cynicism, exasperation, and even distrust. But we ask you to put these aside and help us risk a leap. Help us find enough time for the enormous work that needs doing here. Help us build. Help us shape the future in the name of plain human hope.

C. *Jack Newfield & Jeff Greenfield:* A New Populist Coalition?

Jack Newfield (1939-   ) is a populist-come-lately. Only two years before he co-authored *The Populist Manifesto* (1972) he had tacked on a new introduction to his *A Prophetic Minority* (not a very populist title to begin with) in which he described "the roots" of the New Left as being "cultural rather than political."

What is most radical and self-liberating about the activists is their rejection of the most basic middle-class values of American society. Money and material wealth . . . are unimportant to them. Also unimportant are conventional definitions of patriotism, religion, puritanism, and status. They desire a totally new life-style . . .*

Yet *The Populist Manifesto* is based on the proposition that reform in America must *transcend* matters of "life-style." The concluding chapter of the book contains a rather savage and even personal attack on Charles Reich for arguing what Newfield himself had asserted two years earlier—that "life-styles" are more important than issues.

But it is the 1972 Newfield who concerns us here, and by that time he had gone to the other extreme. He and Jeff Greenfield (1943-   ), a former Lindsay speech-writer, assembled a book which combined some fascinating muckraking with some dubious political assumptions. The muckraking portions, which constitute most of the book, expose some of the leading scandals in the corporate-government sphere: theft by the utilities, bribery by the milk trust, deception by the media, tax evasion by the rich, and so on. The political speculations, however, have a facile ring. The authors would splice together a coalition composed of Bella Abzug, women's lib leaders, the Black Caucus, *and* the lower-middle-class white population.

This is not to discount the possibility of left-right coalitions. The prospects for such alliances may be quite good—if only the New Left will rid itself of those self-appointed leaders and spokesmen who have been so outspokenly hostile to the values of the middle class, especially to the values of the Catholic middle class. Part of the problem is "life-style" again—it is difficult to see Bella Abzug even communicating with the Irish cop in Bay Ridge—but a more serious factor is that certain substantive questions, like busing and abortion, are simply nonnegotiable. They can perhaps be finessed, ignored, or declared off-limits, but never by those who have built their reputations upon them. And this, unfortunately, seems to fit the women's libbers, the Lindsay speech-writers, and the journalists who once made a special point of sneering at "conventional definitions of patriotism, religion, puritanism, and status."

The selection is taken from Ch. 1, in Jack Newfield & Jeff

*Jack Newfield, *A Prophetic Minority* (New York: The New American Library, 1970), p. xvi.

Greenfield, *A Populist Manifesto: The Making of the New Majority.**

The American myth is dying. Things are not getting better. Instead, history seems deranged. We have lost our way.

The Kennedys and King, Evers and Malcolm X are murdered in public, while our sons march off to war, and we watch them burn Ben Tre in our living rooms. Pentagon documents reveal our leaders were liars; our sons come back with track marks on their arms, and throw their Purple Hearts over the White House Wall.

"Things fall apart/the center cannot hold" is true of products and neighborhoods and our moral universe. Our cars can kill; cans of soup are lethal; the telephone breaks down. So does the city's electricity. So do the links between parents and children. The neighborhood of a lifetime imprisons its elderly in their apartments after sunset. And their predators are themselves imprisoned by the heroin in their blood. There is desolation in Eastern Kentucky, where men in their forties look for work that is not there and die of black lung. In Brownsville, Sutter Avenue looks like a moonscape. A geography is drawn in blood: Birmingham, My Lai, Attica, Dallas, Kent State, the Ia Drang Valley.

These are differing evils. But if there is a unified sense of discontent, some impulse to which most Americans would assent, it is that we have lost the power to alter our society because those with power are exempt from accountability. This sensibility —which strikes to the core of America's foundations—has poisoned the wellsprings of trust. "The rich get richer and the poor get poorer." So 62 per cent of white America tell the Harris Poll. "The medium is a false message." So the Vice-President tells the American people. A quarter of the American people abandoned their trust in our government between 1964 and 1970; by the start of this decade, two-thirds of us believed we had lost our national sense of direction; half of us thought we were on the verge of a national breakdown. If a presidential aspirant preaches war, and you vote for the man who promises peace, you have been duped; for the peace-maker has all along been plotting war—and lies to win your assent to that war. So the Pentagon papers tell us.

*(New York: Praeger Publishers, 1972). Reprinted by permission.

Nor is it just the government we have come to doubt. By one measure—a Harris Poll in September of 1971—*every major institution in America* was distrusted by a majority of Americans. The press, business, the courts, Congress, the media, the presidency—*none* of them commanded the respect of the citizenry.

And thus millions of citizens have come to believe that the men and institutions who hold power in this country do not mean what they say: that the Constitution, or a hospital bill, or the label on a can of food, or a *Time* magazine story, or a union pension plan, all falter between the word and the deed. The institutions that govern us—from the presidency to a corporation to a university, a bank, a foundation—do not deserve the legitimacy that is supposed to come with authority. They endure not because they fulfill their purposes, but because they possess power.

This belief is not unique to any single group of Americans. It cuts across divisions of race, sex, class, age, and region. We are infested with the proposition that the rules of the game are not fair; that the fight is fixed; that the key to success in America is power, and that the key to power is the hidden angle, the fix, money.

The core of this manifesto lies in this perception: there are people, classes, and institutions that today possess an illegitimate amount of wealth and power; they use that power for their own benefit and for the common loss. This power, which is at root economic, corrupts the political process and insulates itself from effective challenge.

The fight against this concentration of privilege—open and covert, legal and illegal—is, we believe, the most important political question of this decade. Its goal is a more equitable distribution of wealth and power; its enemy is the entire arrangement of privileges, exemptions, and free rides that has narrowed the opportunity of most Americans to control their own destiny. This fight for fairness is political; it can be won only by organizing a new political majority in America.

There exists a 200-year-old native tradition behind this goal of fairness and equality. It is a tradition that stretches back to Jefferson and Tom Paine, to Andrew Jackson, the muckrakers, George Norris, and Robert LaFollette; it runs through the early organizers of the CIO and the political battles of Estes Kefauver; and it comes down to us today in the campaigns and ideas of Martin Luther

King, Robert Kennedy, and Ralph Nader. It is called populism.
We believe that a new populism, stripped of the paranoia and
racism that afflicted it in the past, can redress some of the key
grievances that have stunted the lives of millions of us. It is a
political movement with a *political* goal. It is *not* a cultural
prescription or a revolutionary nostrum. Far from being a Utopian
dream, the new populism rests on a new majority that is, we
believe, both a necessary and an attainable coalition. It is also the
most important work we have.

Three essential beliefs govern this manifesto, and we state them
bluntly at the outset.

    ONE   Wealth and power are unequally and unfairly
    distributed in America today

After a generation of predominantly liberal, predominantly re-
formist national governments, the concentration of wealth has
increased. In 1949, the richest 1 per cent of the population owned
21 per cent of the wealth. Today, the richest 1 per cent own almost
40 per cent of our national wealth. Income distribution has not
changed for a generation: the bottom fifth of American families get
6 per cent of the national income; the top fifth gets 40 per cent.

This wealth is shielded by private corporate governments,
which are themselves protected by the political process their
wealth helps shape.* These are the corporate enterprises that
pervade our society: General Motors and First National City Bank,
the National Broadcasting Company and Columbia University, the
American Medical Association and the AFL-CIO, Getty Oil and
AT&T. These institutions are often at odds with each other; they
often favor different aspirants to national power and prefer different national priorities. But each holds basic, sometimes life and
death, power over the millions of individuals whose lives they
touch; each of them maintains this power no matter who is elected
to public office; and each believes, first and foremost, in self-

---

*So that we have Henry Jackson, whose servility to the biggest aerospace company in his
state has won him the title of "Senator from Boeing"; and Russell Long, who inherited his
role as protector of the oil industry when Robert Kerr died and Lyndon Johnson left the
Senate; and Congressman Jamie Witten, who is the spokesman for the big corporate
farmers. And so on.

perpetuation and aggrandizement—regardless of what that means for public policy.

These epicenters of power do not win every battle with the public: auto safety laws are sometimes passed, utility rate increases are occasionally denied. But as a general proposition, these groups possess the power to govern themselves and to affect the whole society, and this power is beyond the reach of public or individual redress. No individual who works for a living can avoid taxes; Atlantic Richfield Oil Company paid no taxes for four years although it earned $465 million during that period. No homeowner could hurl his garbage into the street because it hurt his family budget to buy a trash can; the U.S. Steel Corporation has turned Gary, Indiana and countless other communities into open sewers. If a motorist is caught speeding and offers money to the traffic cop, he is guilty of bribery; if doctors are caught participating in the padding of Medicare bills and the AMA spends thousands to stop Congress from legislating reform, it is engaging in public-service advertising.* This imbalance of power is not the result of a conspiracy: such institutions are simply using the power they have to preserve their privileged status in the American hierarchy.

As city planner Charles Abrams first suggested, our economic system is best described as welfare for the rich and free enterprise for the poor. There are $4 billion in federal subsidies every year for big corporate farmers; there are depletion allowances and import quotas to enrich the oil industry; there are expense-account dodges, untaxed foreign bank accounts, and special exemptions for the income from stocks and bonds—all for the rich. Both big business and big labor organizations can hire lobbyists, raise money for political campaigns, and lend out their employees to candidates while keeping them on tax-deductible salaries. The biggest defense contractors—General Dynamics, Lockheed, Boeing—have been virtually subsidized by the Pentagon, as have elitist "think-tanks" such as the RAND Corporation.** And the tax system is itself a major subsidy to the wealthy.

---

*A view certainly held officially. Despite intensive political lobbying by the AMA, the IRS continues to recognize the organization's tax-exempt status for most of its revenues; yet, the Sierra Club had its exemption challenged ostensibly for just such activities.

**As a result of congressional action in 1971, "virtually" and "Pentagon" are no longer necessary modifiers in the case of Lockheed. Now, direct subsidization is the rule. And, in announcing his import surtax in August, 1971, Mr. Nixon specifically exempted Lockheed from its application—another form of subsidy.

Meanwhile, the billions of dollars spent as a result of the reform legislation of the Truman, Kennedy, and Johnson years—on such items as urban renewal, Medicare, the $60 billion highway construction program, the War on Poverty, and aid to education —have made little difference for the forgotten families living on less than $10,000 a year. Administrators profited from these programs, politicians and consultants profited, construction firms profited, but the poor and the nonaffluent did not.

And it is not just blacks or Chicanos or Indians who are victimized by our double-standard economy. Nor is it only those on the poverty level. The majority of Americans are victimized.

White factory workers in Birmingham and Flint still lead frustrated, dead-end lives: the average worker's income is $1,000 less than the Department of Labor says he needs to take care of a family of four, and more often than not his wife also works at a dull, unrewarding job that is nonetheless essential if the family is to make ends meet. The waitress in Cleveland still can't pay her mother's hospital bills, and the law still says her income makes her ineligible for public health care. Old people living on Social Security still have to shoplift cans of tunafish so they can eat. And in New York City, the gross income of 60 per cent of white families is less than $9,400 a year—less, in other words, than a moderate standard of living. So much for the affluent society.

In his famous 1962 commencement address at Yale, President Kennedy argued that the crucial problems of the economy were no longer political or distributive, but had become managerial and technical. We argue the exact opposite.

> TWO   The key to building any new majority in American politics is a coalition of self-interest between blacks and low- and moderate-income whites; the real division in this country is not between generations or between races, but between the rich who have power and those blacks and whites who have neither power nor property.

Until recently, such an alliance seemed impossible, in part because middle-class liberals have persistently defined public issues primarily in terms of race rather than class. "White racism," the Kerner Commission said, was the core of the problem. The OEO bureaucrats did not start any legal-services storefronts in the white sections of Youngstown or South Boston. There were no Model City grants to rebuild the decaying white neighborhoods of Utica or Jersey City. Affluent liberals, living safely behind suburban fences, refused to recognize street crime as an injustice against the old and the poor still trapped in the cities. Middle-class reformers sent their own children to "smart" private schools, and then supported plans that forced white ethnics to bus their children to predominantly black schools where education was inferior. By promising and not delivering to the blacks, and by ignoring the blue-collar worker, the liberals in power during the 1960's managed to anger and polarize both halves of the other America.

But blacks and millions of white workingmen who earn between $5,000 and $10,000 a year do have common problems and share common interests. To get them to recognize this and to act requires that these mutual needs become clearly defined and that programs to meet these needs be offered—*all in terms that benefit both groups*. Despite all the ethnic and racial divisions, blue-collar workers were progressive during the 1930's and 1940's. There is no reason why they can't be again.

We have already noted some of the issues than can unite them. As for the programs, a unifying populist platform might include: stricter industrial safety laws; a 90 per cent tax on inheritance and estates—and tax reforms to help the workingman; free medical care for everyone; public ownership of utilities; limits on land ownership by individuals and corporations; new antitrust laws to go after industrial concentration as well as monopoly; expanded Social Security benefits, including a decent income base for those who cannot work; cable television franchises for civic groups; free and equal access to television for all politicians; strict controls on the profits of banks; and an end to corporate power and control of both the market and the regulatory agencies.

The prospect for this new coalition appears uncertain today. Working-class whites and blacks are separate armed camps in Cicero, Illinois; school buses are bombed in Pontiac, Michigan, in an effort to halt racial busing. In 1968, New York watched as teachers—mostly Jewish—battled parents' groups—mostly black and Puerto Rican—for control of the city's schools. In public universities, on civil-service job lists, in housing, blacks and working-class whites collide, in large part because they are forced to compete against each other for what are, but need not be, inadequate resources. The result is distrust and hostility.

We do not argue that these disputes can be eradicated; racial and cultural hostilities are a fact of life. But we do argue that this competition is in part a consequence of economic concentration—concentration that leaves whites and blacks competing over too scarce public resources. We believe that a redistribution of wealth and power would diminish this combat that turns potential class allies into racial antagonists. If white and black communications workers find wages and promotions inadequate, whom should they blame? Each other? Or the conglomerate International Telephone and Telegraph that turned a profit of $350 million in 1970, and paid its board chairman, Harold Geneen, an annual compensation of $766,000? (Which is more than most Americans earn in a lifetime.) If white and black families are forced to compete against each other for decent housing at a fair price, whom should they blame? Each other? Or banks and insurance companies that finance a glut of new office buildings and luxury apartments and allow realty interests to make a profit out of slum housing?

Blacks and almost-poor whites do not have to love, or even like, each other to forge an alliance of self-interest. The Irish cop on the low end of the middle-income scale living in Brooklyn's Bay Ridge need not embrace the black family in Harlem or the Italian-American homeowner in Corona to know his kids are stuck with the same bad schools, dirty streets, and dangerous parks. The white miner in West Virginia and the Mexican-American migrant worker in Texas share a more important bond than friendship: because they and their families cannot get decent medical care, they will die younger, suffer more disease, and lose more children at birth. In short, the coalition we are describing is based on hard, practical politics. In 1932, Jewish trade unionists and southern segregationists did not love each other, but together they gave ballast to FDR's New Deal. Certainly the jobless youth in Watts and the steelworker laid off his job in Gary have more in common than antilabor millionaires like Senators James Buckley and William Brock III have in common with those blue-collar workers who voted for them.

In 1968, Robert Kennedy, an earthy enemy of war, hunger, and crime, won the votes of both blacks and ethnic whites who had been tempted to follow George Wallace. The organizing work of Saul Alinsky, Ralph Nader, and Msgr. Geno Baroni also indicates the existing potential for this alliance. So do the decisive electoral victories achieved in 1970 by Senators Hart, Proxmire, and Kennedy, by Governor Gilligan, and by Representatives Dellums and Abzug, and the 1971 election of independent populist Henry Howell as Virginia's Lieutenant Governor.

Once cemented, this pact between the have-nots could transform American politics. With the added weight of the burgeoning consumer, environmental, and women's movements, and the millions of new voters between eighteen and twenty-one, an effective political coalition could take power.

> THREE Conceptually and historically, the new populism differs from both the New Frontier and the New Left; it is a synthesis of many radical and some conservative ideas.

The new populism differs from the New Frontier in several distinctive and significant ways. First, it is a *movement*, a broad popular upsurge like the labor movement of the 1930's or today's antiwar movement; it is not a faction yoked to one political party or one charismatic personality. The new populist movement sees winning elections as only half the job because so much power is still locked beyond the reach of the democratic process. It mistrusts the technocrats from the RAND Corporation and the Harvard Business School. It is decentralist and participatory, believing change is generated from below. And, like most of the original populists, it is anti-imperialist in foreign policy.

At the same time, it understands that the New Left in its Weatherman, Panther, and Yippie incarnations has become antidemocratic, terroristic, dogmatic, stoned on rhetoric, and badly disconnected from everyday reality.

The new populism also recognizes that conservatives have been perceptive about such things as the menace of violent street crime, the failure of the welfare system, and the limits human nature places on the abilities of centralized government. Conservatives have been right, too, in sensing the country has lost contact with those human values the ethnic workingman prizes most: family, hard work, pride, loyalty, endurance.

Our basic argument in this manifesto is neither new nor novel. If it seems new, that is because over the last twenty years liberalism lost its vision and its memory, its élan and its program.

For a generation we have watched liberals gain more power and display less liberalism. It began in the early 1950's as liberal politicians and intellectuals dropped everything else to prove their anticommunism. Later in the decade, exhaustion and boredom set in, and political issues were subordinated to sociological concerns with affluence, organization men, suburbia, and mass culture. "The end of ideology" became an intellectual cliché.

During the Kennedy years, an eerie infatuation with management techniques and budgeting expertise—exemplified by Robert McNamara—became the new fashion. Increasingly divorced from a concern with programs, liberals turned these technocratic means into ends, ultimately chaining us by default to a set of distorted policies. So we became mired in a war begun by the anticommunists and the technocrats, and, since 1965, all our energies have of necessity been aimed at ending that war.

But now it is time to return again to the first questions of politics: who holds power—and by what right?

D. *George McGovern:*
   ## "My Stand"*

The life and work of George McGovern (1922-) seem to be cut from the whole cloth of historic populism. He was born in a town of six hundred souls in North Dakota, son of a Methodist minister, subsisting largely on cabbages and potatoes during his impoverished childhood, attending public schools and Dakota Wesleyan, rushing to volunteer in a great patriotic war, emerging

*Remarks at the Jefferson-Jackson Day Dinner at Detroit, *New York Times*, April 25, 1972. Reprinted by permission.

as a hero. Then back to school and a doctoral dissertation on the plight of Colorado miners during their struggle against the Rockefeller interests in 1913-1914. Then his switch from Republican to Democrat because "My study of history convinced me that the Democrats were on the side of the average American." Campaigning on a shoestring (he once had to sell campaign buttons at a picnic to earn his transportation to the next day's rally), he managed to be elected and reelected to Congress in a normally Republican state, and this during the Eisenhower era. In 1960 President Kennedy appointed him director of his Food for Peace program, where he managed at once to feed the poor and make farmers happy by getting rid of surpluses. A year after his election to the Senate in 1962 he began to criticize the Vietnam War, a criticism which escalated along with American involvement. Within the Democratic Party he headed the committee which reformed the rules of nominating conventions so as to allow greater participation by women, minority groups, young people, and unprofessionals.

McGovern's personality adds a final touch to this profile of the populist. Speaking in a Midwestern twang and with little sense of humor or irony, he has about him a kind of simplicity, directness, and empathy for "plain people" ideally suited to a candidate who identifies himself, as McGovern does, with the American populist tradition.

The high point of McGovern's popularity came during the spring primaries of 1972. In Massachusetts, for example, McGovern's support cut across all ethnic, social, and economic lines. He beat his nearest rival by a 5-2 margin and won the endorsement of Boston Brahmins, Irish and Italian blue-collar workers, Harvard intellectuals, and Jewish homeowners in Hyde Park. Despite the brave beginning, however, McGovern was to suffer a resounding defeat by Richard Nixon the following November. The McGovern disaster, it appears in retrospect, underlines a central weakness in populism: a doctrinal flexibility verging on nihilism. From his study of history McGovern knew that historic populism opposed special favors to the rich, imperialist wars, corruption in government, and that it stood on the side of the poor people in their struggles against the rich. What he failed to take into account was that populism has always hedged

these premises with the Protestant work ethic, with uncritical
patriotism during wartime, and with a profound intolerance of
anyone who might seem to condone unorthodox personal behavior. Populism has two faces, one generous and one narrow, one
confident and one cautious, the one full of hope, the other full of
anxiety. Hence one reason why the wooden, mechanical Nixon
was able to win over McGovern, the hyperbolic Dakotan: Nixon
was no populist but he had a sure grasp of populist demonology,
and—with a little help from his friends—he was able to portray his
opponent as the champion of freeloaders, Vietniks, hippies, and
counter-culturists. In 1972 the two faces of populism went to
war, and McGovern was caught in the cross fire.

The following two McGovern selections present two addresses
from his ill-fated campaign.

Prior to the first primary election in New Hampshire, and the
most recent one in Wisconsin, the conventional view of men who
write and read each other's syndicated columns was that the
Presidential candidate elected in 1972 would be the one who clings
most tightly to the center. This view—heavily supported by poll-
sters and analysts of the public mind—held that the American
people wanted not a hard-fought battle over the great issues but a
quiet coronation of the status quo.

I have not found this glorification of the establishment center to
be the mood of the American people. Indeed, most Americans see
the establishment center as an empty, decaying void that commands neither their confidence nor their love.

It is the establishment center that has led us into the stupidest and
cruelest war in all history. That war is a moral and political
disaster—a terrible cancer eating away the soul of the nation. Yet
those who charted its course brand its opponents as too far out to be
electable.

My answer to that is "Nuts!" My platform is to stop the
bombing of the people of Southeast Asia immediately and then get
every American out of Indochina lock, stock and barrel within
ninety days.

The establishment center has persisted in seeing the planet as
engaged in a gigantic struggle to the death between the free world

and the Communist world. The facts are that much of the so-called free world is not free but a collection of self-seeking military dictators financed by hard-pressed American workers. And most of the Communist nations are far more obsessed with their own internal divisions than they are with Washington, London, Bonn or Saigon.

Even so, the establishment center has constructed a vast military colossus based on the paychecks of the American worker. That military monster, now capable of blowing up the entire world a hundred times over, is devouring two out of three of our tax dollars. It inflates our economy, picks our pockets and starves other areas of our national life.

It was not the American worker who designed the Vietnam war or our military machine. It was the establishment wise men, the academicians of the center. As Walter Lippmann once observed: "There is nothing worse than a belligerent professor."

My policy would be to cut the vast waste from our bloated military budget and invest the savings in job-creating enterprises based on a guaranteed job for every man and woman who wants to work.

The Number One economic issue before America today is: jobs and more jobs. This nation desperately needs the labor and talent of every man and woman in this land. Nothing is more wasteful than unemployment.

I pledge without qualification that if I become President I will do whatever is necessary to see that there is a job for every American who wants a job. It is the establishment center that has erected an unjust tax burden on the backs of American workers, while 40 per cent of the corporations paid no Federal income taxes at all last year. I say that is an outrage.

I propose to close $28 billion in tax loopholes for the rich and the powerful and use the savings to reduce property taxes, strengthen our schools and rebuild our cities.

It is the establishment center that tells us we can afford an ABM but we can't afford good health care for the American people. I say that's intolerable.

It is the establishment center that says we can afford a $250-million guaranteed loan to Lockheed but we can't afford a decent retirement income for our senior citizens. And I say that's intolerable.

It is the establishment center that says it's okay to tell the American people one thing in public, while plotting a different course in secret.

I say it's time to end the credibility gap and begin telling the American people the truth. The people of this country are not left or right or centrist. Rather, they seek a way out of the wilderness.

What is needed is a revitalization of the American center based on the enduring ideals of the Republic. The present center has drifted so far from our founding ideals that it bears little resemblance to the dependable values of the Declaration of Independence and the Constitution. I want America to come home from the alien world of power politics, militarism, deception, racism and special privilege to the blunt truth that "all men are created equal—that they are endowed by their creator with certain inalienable rights and among these are life, liberty and the pursuit of happiness."

I want this nation we all love to turn away from cursing and hatred and war to the blessings of hope and brotherhood and love.

Let us choose life, that we and our children may live. Then our children will love America, not simply because it is theirs but because of the great and good land all of us together have made it.

E. *George McGovern:* Come Home, America!*

With a full heart, I accept your nomination.

And this afternoon, I crossed the wide Missouri to recommend a running mate of wide vision and deep compassion—Tom Eagleton.

My nomination is all the more precious in that it is the gift of the most open political process in our national history. It is the sweet

*"Text of Address by McGovern Accepting the Democratic Presidential Nomination," *New York Times*, July 14, 1972. Reprinted by permission.
See preceding Selection D for headnote.

harvest cultivated by tens of thousands of tireless volunteers—old and young—and funded by literally hundreds of thousands of small contributors. Those who lingered on the edge of despair a brief time ago had been brought into this campaign—heart, hand, head and soul.

I have been the beneficiary of the most remarkable political organization in American history—an organization that gives dramatic proof to the power of love and to a faith that can move mountains.

As Yeats put it: "Count where man's glory most begins and ends, and say, my glory was I had such friends."

This is a nomination of the people, and I hereby dedicate this campaign to the people.

And next January we will restore the government to the people. American politics will never be the same again.

We are entering a new period of important, hopeful change in America comparable to the political ferment released in the eras of Jefferson, Jackson and Roosevelt.

I treasure this nomination especially because it comes after vigorous competition with the ablest men and women our party can offer.

Help of Every Democrat

In the months ahead, I covet the help of every Democrat and every Republican and independent who wants America to be the great and good land it can be.

This is going to be a national campaign carried to every part of the nation—North, South, East and West. We are not conceding a single state to Richard Nixon. I want to say to my friend, Frank King, that Ohio may have passed a few times at this convention, but I'm not going to pass Ohio. Governor Gilligan, Ohio may be a little slow counting the votes, but when they come in this November, they are going to show a Democratic victory.

To anyone in this hall or beyond who doubts the ability of Democrats to join together in common cause, I say never underestimate the power of Richard Nixon to bring harmony to Democratic ranks. He is our unwitting unifier and the fundamental issue of this campaign. And all of us together are going to help him redeem the pledge he made 10 years ago: Next year you won't have Richard Nixon to kick around any more.

We have had our fury and our frustrations in these past months and at this convention.

My old and treasured friend and neighbor, Hubert Humphrey; that gracious and good man from Maine, Ed Muskie; a tough fighter for his beliefs, Scoop Jackson; a brave and spirited woman, Shirley Chisholm; a wise and powerful lawmaker from Arkansas, Wilbur Mills; the man from North Carolina who opened new vistas in education and public excellence, Terry Sanford; the leader who in 1968 combined the travail and the hope of the American spirit, Gene McCarthy.

I was as moved as all of you by the appearance at this convention of the Governor of Alabama, George Wallace, whose votes in the primary showed the depths of discontent in this country, and whose courage in the face of pain and adversity is the mark of a man of boundless will. We all despise the senseless act that disrupted his campaign. Governor, we pray for your speedy and full recovery, so you can stand up and speak out forcefully for all of those who see you as their champion.

Well, I frankly welcome the contrast with the smug, dull and empty event which will take place here in Miami next month. We chose this struggle. We reformed our party and let the people in.

A Million-Member Club

And we stand today not as a collection of backroom strategists, not as a tool of I.T.T. or any other special interest, but as a direct reflection of the public will.

So let our opponents stand on the status quo, while we seek to refresh the American spirit.

Let the opposition collect their $10-million in secret money from the privileged. And let us find one million ordinary Americans who will contribute $25 to this campaign—a McGovern "million-member club" with members who will expect not special favors for themselves but a better land for us all.

In Scripture and in the music of our children we are told: "To everything there is a season, and a time to every purpose under heaven."

And for America, the time has come at last.

This is the time for truth, not falsehood.

In a democratic nation, no one likes to say that his inspiration came from secret arrangements behind closed doors. But in a sense that is how my candidacy began. I am here as your candidate tonight in large part because during four administrations of both parties, a terrible war has been charted behind closed doors.

I want those doors opened, and I want that war closed. And I make these pledges above all others—the doors of government will be open, and that brutal war will be closed.

Truth is a habit of integrity, not a strategy of politics. And if we nurture the habit of candor in this campaign, we will continue to be candid once we are in the White House. Let us say to Americans, as Woodrow Wilson said in his first campaign: "Let me inside [the government] and I will tell you everything that is going on in there."

And this is a time not for death, but for life.

In 1968, Americans voted to bring our sons home from Vietnam in peace—and since then, 20,000 have come home in coffins.

I have no secret plan for peace. I have a public plan.

As one whose heart has ached for 10 years over the agony of Vietnam, I will halt the senseless bombing of Indochina on Inauguration Day.

There will be no more Asian children running ablaze from bombed-out schools.

There will be no more talk of bombing the dikes or the cities of the North.

Within 90 days of my inauguration, every American soldier and every American prisoner will be out of the jungle and out of their cells and back home in America where they belong.

Resolution on War

And then let us resolve that never again will we shed the precious young blood of this nation to perpetuate an unrepresentative client abroad.

Let us choose life, not death, this is the time.

This is also the time to turn away from excessive preoccupation overseas to rebuilding our own nation.

America must be restored to her proper role in the world. But we can do that only through the recovery of confidence in ourselves. The greatest contribution America can make to our fellow mortals is to heal our own great but deeply troubled land. We must respond to that ancient command: ''Physician, heal thyself.''

It is necessary in an age of nuclear power and hostile ideology that we be militarily strong. America must never become a second-rate nation. As one who has tasted the bitter fruits of our weakness before Pearl Harbor, 1941, I give you my sacred pledge that if I become President of the United States, America will keep its defenses alert and fully sufficient to meet any danger. We will do that not only for ourselves, but for those who deserve and need the shield of our strength—our old allies in Europe, and elsewhere, including the people of Israel, who will always have our help to hold their promised land.

Yet we know that for 30 years we have been so absorbed with fear and danger from abroad that we have permitted our own house to fall into disarray. We must now show that peace and prosperity can exist side by side—indeed, each now depends on the other.

National strength includes the credibility of our system in the eyes of our own people as well as the credibility of our deterrent in the eyes of others abroad.

National security includes schools for our children as well as silos for our missiles, the health of our families as much as the size of our bombs, the safety of our streets and the condition of our cities and not just the engines of war.

And if we some day choke on the pollution of our own air, there will be little consolation in leaving behind a dying continent ringed with steel.

Let us protect ourselves abroad and perfect ourselves at home.

This is the time.

And we must make this a time of justice and jobs for all.

For more than three years, we have tolerated stagnation and a rising level of joblessness, with more than five million of our best workers unemployed. Surely this is the most false and wasteful economics.

Our deep need is not for idleness but for new housing and

hospitals, for facilities to combat pollution and take us home from work, for products better able to compete on vigorous work markets.

A Job Guarantee

The highest domestic priority of my Administration will be to insure that every American able to work has a job to do. This job guarantee will and must depend upon a reinvigorated private economy, freed at last from the uncertainties and burdens of war.

But it is our commitment that whatever employment the private sector does not provide, the Federal Government will either stimulate, or provide itself. Whatever it takes, this country is going back to work.

America cannot exist with most of our people working and paying taxes to support too many others mired in the demeaning, bureaucratic welfare system. Therefore, we intend to begin by putting millions back to work; and after that is done, we will assure to those unable to work an income sufficient to assure a decent life.

Beyond this, a program to put America back to work demands that work be properly rewarded. That means the end of a system of economic controls in which labor is depressed, but prices and corporate profits are the highest in history. It means a system of national health insurance, so that a worker can afford decent health care for himself and his family. It means real enforcement of the laws so that the drug racketeers are put behind bars for good and our streets are once again safe for our families.

Above all, honest work must be rewarded by a fair and just tax system. The tax system today does not reward hard work—it penalizes it. Inherited or invested wealth frequently multiplies itself while paying no taxes at all. But wages earned on the assembly line, or laying bricks, or picking fruit—these hard earned dollars are taxed to the last penny. There is a depletion allowance for oil wells, but no allowance for the depletion of a man's body in years of toil.

The Administration tells us that we should not discuss tax reform in an election year. They would prefer to keep all discussion of the tax code in closed committee rooms, where the Administration, its powerful friends and their paid lobbyists can turn every effort at reform into a new loophole for the rich. But an election year is the people's year to speak—and this year, the people are going to insure that the tax system is changed so that work is rewarded and so that those who derive the highest benefits will pay their fair share, rather than slipping through the loopholes at the expense of the rest of us.

So let us stand for justice and jobs, and against special privilege. This is the time.

We are not content with things as they are. We reject the view of those who say: "America—love it or leave it." We reply: "Let us change it so we can love it the more."

And this is the time. It is the time for this land to become again a witness to the world for what is noble and just in human affairs. It is the time to live more with faith and less with fear—with an abiding confidence that can sweep away the strongest barriers between us and teach us that we truly are brothers and sisters.

So join with me in this campaign, lend me your strength and your support, give me your voice—and together, we will call America home to the founding ideals that nourished us in the beginning.

From secrecy and deception in high places, come home, America.

From a conflict in Indochina which maims our ideals as well as our soldiers, come home, America.

From the entrenchment of special privilege and tax favoritism, come home, America.

From military spending so wasteful that it weakens our nation, come home, America.

From the waste of idle hands to the joy of useful labor, come home, America.

From the prejudice of race and sex, come home, America.

From the loneliness of the aging poor and the despair of the neglected sick, come home, America.

Come home to the affirmation that we have a dream.

Come home to the conviction that we can move our country forward.

Come home to the belief that we can seek a newer world.

For:

> *This land is your land,*
> *This land is my land,*
> *From California to the New York Island,*
> *From the Redwood Forest*
> *To the Gulfstream waters,*
> *This land was made for you and me.*

May God grant us the wisdom to cherish this good land to meet the great challenge that beckons us home.

VI. LEFT-RIGHT ECUMENISM

"Left" and "right," we have seen, are elusive categories in the history of American populism. On some matters, at least, both of these "fringes" had more in common with one another than either shared with the "vital center." Both invoked the myth of America's revolutionary past. The rhetoric of both was closer to Jefferson and Jesus than to either Edmund Burke or Karl Marx. Both were filled with what Richard Hofstadter called "absolutist enthusiasm," which they castigated American society for lacking. (What was "moral decay" to right-wing populists was "spiritual emptiness" to the New Left.) Both sides attacked the managerial liberalism of the New Frontier and the manipulative liberalism of the Great Society. Both sides declared themselves enemies of the ultra-rich. Both sides distrusted intellectuals in the pay of the government. Both sides singled out the term "bureaucrat" as a symbol of conspiracy—a conspiracy not only against democratic government but against simplicity, innocence, and spontaneity, virtues which they associated with an older America.

On more specific issues both sides resented the hypocrisy of liberals who prescribed racial integration from privileged sanctuaries, destroyed old neighborhoods by ill-conceived planning, called for the punishment of the immediate perpetrators of war crimes but not the ultimate decision makers who sent them into battle. Both sides decried tax loopholes and other privileges for the rich.

Why not get together then? Why not "a hip coalition of right and left"? This was the proposal of the novelist Norman Mailer, who then proceeded to put it to work by running for mayor of New York with Jimmy Breslin, a writer from the sidewalks of New York who speaks the language of the Irish working class.

Their candidacy was probably intended as a means of dramatizing the cause of populism—their slogan was "power to the neighborhoods!" But other, more serious, candidacies of the sixties and seventies helped to promote the belief that right-left coalitions might be more than a theoretical possibility. Robert Kennedy in the Indiana primary of 1968 received a number of blue-collar votes which were later diverted to the "right-wing" George Wallace. In 1972 the "left-wing" Daniel Walker (who was responsible for the report on the 1968 Democratic Convention which talked about a "police riot") emerged as a Democratic victor in the Illinois gubernatorial race; part of the reason, surely, was the incumbent Republican's unpopular income tax, but Walker had also taken his own name seriously enough to walk all over the state, stressing person-to-person contact.

But ecumenism implies more than coalition-building. More importantly, it implies understanding and mutual respect. The seventies in America may be a decade when those who have classified themselves as "left" realize how estranged they have become from the broad masses of Americans. Andrew Greeley, a priest-intellectual, has contended that his fellow-intellectuals have become a kind of self-centered ethnic group, complete with all manner of devices which prevent them from understanding outsiders. Peter and Brigitte Berger, two shrewd sociologists, have predicted that the "greening" of America movement will culminate in its "bluing"—an energetic working class will take the places vacated by an exhausted liberal elite. Even Newfield and Greenfield, as we have seen, have rediscovered the lower-middle class, "middle-class values" and all, and repudiated the snobbism of Consciousness III.

It is best not to minimize the difficulties standing in the way of left-right ecumenism. Defense spending, busing, and abortion remain among the serious substantive differences, all aside from life-styles. And yet—surely, one hopes, surely, in an age when the Chinese People's Liberation Army Band plays "Home on the Range" to a visiting American President, the American people can move toward healing the cultural and ideological wounds within their own nation.

Saul Alinsky:
Organizing the Middle Class*

The late Saul Alinsky (1909-1972) combined the idealism of the left with the toughness of the right. He possessed compassion for the unfortunate without the kind of guilt stigmatized as "bleeding heart" by the less-unfortunate. A veteran of the radical movement in the thirties and CIO-organizing in the forties, Alinsky first brought his own name into prominence as an organizer of poor whites in the slums of Chicago. He forged a coalition of workers, small merchants, union leaders, and churches to win concessions from City Hall; he left behind a vigorous self-help organization in the area. During this period, in the late forties, Alinsky set a pattern which left-right ecumenists might study: He was never averse to militant tactics—boycotts and sit-ins were among his favorites—but he used them in the context of a familiar American value system. Alinsky was a master of the lower-middle-class vernacular. Thus, when he helped organize a black ghetto in Rochester, New York, during the 1960's his organization was called FIGHT: Freedom, Integration, God, Honor, Today—a roll call of values which combine reform with tradition. Alinsky was a Jew, an agnostic, and a militant, but he won the support of such unlikely patrons as Marshall Field, the millionaire philanthropist, and the Roman Catholic hierarchy in America. In the selection we see part of the reason for Alinsky's broad appeal: his simple, homely common sense.

Organization for action will now and in the decade ahead center upon America's white middle class. That is where the power is. When more than three-fourths of our people from both the point of view of economics and of their self-identification are middle class, it is obvious that their action or inaction will determine the direction of change. Large parts of the middle class, the "silent major-

*From Saul Alinsky, "The Way Ahead," in *Rules for Radicals* (New York: Random House, 1971). Reprinted by permission.

ity," must be activated; action and articulation are one, as are silence and surrender.

We are belatedly beginning to understand this, to know that even if all the low-income parts of our population were organized—all the blacks, Mexican-Americans, Puerto Ricans, Appalachian poor whites—if through some genius of organization they were all united in a coalition, it would not be powerful enough to get significant, basic, needed changes. It would have to do what all minority organizations, small nations, labor unions, political parties or anything small, must do—seek out allies. The pragmatics of power will not allow any alternative.

The only potential allies for America's poor would be in various organized sectors of the middle class. We have seen Cesar Chavez' migrant farm workers turn to the middle class with their grape boycott. In the fight against Eastman Kodak, the blacks of Rochester, New York, turned to the middle class and their proxies.

Activists and radicals, on and off our college campuses—people who are committed to change—must make a complete turnabout. With rare exceptions, our activists and radicals are products of and rebels against our middle-class society. All rebels must attack the power states in their society. Our rebels have contemptuously rejected the values and way of life of the middle class. They have stigmatized it as materialistic, decadent, bourgeois, degenerate, imperialistic, war-mongering, brutalized, and corrupt. They are right; but we must begin from where we are if we are to build power for change, and the power and the people are in the big middle-class majority. Therefore, it is useless self-indulgence for an activist to put his past behind him. Instead, he should realize the priceless value of his middle-class experience. His middle-class identity, his familiarity with the values and problems, are invaluable for organization of his "own people." He has the background to go back, examine, and try to understand the middle-class way; now he has a compelling reason to know, for he must know if he is to organize. He must know so he can be effective in communication, tactics, creating issues and organization. He will look very differently upon his parents, their friends, and their way of life. Instead of the infantile dramatics of rejection, he will now begin to dissect and examine that way of life as he never has before. He will know that a "square" is no longer to be dismissed as such—

instead, his own approach must be "square" enough to get the action started. Turning back to the middle class as an organizer, he will find that everything now has a different meaning and purpose. He learns to view actions outside of the experience of people as serving only to confuse and antagonize them. He begins to understand the differences in value definition of the older generation regarding "the privilege of college experience," and their current reaction to the tactics a sizeable minority of students uses in campus rebellions. He discovers what their definition of the police is, and their language—he discards the rhetoric that always says "pig." Instead of hostile rejection he is seeking bridges of communication and unity over the gaps, generation, value, or others. He will view with strategic sensitivity the nature of middle-class behavior with its hangups over rudeness or aggressive, insulting, profane actions. All this and more must be grasped and used to radicalize parts of the middle class.

The rough category "middle class" can be broken down into three groups: lower middle class, with incomes from $6,000 to $11,000; middle middle class, $12,000 to $20,000; and upper middle class, $20,000 to $35,000. There are marked cultural differences between the lower middle class and the rest of the middle class. In the lower middle class we encounter people who have struggled all their lives for what relatively little they have.

With a few exceptions, such as teachers, they have never gone beyond high school. They have been committed to the values of success, getting ahead, security, having their "own" home, auto, color TV, and friends. Their lives have been 90 per cent unfulfilled dreams. To escape their frustration they grasp at a last hope that their children will get that college education and realize those unfulfilled dreams. They are a fearful people, who feel threatened from all sides: the nightmare of pending retirement and old age with a Social Security decimated by inflation; the shadow of unemployment from a slumping economy, with blacks, already fearsome because the cultures conflict, threatening job competition; the high cost of long-term illness; and finally with mortgages outstanding, they dread the possibility of property devaluation from non-whites moving into their neighborhood. They are beset by taxes on incomes, food, real estate, and automobiles, at all levels—city, state, and national. Seduced by their values into

installment buying, they find themselves barely able to meet
long-term payments, let alone the current cost of living. Victimized by TV commercials with their fraudulent claims for food
and medical products, they watch the news between the commercials with Senate committee hearings showing that the purchase of
these products is largely a waste of their hard-earned money.
Repeated financial crises result from accidents that they thought
they were insured against only to experience the fine-print eva-
sions of one of our most shocking confidence rackets of today, the
insurance racket. Their pleasures are simple: gardening a tiny back
yard behind a small house, bungalow, or ticky-tacky, in a
monotonous subdivision on the fringe of suburbs; going on a
Sunday drive out to the country, having a once-a-week dinner out
at some place like a Howard Johnson's. Many of the so-called hard
hats, police, fire, sanitation workers, schoolteachers, and much of
civil service, mechanics, electricians, janitors, and semi-skilled
workers are in this class.

They look at the unemployed poor as parasitical dependents,
recipients of a vast variety of massive public programs all paid for
by them, "the public." They see the poor going to colleges with
the waiving of admission requirements and given special financial
aid. In many cases the lower middle class were denied the opportunity of college by these very circumstances. Their bitterness is
compounded by their also paying taxes for these colleges, for
increased public services, fire, police, public health, and welfare.
They hear the poor demanding welfare as "rights." To them this is
insult on top of injury.

Seeking some meaning in life, they turn to an extreme
chauvinism and become defenders of the "American" faith. Now
they even develop rationalizations for a life of futility and frustration. "It's the Red menace!" Now they are not only the most
vociferous in their espousal of law and order but ripe victims for
such as demagogic George Wallace, the John Birch Society, and
the Red-menace perennials.

Insecure in this fast-changing world, they cling to illusory fixed
points—which are very real to them. Even conversation is charted
toward fixing your position in the world: "I don't want to argue
with you, just tell me what our flag means to you?" or "What do
you think of those college punks who never worked a day in their

lives?'' They use revealing adjectives such as ''outside agitators'' or ''troublemakers'' and other ''When did you last beat your wife?'' questions.

On the other side they see the middle middle class and the upper middle class assuming a liberal, democratic, holier-than-thou position, and attacking the bigotry of the employed poor. They see that through all kinds of tax-evasion devices the middle middle and upper middle can elude their share of the tax burdens—so that most of it comes back (as they see it) upon themselves, the lower middle class.

They see a United States Senate in which approximately one-third are millionaires and the rest with rare exception very wealthy. The bill requiring full public disclosure of senators' financial interests and prophetically titled Senate Bill 1993 (which is probably the year it will finally be passed) is ''in committee,'' they see, and then they say to themselves, ''The government represents the upper class but not us.''

Many of the lower middle class are members of labor unions, churches, bowling clubs, fraternal, service, and nationality organizations. They are organizations and people that must be worked with as one would work with any other part of our population—with respect, understanding, and sympathy.

To reject them is to lose them by default. They will not shrivel and disappear. You can't switch channels and get rid of them. This is what you have been doing in your radicalized dream world but they are here and will be. If we don't win them Wallace or Spiro T. Nixon will. Never doubt it that the voice may be Agnew's but the words, the vindictive smearing, is Nixon's. There never was a vice-president who didn't either faithfully serve as his superior's faithful sounding board or else be silent.

Remember that even if you cannot win over the lower middle class, at least parts of them must be persuaded to where there is at least communication, then to a series of partial agreements and a willingness to abstain from hard opposition as changes take place. They have their role to play in the essential prelude of reformation, in their acceptance that the ways of the past with its promises for the future no longer work and we must move ahead—where we move to may not be definite or certain, but move we must.

People must be ''reformed''—so they cannot be deformed into

dependency and driven through desperation to dictatorship and the death of freedom. The "silent majority," now, are hurt, bitter, suspicious, feeling rejected and at bay. This sick condition in many ways is as explosive as the current race crisis. Their fears and frustrations at their helplessness are mounting to a point of a political paranoia which can demonize people to turn to the law of survival in the narrowest sense. These emotions can go either to the far right or totalitarianism or forward to Act II of the American Revolution.

The issues of 1972 would be those of 1776, "No Taxation Without Representation." To have real representation would involve public funds being available for campaign costs so that the members of the lower middle class can campaign for political office. This can be an issue for mobilization among the lower middle class and substantial sectors of the middle middle class.

The rest of the middle class, with few exceptions, reside in suburbia, living in illusions of partial escape. Being more literate, they are even more lost. Nothing seems to make sense. They thought that a split-level house in the suburbs, two cars, two color TVs, country club membership, a bank account, children in good prep schools and then in college, and they had it made. They got it—only to discover that they didn't have it. Many have lost their children—they dropped out of sight into something called the generation gap. They have seen values they held sacred sneered at and found themselves ridiculed as squares or relics of a dead world. The frenetic scene around them is so bewildering as to induce them to either drop out into a private world, the nonexistent past, sick with its own form of social schizophrenia—or to face it and move into action. If one wants to act, the dilemma is how and where; there is no "when?" with time running out, the time is obviously now.

There are enormous basic changes ahead. We cannot continue or last in the nihilistic absurdities of our time where nothing we do makes sense. The scene around us compels us to look away quickly, if we are to cling to any sanity. We are the age of pollution, progressively burying ourselves in our own waste. We announce that our water is contaminated by our own excrement, insecticides, and detergents, and then do nothing. Even a half-witted people, if sane, would long since have done the simple and

obvious—ban all detergents, develop new non-polluting insecticides, and immediately build waste-disposal units. Apparently
we would rather be corpses in clean shirts. We prefer a strangling
ring of dirty air to a "ring around the collar." Until the last, we'll
be buried in bright white shirts. Our persistent use of our present
insecticides may well ensure that the insects shall inherit the
world.

Of all the pollution around us, none compares to the political
pollution of the Pentagon. From a Vietnam war simultaneously
suicidal and murderous to a policy of getting out by getting in
deeper and wider, to the Pentagon reports that strained even a
moron's intelligence that within the next six months the war would
be "won," to destroying more bridges in North Vietnam than
there are in the world, to counting and reporting the enemy dead
from helicopters, "Okay, Joe, we've been here for fifteen minutes; let's go back and call it 150 dead," to brutalizing our
younger generation with My Lais but ignoring our own principles
of the Nuremberg trials, to putting our soldiers in conditions so
conducive to drugs that we stand forth as freedom's liberating
force of pot. This Pentagon, whose economic waste and corruption
is bankrupting our nation morally as well as economically, allows
Lockheed Aircraft to put one-fourth of its production in the small
Georgia country town of the late Senator Russell (a powerful man
in military appropriation decisions), and then transmits its appeals
for federal millions to save it from its financial fiascos. Far worse
is the situation in the late Representative Mendel Rivers' congressional district—he of the House Military Affairs Committee
—with the phenomenal pay-offs of every kind of installation from
corporations vying for Pentagon gold. Even our solid-state mental
vice-president described it in a way he thought was amusing but is
tragic beyond belief to any freedom-loving American.

> . . . Vice President Agnew praised Mr. Rivers for his
> "willingness to go to bat for the so-called and often
> discredited military industrial complex" as 1,150 gen-
> erals, Congressmen and defense contractors applauded
> in the ballroom of the Washington Hilton Hotel.
> . . . Mr. Agnew said he wanted "to lay to rest the
> ugly, vicious, dastardly rumor" that Mr. Rivers, whose

Charleston, S.C., district is chock full of military instal-
lations, "is trying to move the Pentagon piecemeal to
South Carolina.

"Even when it appeared Charleston might sink into
the sea from the burden," said the Vice President, Mr.
Rivers' response was, "I regret that I have but one
Congressional District to my country to—I mean to give
to my country."

—*New York Times*, August 13, 1970

This is the Pentagon that has manufactured nearly 16,000 tons
of nerve gas, why and what for being unclear except to overkill the
overkill. No one has raised the questions, who got the contracts?
what it cost? where the pay-offs went? Now the big question is how
to dispose of it as it deteriorates and threatens to get loose among
us. The Pentagon announces that the sinking of the nerve gas is
safe *but from now on they will find a safe way*! The obvious
American way of assuming personal responsibility for one's action
is utterly ignored—otherwise, since the Pentagon made it, it
should keep it, and have it all stored in the basements of the
Pentagon; or, since the President as Commander-in-Chief of our
armed forces believed that the sinking in the ocean of the 67 tons of
nerve gas was so safe, why didn't he attest to his belief by having it
dumped into the waters off San Clemente, California? Either
action would at least have given some hope for the nation's future.

The record goes on without any deviations toward sanity. The
army chose the final day of hearings of the President's Commission investigating the National Guard killings at Kent State, to
announce that M-16 rifles would now be issued to the National
Guard. The President's Commission report is doomed not to be
read until after the bowl games on New Year's Day by a President
who watches football on TV the afternoon of the biggest march in
history on Washington, Moratorium Day. There are our generals
and their "scientific" gremlins who after assurance of no radioactive menace from the atomic tests in Nevada now more than a
dozen years later have sealed off 250 square miles as "contaminated with poisonous and radioactive plutonium 239." (*New York
Times*, August 21, 1970.) This from the explosions in 1958! Will
the "safe" disposition in 1970 of the nerve gas still be as "safe" a

dozen or less years from now? One can only wonder how they will seal off some 250 miles in the Atlantic Ocean. We can assume that these same "scientific" gremlins will be assigned to the disposition of the thousands of tons of additional stockpiled nerve gas of which approximately 15,000 tons are on Okinawa and to be moved to some other island.

Compound this with a daily record of now we are in Cambodia, now we are out, now we are not in it just over it with our bombers, we will not get involved there as in Vietnam but we can't get out of Vietnam without safeguarding Cambodia, we're doing this but really the other, with no other clue to all this madness except the half-helpful comment from the White House, "Don't listen to what we say, just watch what we do," half-helpful only because either statements or actions are sufficient to make us freeze into bewilderment and stunned disbelief. It is in such times that we are haunted by the old maxim, "Those whom the gods would destroy, they first make ludicrous."

The middle classes are numb, bewildered, scared into silence. They don't know what, if anything, they can do. This is the job for today's radical—to fan the embers of hopelessness into a flame to fight. To say, "You cannot cop out as have many of my generation!" "You cannot turn away—look at it—let us change it together!" "Look at us. We are your children. Let us not abandon each other for then we are all lost. Together we can change it for what we want. Let's start here and there—let's go!"

It is a job first of bringing hope and doing what every organizer must do with all people, all classes, places, and times—communicate the means or tactics whereby the people can feel that they have the power to do this and that and on. To a great extent the middle class of today feels more defeated and lost than do our poor.

So you return to the suburban scene of your middle class with its variety of organizations from PTAs to League of Women Voters, consumer groups, churches, and clubs. The job is to search out the leaders in these various activities, identify their major issues, find areas of common agreement, and excite their imagination with tactics that can introduce drama and adventure into the tedium of middle-class life.

Tactics must begin within the experience of the middle class, accepting their aversion to rudeness, vulgarity, and conflict. Start them easy, don't scare them off. The opposition's reactions will provide the "education" or radicalization of the middle class. It does it every time. Tactics here, as already described, will develop in the flow of action and reaction. The chance for organization for action on pollution, inflation, Vietnam, violence, race, taxes, and other issues, is all about us. Tactics such as stock proxies and others are waiting to be hurled into the attack.

The revolution must manifest itself in the corporate sector by the corporations' realistic appraisal of conditions in the nation. The corporations must forget their nonsense about "private sectors." It is not just that government contracts and subsidies have long since blurred the line between public and private sectors, but that every American individual or corporation is public as well as private; public in that we are Americans and concerned about our national welfare. We have a double commitment and corporations had better recognize this for the sake of their own survival. Poverty, discrimination, disease, crime—everything is as much a concern of the corporation as is profits. The days when corporate public relations worked to keep the corporation out of controversy, days of playing it safe, of not offending Democratic or Republican customers, advertisers or associates—those days are done. If the same predatory drives for profits can be partially transmuted for progress, then we will have opened a whole new ball game. I suggest here that this new policy will give its executives a reason for what they are doing—a chance for a meaningful life.

A major battle will be pitched on quality and prices of consumer goods, targeting particularly on the massive misleading advertising campaigns, the costs of which are passed on to the consumer. It will be the people against Madison Avenue or "The Battle of Bunkum Hill."

Any timetable would be speculation but the writing of middle-class organization had better be on the walls by 1972.

The human cry of the second revolution is one for a meaning, a purpose for life—a cause to live for and if need be die for. Tom Paine's words, "These are the times that try men's souls," are more relevant to Part II of the American Revolution than the beginning. This is literally the revolution of the soul.

The great American dream that reached out to the stars has been lost to the stripes. We have forgotten where we came from, we don't know where we are, and we fear where we may be going. Afraid, we turn from the glorious adventure of the pursuit of happiness to a pursuit of an illusionary security in an ordered, stratified, striped society. Our way of life is symbolized to the world by the stripes of military force. At home we have made a mockery of being our brother's keeper by being his jail keeper. When Americans can no longer see the stars, the times are tragic. We must believe that it is the darkness before the dawn of a beautiful new world; we will see it when we believe it.

Epilogue

This volume has provided selections from several varieties of populism, beginning with the Enlightenment populism of Jefferson and Paine, extending through the period in the nineteenth century more commonly associated with Populism, tracing its path through the twenties and thirties, and ending with an examination of more recent strains of "left" and "right" populism. The controlling thesis of this anthology is that populism is not merely a historical phenomenon in America—something to be dusted off and studied as part of a particular period—but a perennial, if partly unconscious, political tradition, one which continues to shape our thinking about candidates and coalitions.

When George McGovern ran a campaign for President on the combined themes of domestic evangelism and international disengagement, he contrived—some thought rather too obviously—to reach back into America's populist heritage. When Richard Nixon countered with a campaign stressing social puritanism and the work ethic, he appealed to another side of this tradition. When it later became clear that Nixon's campaign also involved the use of some distinctly un-populist tricks, including sabotage and espionage, the American people were angry but not particularly shocked. In May, 1973, a Gallup poll revealed that a clear majority of those sampled found "little difference" between the corruption of the Nixon Administration and that of other administrations over the past twenty-five years. *All* political leaders, said Jefferson, are wolves. To liberals, who had gotten used to seeing them as shepherds, this judgment seemed overly harsh; but not to the majority of Americans.

If the word "populism" is broad enough to cover both Nixon and his 1972 opponent, if it includes both McGovern and Wallace, along with several other odd couples, the question has to be asked whether it really has any meaning. Nets this wide have a way of catching everything—fish, water, seaweed, and sand.

The problem was anticipated in the Introduction, and the way of dealing with it was to contrast populism with other reform ideologies, such as socialism and liberalism, in order at least to get a clearer idea of what populism is not. Despite its many different varieties, populism contains certain common features setting it aside from other "isms." Some of these features were described in the Introduction.

Yet the question can still be asked: What political relevance does all this have? What kind of practical, operational meaning is there in the conclusion that George Wallace, C. Wright Mills, Joe McCarthy, and an undetermined number of SDSers were all populists in some respects? Is it very likely that we could ever build a political alliance of such types? Could we so much as get them in the same room?

Hardly. *They*—the personalities themselves—could probably never be reconciled. But suppose the line of questioning were put this way: Are the responses which each of these personalities elicited from Americans necessarily incompatible? Was it necessarily illogical for one who voted for Robert Kennedy in the 1968 primaries to have voted for Wallace in the general election? Or for a worker to have voted Republican in 1972? Or for people to swing back and forth between what intellectuals call "progressive" and "reactionary" solutions to social problems?

If any point has been stressed in this volume, it is that these labels do not do justice to the complexity of the American mind. Americans are neither progressive nor reactionary, but populistic. They are quite prepared to approve bold new initiatives in social welfare, including family allowances and income supplements —but not to hand out money to people *unwilling* to work. They want serious tax reforms, including the elimination of loopholes for the rich—but not a classless society. They harbor a deep distrust for politicians—but they abhor anarchy.

Those who can find nothing but contradiction and bourgeois hypocrisy in these combinations should find another vocation than politics. Americans are what they are. After ten years of scolding by prophets, they went ahead and reelected Richard Nixon. But those who can reconcile these combinations—those, in fact, who share the views contained in them—may find in them the ingredients of a new populist alliance.

Populists do not have to assume, as the liberals used to, that Americans want only incremental changes. The results of public opinion polls suggest that Americans will welcome sweeping reforms in environmental protection, tax laws, gun control, social welfare, consumer protection, antitrust action, and interracial justice. The question is not the degree of change but the context in which change is proposed. The question is whether the appeal is going to be made in the context of respect for America, for all its people and for the best of its traditions, or in the name of the Third World, black liberation, counterculture, and the international youth movement.

Populism, still viable after two hundred years, offers the possibility of reconciling reform and patriotism. It could give both a better name.